Thought-provoking and emotionally resonant, the book sheds light on the complex issue of addiction and its impact on families, with characters so well-drawn we feel like we're living through the experience with them. A must-read for anyone who's been touched by addiction and seeks to understand the power of forgiveness, healing and redemption.

DENISE BARON, Ayurvedic practitioner and
wellness expert, Wellness 360

One of the most powerful messages of this memoir is its emphasis on the importance of compassion and understanding in healing family relationships. The author demonstrates that, no matter how destructive the effects of addiction may be, there is always hope for healing and renewal. By embracing the principles of recovery and working together as a family, even the most shattered relationships can be mended or transformed into something stronger and more resilient. Highly recommended, with honor.

ASHLEY B. COOK, M.Ed., LPC, LMHC, NCC, ABC
Therapies, Mind & Life Empowerment

What was most interesting to me was the author's family karma, the patterns of alcoholism and abuse passed down from generation to generation. But talents are also passed down. Although Kennerly's dad, a clever writer with a gift for word play and a sharp mind, lacked the self-discipline, fortitude, and support to become a published author, his legacy lives on through his daughter's strength, wit, and commitment to sobriety — and having his and her voices be heard.

DJUNA WOJTON, spiritual healer, astrologer, and
author of *Karmic Healing* and *Karmic Choices*

letters from east of nowhere

letters from east of nowhere

Daddy's Words to Live, Drink & Die By: A Memoir

F. Kennerly Clay

contents

"To write a letter is to send a message to the future;
to speak of the present with an addressee who is not there,
knowing nothing about how that person is (in what
    spirits, with whom)
while we write and, above all, later:
while reading over what we have written.
Correspondence is the utopian form of conversation
    because
it annihilates the present
and turns the future into the only possible place for
    dialogue."
—Ricardo Piglia, Respiración artificial

"The only way of knowing a person is to love them without
    hope."
—Walter Benjamin

To Jimmy, Shannah, TJ and Jeffrey:
We were all meant to be here.

And to my mother,
who carried that weight a long time:
You done good, Mama.

one
unlikely legacy

"An outlaw can be defined as somebody who lives outside the law, beyond the law and not necessarily against it."
— Hunter S. Thompson

My father's mugshots are strewn all over the internet, permanently recording the places he got arrested for being drunk and disorderly the last 15 years of his life. He wore out his welcome with cops and with family in places like Brunswick, Maine; Greenville, Maryland; Charlotte, North Carolina; and Vero Beach, Florida.

In one forlorn photo, his green eyes bleary and a little worse for wear, his hair is still kempt. In another, his face is bloated and unshaven, and his hair has gotten long. He looks rough.

My sister Shannah cringes at these photos out there for the world to see.

Me? I kinda like it.

It's as though my father's stubborn stance against any form of oppression or persecution has prevailed in some way, and now he's immortalized like his favorite outlaw heroes, the fictitious western cowboy Josey Wales and the real-life Beat author Neal Cassady.

Daddy shows no remorse in these pictures. His weary look seems to be saying what had been said many times before, that all he wanted was to be left the hell alone so he could live life on his terms—even if that meant drinking it away.

The letters

East of Nowhere is the novel my father—Francis Edward Clay, Jr., better known as Ed, and alter egos he took on, like Eddie Armadillo, Barry Dingle, and Sergeant Thrillhammer—never finished writing. He scrawled pages and pages of it as he made his way to Maryland, Texas, Colorado, California and back. He was convinced it would be a best-seller. It was full of Kerouacian hedonistic delights, all told in my father's particular way, but for those of us who occasioned upon a page here and there, it was mostly undecipherable and raunchy. I remember some scene involving lewd, drunken sex with Mexican women. Ultimately, just about every portion of the unfinished novel was stolen in a hobo bag along with what little my father possessed at the time.

Perhaps it could have been a good book, if Daddy had been a different version of himself, not the one beleaguered by alcohol and a lifetime of regrets he said he never had. He was a decent writer, after all—philosophical, perspicacious, amused by it all. But that version of my father never made it into a book. Instead, he flexed most of his writing muscle in letters, many of them to me.

The ones to me began early, since we were the first family he left. I was born at the height of the hippie era, and after my parents split up, my father went on to remarry and have four other children. The first, Jimmy, arrived when I was seven years old, followed by Shannah a year later. The youngest two boys, TJ and Jeffrey, arrived when I was 14 and 15 years old. When I was a kid, they were my "half-siblings," but we've long since dropped the half crap. I always refer to them as my brothers and sister. Aside from Clay humor in common, we each followed my father's lead—genetically and environmentally—becoming alcoholics ourselves and carrying our own daddy-baggage around for occasional display.

Among the dozens of letters I've saved from my father is a giant postcard Daddy sent me as a kid. It is of the Empire State Building and it's cut out in the same shape, from back when he was trucking in and out of New York City. After high school, his letters arrived at my own Manhattan addresses, from my first year in fashion school to right before I moved out to San Francisco, my birthplace and his old stomping grounds, to finish my bachelor's degree at the University of San Francisco. He would write, then I would write, and back and forth it always went.

I recently noticed for the first time that Daddy wrote upside-down peace signs on the back of envelopes in later years, just like my mother still does. "Turn peace up."

I have bundles of letters addressed to me from Daddy when I lived in Kobe, Japan. I spent three years there teaching English and wrote prolifically to friends and family. Later, he and I had weekly letter exchanges when I landed in Philadelphia and was engaged.

After I got married, every letter he ever wrote to me was addressed to Mrs. Kennerly Phillips, Mrs. Kirk D. Phillips, or some variation thereof. Given that I never changed my maiden name, my father was one of very few people who ever addressed me like that. I wonder if he wanted to honor my husband in some way, perhaps thinking Kirk would see the letter when it arrived.

At some point, after he became completely untethered, he would sign off with pseudonyms. "I love you," he wrote in 1990, followed by the name "Pancho." Later, in Florida, he became Tony Turtle, and eventually the Reverend Eddie Chowan, named after the river that ran near the old Clay farm in Harrellsville, North Carolina.

Carolina Sunrise

The Chowan flowed like a razor
I rowed it,
For dear life.
I took its
Name
There is a

Going back
Always.
"Shure."

Since I've gone through so many of Daddy's letters these past few years, I appreciate how much letter writing was a part of our lives not that long ago. And some people's letters you saved because they were just so good. For me, it wasn't just what Daddy wrote—it was how he wrote it.

He randomly switched between capital and lowercase letters, but all written very neatly across the lines. Certain letters always seemed to be in caps, like E and R and N, a particularly obstinate bunch, demanding to be capitalized, even in the middle of a sentence. No one could tell *them* what to do—just like Daddy.

Sometimes he transitioned to cursive for no reason, but clean print was his main style. And whenever he began a letter, if there were any throat-clearing or small talk to be had, it was usually written in clever form to amuse.

- "The splendiferous view from my jail cell ..."
- "Greetings from the southwest baboon's asshole..."
- "I thumbed for six weeks and 10,000 miles..."

He wrote stories in these letters, stories that you were never quite sure were true but were just plausible enough to *maybe* be true. Like the letter he sent to Jeffrey about playing an afternoon of pool with a one-armed midget whose car bumper sticker read, "If you drive too close, I'll flick a booger on your windshield!" Or the story about slipping on bear shit while hunting as a boy (TJ later figured out that one was made up). And did Daddy and Grandfather really go on a six-figure Vegas binge? Or the one he told Jeffrey about having a box-cutter held to his throat in San Francisco, then pushing the guy out a third-story window (Jeffrey mused it may have been the only time our father went looking *for* a cop).

Daddy sent poems he'd written (*East of Nowhere*, in fact, began as a poem) and he wrote dirty limericks. His fine vocabulary made for expressive, engaging writing, and he was well-read and culturally attuned. Even today, I look things up online that I never knew the meaning of at the time.

He'd tell me stories of me as a baby and would reference my mother and our former life in California. There was always this abiding love and approval of me in his letters. In fact, my father never disapproved of any of us, for who we were or for anything we did. Quite the contrary, he *championed* us—in direct contrast to the lifelong, overt disapproval of his own father.

My sister Shannah and my youngest brother Jeffrey and I had each saved many of our letters over the years and talked about putting a book together at some point. We thought we'd gather up the letters and select the ones that had some wit and wisdom to impart to future generations, then determine how much we'd be willing to reveal about our dad. After all, our children would be reading this stuff. But to imagine a cleaned-up version of our father was laughable, and it was impossible to pick and choose pieces of the story. Here was a man with an education and a family and people who loved and cared about him, yet at mid-life found himself jobless, homeless, hitchhiking inebriated across the country, getting his teeth knocked out God knows how. Then out of the blue, he'd send a letter from East of Somewhere that was clear as day, perennially optimistic, never cynical, always full of warmth and good wishes for his children.

Daddy had this uncanny ability—and I suppose the great genetic good fortune—of being able to clean up right good once his hair was combed and his shirt tucked in (which it always was). As my brother TJ remembers, "He was always tan, always generally better looking than he had any right to be"— and by the looks of him you'd never know what a whirlwind of shit he'd created and survived.

Discomfort zone

At some point, it became clear to me that a larger story had to be told. Splicing together a bunch of letters and commentary without context wouldn't tell the real story.

But immediately I recognized there would be risk involved. Risk that I'd have to give up something of my carefully preserved relationship with my father. Risk that I'd have to tell the truth about some things and take a chance on hurting people's feelings.

As I started to realize what was at stake, I saw how suppressed I was about revealing my own life story. I grew indignant: Why on earth should I be so afraid to tell my *own* story as an adult woman while I had to live this family's life all those years?

I became eager to push past the perceptions my siblings had of our father, and past my own while I was at it. So, I started to ask other family members and friends to share about him, starting with his first cousin, who was really dear to him. She revealed aspects of who he was as a child, and in the safe space of their lifelong friendship, she was the only one to whom he ever squarely admitted the grip alcohol had on him. Conversations with an old friend of his from college provided a melancholic glimpse into who Daddy was as a young man and over fifty years of friendship.

I also didn't want this to be just my story about my father. I wanted to give voice to my three brothers and sister, doing my best to imagine their lives in relation to him. I know that I have at times here been so insistent upon making my own story known that I may have quieted theirs. That was not my intent; it is simply overcompensation for what never was.

From a very young age, I had developed a protective bond with Daddy, since he and my mother were divorced for as long as I could remember.

Sharing my relationship with him out loud makes me feel like I'm going to lose something of what we had. Fear—no, more like terror—creeps into my chest and throat, threatening to strangle my entire existence. My relationship with my father, I have discovered, is profoundly visceral because when I start going deep, everything hurts.

Hurts like the time I was two years old and my mom yelled at him over the bookshelves. I've had this memory my entire life that I always equated with their final straw. Daddy wasn't building something the way she wanted with cinder blocks and slabs of wood. She got mad and yelled. He yelled back and stormed out of the house. It's only in the last few years that I figured out why the memory was so deeply ingrained and painful for me: He never said goodbye.

So I have given myself permission to hold back nothing. No feelings spared. No secrets withheld. This is life the way I remember it, this is all of us coming through it all pretty darn well, and this is our dad who was, well, our dad, and I can't think of any other dad I would rather have had.

"East of Nowhere" '98-'99
Give me somewhere removed
from nowhere
Gotta' have another chance.

Give me nowhere removed
from somewhere
Where went romance?

It's only me, It's only you.
East of Nowhere.
Nowhere to go.
Fiery furnaces amok in smoke
Caboose on runaway freight.

East of Nowhere
I [ ] your hands

Lowlands like glue,
Maybe a different job to do.
Perhaps dying with you.

Back to somewhere like
ancient shoe
Ideas clingling in
abstract blue
Give to me and ten-fold to you.

We walk like prehistoric
as once we were
Poaching for at random
and called a jolly crime,
Who'll ever know
me or you? East of Nowhere?

The Penthouse burns
in smoky chartreuse
There is no notice but mine
and I won't tell.
What is the use?

East of Nowhere, true law
in broken thumb
Hob-nailed boot on carcass
Money running through all
like greased lightning.
God forgive me — A .38 is a necessity,
I will live with quiet fury.

The original "East of Nowhere" poem that spurred
writing of early chapters of my father's unfinished
novel

left unsung

"Where words leave off, music begins."
— Heinrich Heine

December 8, 1980. The day John Lennon was shot in front of the Dakota residence where he and Yoko and Sean lived in New York City. Until that day, I had been only vaguely aware of the Beatles. *Yellow Submarine* was one of my first LPs when I was seven years old, along with The Who's *Tommy*. But on that day, when I saw my mom crying and I heard the news all over the radio about this rock icon being murdered, I knew it was something awful, much bigger than the death of the person. It was the silencing of a voice and a generation.

Yoko had called for a vigil to be held that night in Central Park, and although we were four and a half hours away on the Eastern Shore of Maryland, my mother lit candles and turned out the lights, and we sat together in quiet solemnity, sending prayers to Yoko and mourning the loss of Yesterday, when all our troubles seemed so far away.

I'm pretty sure my mother called my father at some point during that time. The music of the 1960s was integral to their early life together. They had shared pain. And as with anything that I saw as a child that brought my parents together in some way—even though they'd been apart since I was so little—I grabbed onto it, teased it out, made it part of me, because I was a part of the "them" that no longer existed except in the recesses of memory, which they would both share with me from time to time.

My mother had more than 400 albums, all in alphabetical order by artist, from The Allman Brothers to Warren Zevon, lined up on four horizontal levels of shelving. I went to the Bs to look for The Beatles and found titles like *Abbey Road, Let it Be, Magical Mystery Tour, Revolver, Rubber Soul, Sgt Pepper's Lonely Hearts Club Band,* and the *White Album,* all in alphabetical order by artist, then title. As I had been trained to do, I carefully pulled out the album before *Abbey Road* (that was the way you marked your place to ensure the records got put back in order) and slipped it off the shelf. I pulled the paper sleeve from within the record cover, then guided the record out of the sleeve carefully between my thumb and middle finger, touching the round paper label in the center and never the vinyl itself. I positioned the album hole over the spindle, side one up, glided the arm from right to center to hold it in place, then pushed the button that released the album with a smooth *clack!* The needle arm lifted, jerked slightly, then hovered over the lines of the first track and descended with that familiar crackling sound and first moment of silent anticipation: "Come Together."

By the time I got to "Golden Slumbers," tears were rolling down my face for something I couldn't quite grasp. Music and memories that weren't even mine spoke history that were, in fact, a part of me. I devoured The Beatles for days. This was just after the release of *Double Fantasy,* so Lennon songs were playing constantly on the radio. Back then we would read the album inserts cover to cover, memorizing the lyrics, playing albums on repeat until they got into our bones. Every time Lennon's voice sang about beautiful, darling Sean, my heart ached for his kid and the wife he left behind. I, too, had been separated from my father, not in the same way of course, but that sort of thing breeds empathy.

When I went off to summer camp in Vermont over the next few years, I took with me a handful of cassette tapes I'd discovered in a black vinyl crocodile pattern carrying case on the bottom of my mother's album shelves. These cassettes had my father's writing on them. It was like discovering lost treasure, relics of him I'd never known about but was now ready to discover. Buffalo Springfield. Crosby, Stills, Nash & Young. The Doors. Old homemade tapes where, if I listened carefully, I could almost hear my father there in the background, inhaling a fat joint in San Francisco, immersed in sweet smoke and music, the lyrics speaking through him like a message to me 12 years later.

"Tell me why," Neil Young crooned. Every time I heard the line about making arrangements with yourself, it was as though the lyrics were written about my father. I imagined myself singing those words to him, now that I was getting older and could see things more clearly, or I could imagine him singing those words about himself, bemused perhaps at how he ended up where he was in life.

I remember playing that "After the Goldrush" tape over and over at camp one summer, giving into melancholy and latching on to the lyrics that threaded through our distant lives. I now understood that "Only Love Can Break Your Heart" and wondered if the world that fell apart was the one we once shared.

Those songs dug into my soul, bonding me with my father even though we hardly saw each other.

The front door knocker smacked twice, a little after one o'clock one day when I was maybe eight years old. I bounced out of the living room chair where I'd been sitting, bored out of my mind, waiting, and took a deep breath. Without looking to see who it was, I clacked the bolts open, expectantly.

"Hey, Pooh Doll," Daddy said as he ducked through the doorway, bringing with him a waft of Old Spice I wished would never leave. I could feel him sizing me up as he smiled in disbelief. I knew I'd gotten taller. It'd been what, three months since he last saw me? He stooped down to embrace me with a loud whisper and a hint of Miller beer on his breath. "Sure is good to see you." Daddy's arms were long and encompassing, though his hugs always felt apologetic, for much more than being late.

Never mind he was supposed to be here two hours ago. He was just in from back-to-back weeks of being on the road, driving a big rig halfway across the country and back again. I figured he was tired, with a familiar pang of sympathy that bubbled up when I thought of my father and hard work and two families. I said nothing about his lateness because I understood. I *always* understood.

I was able to see clearly from a pretty young age the strains of life, the dynamic of ex-wife and divorced kid vs. new wife and new kids. Not enough time or money to go around, working his ass off all the time. The bind he was in was obvious. For many years, my mother covered for him on the latenesses and no-shows, trying to protect me. What was really going on was that he was either drinking and incapacitated, or he was spending what little free time he had with his current family, and by the time that happened, he had tied one on, or it was too late to drive all the way down to see me and then drive back in time to be in his truck the next day.

Except for the tantrums I threw for my mom when Daddy didn't show up, I didn't allow myself to dwell on it. What was anyone to do about any of it? What would I fight for? Create more challenges for my father than already existed? I took what I could get, kept my mouth shut, and buried any grievances. Even though I fully understood he'd made his own choices in life, I mostly felt pity and sadness for my father, and I was quick to defend him, a protectiveness I carried into adulthood.

Behind the bleariness of fourteen-hour trucking shifts and alcohol, my father's eyes were true green, not just hazel, and warm and kind, the way that shows up in some people's eyes. I rarely made eye contact with him, though, as a kid. We only had a few hours together at a time, the first part of which I'd have to get over the shyness of not having seen him for a while. Looking him square in the eye would have been too confronting.

In later years, I longed to look into his eyes, to be connected, but by then his eyes had become a bit shifty. If I caught his gaze for too long, we'd both know he'd been drinking, then I'd look away to spare him the embarrassment of my knowing and judging.

The same thing happened with promises he'd make to me. He knew and I knew they were not going to happen, but if we never locked eyes, we could pretend that he was going to deliver. I could allow him to experience his own good intentions without overtly doubting him.

"Hello, Du-WARD," my mom drawled playfully, stressing the second syllable of Edward like "card," cordial as always. She looked pretty, with loose, dark brown curls and big, gold hoop earrings. Barefoot, she was tiny next to him.

To my surprise, he pulled her in and gave her a perfectly platonic kiss on the forehead. This made me momentarily uncomfortable, as I knew he would never have done that in front of his current wife. I also knew there wasn't a chance in hell that my parents would get together again. But something about that little show of affection showed me that love had been there between them. Once.

In one of my baby-book pictures, the three of us are sitting on a picnic blanket in Golden Gate Park. I'm about a year old, and Mom is smiling, peering out through round-lens hippie glasses, long dark hair cascading down to her waist. Daddy seems happy and in the moment with us. You can make out his trim sideburns and boyish features. I had seen this photo throughout my life and always sensed this was a time when love really did live between my parents. In that captured moment, it appeared like we were a real family—a whole unit—the way it once was, but hardly ever would be again.

I always joked with some amount of cynicism when telling people about having been a product of the San Francisco scene. "My parents just missed the Summer of Love—it was kind of metaphorical," I'd say. Daddy had arrived just after, in fall of 1967. I was born a year later, and then in August of 1969 my parents were wed in Golden Gate Park. In 1970, we were on our way back to the East Coast, and by 1971 or 1972, Daddy was headed to Florida looking for work.

Us as a family, Golden Gate Park, 1969

Because I was so young when my parents split up, I didn't have to go through what an older child would. I wore their divorce like a badge of honor in the 1970s, long before all the other kids started wearing it. As I got older, I could observe my parents' faults—my mother's controlling behaviors, for example, and my father's lack of responsibility—while they individually shared with me their reasons for not having been able to make their relationship work.

Your mother is incredibly smart but she has no common sense. I loved her but we just couldn't live together.

After your father got drunk and wrecked my car, that was pretty much the end of it. Although I should've seen the writing on the wall when he was pissing out the window of our house in San Francisco.

Even worse, my mother added, was him pissing down the inside wall of their two-year-old's bedroom in Maryland a couple years later.

If I were to imagine them together for even a split second, a shit-storm would pop up in my young mind so fast I'd look away before the tape reel could play out in my head. I could see my father sauntering away, yelling over his shoulder, "Kiss my cornbread ass!"

And my mother using all the English language expletives in one breath, "Goddamnmutherfuckingsunnuvabitch, just take your shit and get out!"

The storyline became cemented even more once my mother got sober when I was in high school, and still more five years later when I did. Everything then was seen and talked about through the lens of greater sanity but filtered with righteousness and disdain. Suffice it to say, throughout my entire life, I not only never entertained the notion of my parents being together again after they had split up, I knew that it would be a terrible idea. In fact, through my mother's telling of events, it never seemed like their being together was a great idea in the first place. Mostly because of the alcohol.

Music continued to keep the lines of communication open between Daddy and me. For my twelfth birthday, he brought me a Walkman cassette player with headphones. For my fourteenth, an all-in-one turntable with radio and cassette. My gifts to him were often record albums my mom knew he would appreciate, like the latest Eric Clapton, or Bob Dylan's *Slow Train Coming*.

"You gotta suhvvv some-bodday," Daddy would croon like the Black gospel backup singers, then half-laugh, amused at himself. It always seemed like something witty was yet to come, so I often giggled along, teetering there on the precipice, finding the funny in just about everything, just like my father did.

If we were out somewhere and observed the odd behavior of a random stranger, or we happened to eavesdrop on somebody's conversation, taken completely out of context, Daddy would toss his head back.

"Hideous!" he'd say, with that half-laugh, or sarcastically, "Outstanding! Yes, just outstanding!" Just being around Daddy being amused was the funniest thing of all.

The times we were together with family, Daddy and my Uncle Ray would banter back and forth, bullshitting and cutting up, teasing my grandmother about something inane and watching her feign offense, their giggles turning into howls because the more she said in her oh-so-polite, slightly clueless-but-not-really, sing-songy Virginia way, the unintentionally funnier it all became. She was especially mock-offended by farting, often demonstrated around the dinner table and a topic of much conversation that we all took great delight in. Just listening to my father and Uncle Ray jesting back and forth and giggling was funny enough. Uncle Ray says he'll never forget my dad's "hee-hee-hee!" giggle before the outright laughter, "like an uncontrollable laugh from the heart." Makes me realize there's some things I'll never laugh about again in quite the same way, because the people who made it so hilarious aren't here anymore.

Uncle Ray, Daddy, Mammonk, Grandmother, Jimmy
and Shannah

I remember my father's sheer delight when he heard I was reading J.D. Salinger's *Catcher in the Rye* in school, saying it was one of his all-time favorite books. Literature, too, became a shared interest. In high school, I was soon drawn to Kerouac novels from my mom's bookshelves, where I knew I was drinking from the same fountain as my father. In my mother's paperback collection, I discovered the likes of Carlos Castañeda, Henry Miller, Ken Kesey, and Anais Nin. Years later, my father turned me on to Richard Brautigan, another late-Beat generation writer with a collection of short stories, including one haunting one called "The Abortion" set in San Francisco in the 1960s. Brautigan had been a voice for the Summer of Love, and parts of his top-selling book, *Trout Fishing in America*, were first published by Lawrence Ferlinghetti, the legendary proprietor of the City Lights bookstore where the Beat poets and authors all hung out. Ferlinghetti was still there during my time in San Francisco and for many years after. He died in February 2021 at 101 years old. My father preceded him in 2011 at age 64.

Remember - Melville died in a fetid hotel room. Poe on the streets of Baltimore. Clay on the highway. Be like Henry Miller. Never stop putting it all down.

As I grew into adulthood, my mother, too, made musical references that became part of the narrative of an earlier time.

"This song was out when your father and I were breaking up," she said to me, driving in the car one day and listening to Carole King's "It's Too Late."

As my mom drove along and sang in tune with the radio cranked, I internalized the lyrics as apropos of their relationship. To this day, I call it my mother and father's break-up song.

And sometimes it was just listening to rock-n-roll. Maybe Jefferson Airplane on the radio and Grace Slick belting out the first lines of "Somebody to Love" would trigger a concert memory or a San Francisco vignette of life when I was a baby and my parents were still together. Through these fragments of memory and song lyrics that ran deep, resurrecting an earlier time and place and continuously speaking to me, I cobbled together my own life story. Music was mortar holding everything together, always there in the background.

I really disapprove of your reading Brautigan. Then, not again, you shouldn't miss him altogether. Incidentally, his 2nd wife was Japanese and some of his poems and lamentations are based in Tokyo. (His funniest work by far is 'Confederal General from Big Sur.') I think you can easily find his stuff in Japan. Glad I didn't strike out there.

— March 2, 1997

three
come gather 'round people

"The thing the Sixties did was to show us the possibilities and the responsibility that we all had. It wasn't the answer. It just gave us a glimpse of the possibility."
— John Lennon

My parents met at a political action meeting—Students for Liberal Action, or SLA, as my mom recalls—about the Vietnam War. It was the fall of 1965, and my father was in his first year at William & Mary, the second oldest college in the country, in Williamsburg, Virginia, and my mother was soon to graduate. (Which would have made her just 22 and he just barely 18. *Christ!* Still letting this sink in every time I think about it.) Daddy had grown up in nearby Newport News, while my mother hailed from Maryland's Eastern Shore. Back then, the Chesapeake Bay Bridge Tunnel hadn't been built yet, so her trips down to college involved taking long ferry rides from the southern tip of Virginia's Eastern Shore to mainland Virginia, around Norfolk.

Volume 55, Number 26   College of William and Mary, Williamsburg, Virginia   Friday, May 6, 1966

Struck by my father's tall and lean form sitting there along the wall at the meeting, it was hard for my mom not to notice his dark, wavy hair and all around good-lookingness. My father carried himself with a confidence that drew people in. My brother TJ called it something like being a man of the people, someone who could converse with anyone, anywhere, about anything. My mother's green eyes must have met my father's at some point, and they hit it off and were soon seeing each other. Daddy had a tiny bit of a lisp, my mom says, though I can't remember this about him at all.

(Random fact: Only two percent of the world's population have green eyes!)

They found they had a lot of mutual friends who were also protesting the war and getting into the music scene. Daddy had a little Volkswagen Bug at the time, and according to his college friend Dick Losh, "Ed was the man with the resources" back then, giving everybody rides in that Volkswagen. My mother, on the other hand, found it challenging to make

This Week On Campus

Students for Liberal Action, in conjunction with the Williamsburg-James City County League of Women Voters, are co-sponsoring a voter registration drive tomorrow.

Any students interested in helping should meet at 1 p. m. in Room D of the Campus Center. Students who own cars are specifically urged to help.

Students for Liberal Action (SLA) meetings listed in *The Flat Hat*, William & Mary's campus newspaper out in the backseat with a six-foot-tall man. For work on the side, Daddy was the night check-in guy at a motel.

While drinking was a huge part of their relationship from the very start, my mother conveys just how much the music and experience of being part of a movement were integral to their bond. Not to mention, they were bolstered by mutual friendships.

"Our friends were all partying like we did and felt the same way, politically. There was no isolation or feeling that we were different or outcast. We were part of the new world order," she continues, quoting Jim Morrison. "It was like, 'We want the world, and we want it NOW!'" (For any conspiracists, "new world order" in this context was often used to refer to "revolution" and counterculture in the 1960s.)

The summer of 1966, after my mother graduated from William & Mary, she and my father and their good friend Steve Skinner shared a cozy apartment on Richmond Road in Williamsburg.

"It had a little balcony," she reminisces. "You could sit out there and take the air. It wasn't that huge of a place, but we made out. Ed worked all night, but whenever he was off, we stayed up all night and played gin rummy and listened to the wonderful '60s music that was out—Bob Dylan, the Rolling Stones. Everything on record players, of course."

My mom will never forget the day my paternal grandparents came storming in. My Grandfather Clay's words still echo in her ears all these years later. *"Y'all are livin' like white niggahs!"*

It's still inconceivable to me just how blasphemous it was for a couple of unwed college kids to shack up in 1966 in Williamsburg. But my grandfather's response was a stark reminder of just how big the gap was between generations—or at least between my grandparents and the hippie culture my mom and dad were becoming a part of. In fact, the term "generation gap" was coined in the '60s to describe that very phenomenon of distance between the beliefs and cultural norms ascribed to by young people vs. their parents. Incidentally, my mother's parents were equally conservative, though not in the Southern way, and were none too pleased either with the freewheeling lifestyle on the horizon.

People of their generation and upbringing were still very much about appearances, reputation, and propriety. My parents, on the other hand, didn't live under that guise at all. Living together was a total non-issue; they had no self-consciousness about it. The notion of living in sin—whether sin of the deeply religious kind or sin of the "don't-make-us-look-bad" kind—meant nothing to them. Sin itself didn't even register.

Contemplating that gaping divide, I always had it as mere coincidence that my grandparents on both sides were particularly conservative and against the union of my parents. It has taken a lot of thought and reflection for me to recognize just how radically different things were for parents of that era whose children were of the counterculture. The psychological limitations of my grandparents—that inability for them to grasp or relate to what was happening with hippies and the Civil Rights movement and anti-Vietnam War activism—accentuated by a desperate need to hold on to the last vestiges of 1950's wholesomeness must've been excruciating. In less than two decades, my grandparents would have heard the swoony melodies of their day turn into loud rock-n-roll and protest songs. Suddenly, music took on all kinds of meaning that would expose any shallow, smarminess of previous generations, and all those nice-looking kids with crewcuts would soon become long-haired, bearded hippies smoking weed. Talk about beyond their command—an old world rapidly aging. I'm sure it was all a bit much.

When I try to relate to their parental freak-out, I reckon it's something akin to when I'm having a batshitcrazymom day, like when my son locked himself in his room the night he was supposed to go for his Boy Scout rank interview and I had a deadline and it was the holidays and I'd had about enough of this bullshit and my husband's, too, for that matter, so fuck this and I kicked the door in. Oh yeah, totally, I muse, in retrospect, I can pretty much see why any mom of any generation did any crazy-ass thing, like storming into the Williamsburg apartment to break up that hippie love fest and pot-smoking den of sin. Or in the case of my maternal grandmother, changing the wedding date in the date book so everyone would think the grandchild (me) had been born after marriage, not out of wedlock—as if anybody ever went back through the date book and gave half a shit.

In addition to their respective conservative upbringings, I have also pointed out to my mother that she and my father were both the firstborn children of three siblings and came from families where they were never accepted for who they were. There must've been something about that, and the perfect storm that was the 1960s, but it's nothing that she or my father recognized during their time together.

Botched elopement

When my mother went off to Europe for a few weeks at the end of the summer of '66, she realized just how much she had fallen for my father. On her return in September, she landed a job as a teacher's assistant at an elementary school, and she and my father got their own place together. By spring of 1967, there was some talk about getting married, although my mother says they weren't sure how to go about it. In Virginia, you had to get a blood test, and there was a waiting period she thinks had something to do with disease. So instead, they hopped in Daddy's car and went off to North Carolina to get married, but when they got there, everything was closed. "Besides, we were both drunk and had driven all night, so that fell through," she says.

Sitting across the table from my mother at a cafe in Wayne, Pennsylvania, I'm hearing this chronological telling of my parents' early life together for the first time. I'm on my second latte, hanging on her every word. I had heard bits and pieces, highlights, my father's version of something or my mother's telling of the same. But now that I'm getting this collective history, I realize for the first time just how much I long to give voice to what they had as a couple before I came along, and before the other marriage and kids. It's as though everything that happened between my parents was discounted because we were the divorced ones, my mother and me. My experience and understanding of their life together were suppressed for the sake of his other family, not because anybody made me do that, but it just seemed like that's what had to be done. Only between themselves and with me could they exchange stories, laughs, and memories.

To even put the words down, I have to summon courage from places I've never had to before to let my own experience and knowledge of my parents and their lives and my birth be freely expressed without hesitation or concern for how it might affect anybody else. Maybe it matters far less to others and is merely the residual concern of a child who learned to be careful about such things from an early age—fearful of offending, of creating jealousy or strife, of rocking the boat more than it was already being rocked.

After their botched elopement, my mother says she and my father started to drift apart. He had become good friends with Dick Losh, and a lot of drugs started entering the picture, according to my mom.

"I was feeling frozen out," she says.

Leaving the cuckoo's nest

"I was able to find Dick Losh to interview for the book." I'm bubbling on the phone, excited to share with my brother Jeffrey. "You know, Daddy's friend in Colorado."

"Who?"

"Dick Losh, you know, they rode motorcycles across the country to California together."

"Never heard of him."

"Wow." I'm trying to process how it is that my youngest brother doesn't know who Dick Losh is, given that my father was still traversing the country by thumb and stopping off in Colorado in his later years. "Well, they were the best of friends for like 50 years."

Surely, Daddy would have mentioned him at some point. I'm guessing if the stories were to start coming out, "the guy he lived with in Maine in the same town you live in," for example, there would be some recognition, but that earlier chapter was left untold or unasked about. I can't tell which. And maybe it doesn't matter anyway, except it's the part I came from.

Which makes my conversation with Dick, a personal injury attorney in Denver, even more satisfying. Dick Losh. A name I grew up with. His name would come up when my mom and I were visiting mutual friends when I was a kid. Or in later years, my grandmother would mention he had called her house asking for my father. A connection. Someone who tied us all together, even though we weren't together anymore.

Dick launches into earliest memories of first meeting my father. "Your father had the coolest record collection of anyone I'd ever met.

Donovan's *Universal Soldier*. Rolling Stones. Ed knew more about music and the counterculture of the day than anyone else I spoke with. He was up to date on everything, from the lyrics to songs by Dylan and the Stones, the Beatles and so many others, all the way to the important issues of the time, as expressed by various groups of folks speaking out against the government."

Dick lists civil rights activists down the line. The Student Nonviolent Coordinating Committee (SNCC) with Stokely Carmichael, H. Rap Brown, the Black Panthers, Eldridge Cleaver, Angela Davis, and the Chicago Seven, who were arrested during the 1968 Democratic National Convention for stoking anti-Vietnam war protest in Chicago. Renowned activists Abbie Hoffman and Jerry Rubin, along with David Dellinger, Rennie Davis, Tom Hayden, John Froines, and Lee Weiner were brought to trial for crossing state lines to incite riot and countercultural protests against the Vietnam War, among other things. (The Netflix original *The Trial of the Chicago 7*, out in 2020, tells the story.) Ultimately, all convictions were reversed on appeal.

Rennie Davis, one of the seven, died in February 2021. My parents were good friends with his brother Bob and wife Lynne.

"Your father definitely had his ear tuned to what was happening," Dick continues. "Besides that, he was just a lot of fun to talk to and joke around with. He was generous to a fault, and a very good person."

Here, Dick recalls, just as my mother had mentioned, my father had a lisp. "It may have been something that held him back a bit."

At the time they were all in college at William & Mary together, the dean of the school was Carson Barnes, a relative of my father on my grandmother's side.

"He didn't care much for me," Dick says, telling the story about how he and his buddy were wrestling outside the girls' dorm when the campus cops came along and busted them. "My buddy was graduating, going into the military, and I was in summer school. The dean told me not to come back on campus, but I told him I still had to come back to take a literature class and final exams." Dick quit school after that.

The streets of Williamsburg were also a bit of a drag.

"We were kind of bad boys, always getting hassled by the cops. I got busted and went to jail for sitting on the curb with a Black gal named

Maria (who lived with Mary Renfro and her boyfriend Rick). Maria was also a committed virgin who didn't want any romantic relationships. All I wanted to do was sit and talk to her, and the cops couldn't stand it." (My mother remained friends for many years with Mary Renfro, who passed away in 2008 from leukemia.)

Sometime after leaving school, Dick joined up with my father, who by then was working at Eastern State Hospital in Williamsburg, where my grandmother was a psychiatric nurse.

"We were psychiatric attendants, wore the white uniforms, had a wad of keys, the whole deal. People were in locked wards, and you had to restrain them and put them in seclusion, in straightjackets. It was shock treatments galore. This was before privacy as well. Some you'd meet on the street, you'd think they were normal."

This is the first time I'm hearing details of the hospital stint and the basement apartment Dick and my father ended up sharing in Williamsburg. The guy upstairs' father was one of the founders of Colonial Williamsburg.

"The landlord would try to lure us with a cheap six-pack of beer and some hot dogs and eggs," Dick laughs. "The old boy was nuts, but we put up with him."

Late at night, Dick and my father would come home cracking up about things that went on in the hospital.

"I'd be mopping floors, and some people would be walking around all night like zombies. There was one fella standing there in his mid-20s, doofy as they come, whether from meds they had him on or from an underlying disorder, and he would say, '11,000'—and he'd have this huge grin on his face. We were always wondering, 11,000 what? Money? 11,000 what?!"

Published in 1962, Ken Kesey's *One Flew Over the Cuckoo's Nest* provided a glimpse into the world of mental institutions of that era and the use of electroshock therapy—particularly for schizophrenia—although it was often used as a fear and control tactic on other patients because it would induce convulsions. Today, electroconvulsive therapy or ECT has been modified but is still effective in treating certain behavioral and mental health disorders.

In the '60s, talk therapy had barely emerged, and the only other option was for patients to be totally doped up. Dick conjures the memory of a guy who looked like Gollum from *Lord of the Rings*. "Talking to himself nonstop, up and down the halls, driving people crazy. 'I'd do like Primo Carnera,' he'd say, referring to this prize fighter, 'right across the jaw!' He wouldn't shut up, so they doped him up on meds just like the movie. Another tiny guy was totally mentally deranged and breaking out of restraints and slashing his own throat. They shocked him a bunch of times. I saw one ECT that really worked, a guy who had slashed his own throat. It brought him back from being suicidal."

I imagine my father having borne witness to all of this, more horrifically real perhaps than the story about pushing a guy out a third-floor window in San Francisco after having a box-cutter held to his throat.

When I contacted the San Francisco police and requested any reports with my father's name or myriad addresses going back to 1998 (presumably this scuffle was in his uber-vagabond later years), I was unable to verify the tale. But slashed throats in a mental institution? My admiration swells.

With the previous arrest charge from fraternizing with a Black woman, plus the draft coming after him since

Students Write To Dean Rusk

To the Editor:

A William and Mary student has written the following letter to Secretary of State Dean Rusk:

"Dear Sir: As a student at the College of William and Mary, Williamsburg, Virginia, I noted with interest your scheduled 'Prelude to Independence Address' here in Williamsburg, on May 28, 1966.

I am among not a few students dissatisfied with what appears to us to be the hypocritical tenor of the United States government's policies, both foreign and domestic, but principally the first.

We wonder, what is your opinion of genuine public protest? We are not interested in histrionics nor in harrassment, but in demonstrating our concern for the present and future of the world you will leave us.

Would you object to an orderly demonstration at your speech in protest of our policy in Viet Nam? Have you concrete suggestions regarding such a protest? This means, most importantly for us, would you be able and willing to speak to students here in the College, to discuss our objections?

Thank you. Sincerely, Mary Ellen Wilkinson."

We are interested in activating student opinion on this matter. Essential to any consensus is the free expression of students' views, and we hope the student body will respond with serious deliberation.

Mary Renfro
Steven Skinner
Mary Ellen Wilkinson
Phyllis Morse
Stephen H. Snell
Wendy Fairbank

Letter to William & Mary dean, from friends of my parents

he'd dropped out of school, Dick says, "We were feeling like outcasts, culturally disenchanted. Neither of us could stand the thought of going back to our hometowns, and the Williamsburg stuff seemed so picayune. We needed to strike out and have new experiences."

They decided they needed to go out to San Francisco and check out the hippie scene.

The abandoned Chronicle Hotel at 934 Mission Street between 5th and 6th Streets in the South of Market neighborhood of San Francisco. Source: Beyond My Ken, CC BY-SA 4.0, via Wikimedia Commons

---

On October 2nd, 1967 at 8:30 am a broke and weary motorcyclist from Virginia rode into Tenderloin, mailed a $50

Western Union check, ate a $1.50 Chinese lunch, checked into the Chronicle Hotel, and embarked on a 'new life.' There were tomatoes to be picked in Milpitas if you could stand the ride; easy 50 miles southeast but everyone came back tired and drunk and $8.00 to $20.00 wealthier. This was the land of opportunity for an undereducated, draft-eligible, ex-student, ex-psychiatric attendant, ex-Vista reporter, ex-motel manager, and ex-boyfriend. Fifty-five weeks later, a child to be famous got lucky anyway. To her I write.

— April 1992

While digging through letters from my father, I ask my mom to see if she has any left. I'm thinking one or two would be cool, just to see how he wrote when he was younger and what window it would provide into who he was at that time. One day on the phone with me, my Mother the Organizer (who saves every goddamn thing under the sun, alphabetically, chronologically, anal-retentively, like the perpetual Virgo that she is) announces she has found some letters my father wrote to her. In fact (no surprise) they're filed in chronological order, going all the way back to 1965, when my father first wrote to her on Christmas break from college. The letters, my mother reports, continue up through 1978, when I would have been about 10 years old. I vow never to hassle my mother again about saving too much crap around the house.

In what must have been the first missive my father ever wrote to my mom, Daddy was chatty. "Getting a haircut Saturday but please don't follow suit and destroy those flowing strands," referring to my mother's beautiful, long dark hair. He was writing "to the sound of Bach's concerto in C Minor." (Was he trying to impress her, I wonder, or did he always have Bach playing in the background?) In another letter when my mom was away in Germany, Daddy wrote of tough times he was going through. His Uncle Cecil had been shot down in an Air Force transport plane over Formosa en route from Saigon. There was no trace of him or the other four men in the wreckage. (A news clipping I have in my possession from my Grandfather Clay's things years later has a photo of Uncle Cecil, and the headline reads: "Sgt. Clay Made the Greatest Sacrifice - Harrellsville man served in two wars before losing life.") Mom and Daddy's roommate Steve Skinner was dealing with his own heavy blow, having just found out his mother had been diagnosed with a malignant lump in her left breast. Not to mention, the landlord had leukemia and could die at any time. My father and Steve were both pining for my mother to come back.

Annie, I miss you very much; if you cannot locate me in town early next year—check the alcoholics' ward at Eastern State Hospital. I am filled with grief and loneliness which I cannot describe, I now close. I love you, Ed

four
love-haight
relationship

"The one thing we can never get enough of is love. And the one thing we never give enough of is love."
— Henry Miller

My mom remembers my father and Dick Losh leaving for San Francisco. She had just left her elementary school teaching job in the summer of 1967 and gotten a job teaching in Newport News. My father took her all dressed up for the job interview on the back of his motorcycle. When she landed the position, my Grandfather Clay, who was a car salesman, got her a Chevrolet so she could get back and forth to Williamsburg.

I have never imagined my parents doing such mundane things together, just going about daily life. It was always tales of outdoor concerts in Golden Gate Park or the drunk agnostic priest at the wedding or the woman who tried to kidnap me at the Altamont Speedway Free Festival. I wonder how my mother and father got along during those other times. Were they ever good together, in spite of the drinking?

"I gave your father some kind of girdle for riding long distances," my mother recalls, of seeing the guys off on their respective Harleys. "I was really smitten. I didn't like my new teaching job much either."

As they made their way out west, my father and Dick camped out at night along the side of the road, then bounced up early each morning, packed up, and kept going. Young, free, and California-bound. My mind fills in the gaps, imagining my freewheeling father before my mother showed up a month later on his doorstep in San Francisco. Whatever Dick might have known about that, he didn't say.

"I wasn't nosey with him and he wasn't nosey with me, and that's probably why we got along so well. For the most part, I think he was genuine, although he had an evasive side to him if you got a little too personal or he wanted to keep certain things to himself."

Dick reminisces about getting a job at the Harley-Davidson place in San Francisco.

"One of the best jobs in my life," he says.

Harley-Davidson delivered printed matter around town, so every day, Dick waited on the sidewalk for when other drivers reported in sick or hungover.

"I'd get to ride a trike-wheel Harley all over the city and get paid at the end of the day, then I'd stop at the grocery store and have a taco or whatever."

Sometime in November of 1967, my mother decided to use her teacher days to book a flight to San Francisco. She arrived—unannounced—at my father's address with all of her luggage.

"I just camped out on his doorstep and waited for him to come home from work, I guess," she chortles, as only my mother can do at her own inanity. "He was happy to see me, but it was apparent he had been having a relationship with some 15-year-old girl who shot amphetamines in her legs."

From here on my mother always calls her "The 15-year-old Who Shot Amphetamines in Her Legs." Nonetheless, my father and mother spent a "riotous and amorous weekend" together. My mother called into school on Monday to say she was hung up and couldn't get back on time, that she'd get another flight the next day.

"I was totally miserable and in love—and drinking heavily."

Back in Williamsburg, Mom tried to hitchhike out to California one night, inebriated, but it didn't go well.

Then a letter arrived from San Francisco dated December 15th in which Daddy reports he's been turned on for four straight nights with "real groovy grass," possibly referring to Numero Uno, my mother elaborates, a particularly strong marijuana that was going around at the time.

"Half a joint annihilates the normal skull," Daddy wrote, also musing about goddesses, walruses, padres (his parents), sis (my Aunt Sally, who was in a horrible, abusive relationship), cold, and *mulla*.

Writing of the San Francisco music scene, he'd heard live bands like The Byrds, Electric Flag, B.B. King, The Chambers Brothers, and Tim Buckley. He was reading Rod McKuen and sent along a quote from Richard Fariña, singer/songwriter and author of *Been Down So Long It Looks Like Up to Me*, the cult classic that spoke to a generation of hippie college students who shirked that which came before.

I'd heard music like "Bold Marauder" by Richard Fariña and his wife Mimi (whose sister is Joan Baez) on those long-lost tapes I discovered at my mom's house when I was a kid. Curious now to see what was speaking to my father at the time, I look up the book online. The back cover of the Four Square / New English Library 1968 edition reads:

"This book is like a trip on LSD: a wild, irreverent, sexy joyride through the world of the Hippies.

Meet Gnossos. Who's Gnossos? He's a long-haired, pot-smoking hipster who loathes convention, seeks for kicks, lusts for girls— and never for a moment stops playing it cool.

This comic work of genius which has become an Underground classic and is now published in Britain for the first time, really tells it how it is, baby!"

My father's own lusting for girls may have discouraged my mother from coming for the holidays: "Too goddamned much money to squander to visit someone who is virtually oblivious to his past."

Hint one—but my mother missed or chose to ignore it.

Too stoned to write more, Daddy mentioned riots on campuses all over California, mused whether dolphins were more intelligent than humans, and left my mother with a poem about stallions.

Another letter arrived in January.

January 21, 1968.

"Hippie Hill Poem"

Long drums
25 black Africans
Dogs
Prostrate bodies of stoned people
Warm sun more striking than golden cheese
My own head a whirling cistern
I am hopelessly transfixed—I cannot hope to move
More than 1000 heads sprawled on the soft green about
    the hill

Paralized as such, I will endeavor to write you, saying only what must be said.

My father was writing to let my mom know that his mother would be coming out in seven days, on the 28th, and would be staying at his apartment for four to six weeks. There's no way my mom could come at the same time, and he told her she should wait until March.

De-selective Service

As I read this aloud sitting across from my mother, I'm like, "How on earth is he going to get it together in seven days?" Just knowing my father's drinking habits in later years, I can't imagine this coming to fruition in the earlier ones. "And how on earth is he going to keep it together for six weeks?"

"Just wait till you read the next page," says my mother. "You have no idea."

My mother had already had her taste of his parents' disapproval of the relationship back in Williamsburg, and my paternal grandparents had already gone to great lengths to get her own parents involved several times around whatever impropriety was seriously yanking their chain. So, my mother wasn't exactly advertising the fact she was going out to San Francisco, and my father sure wasn't letting anyone know.

17 days later another letter arrives. It reads:

Better shed any evidence you happen to have around of grass. Grizzly scene here. My mother went snooping into every nook and cranny of the apartment; read nine letters, all from Dick [Losh] and you, as well as discovering the jar of seeds and stems (which I destroyed immediately). You know, and no doubt, have felt the repercussions of her discovery. She called the Oakland Examination...my file is being mailed to my father. Jesus on a crutch! I suspect apartment will be placed under surveillance and I will be recalled by the SS [Selective Service] for another examination. I am feeling mildly suicidal. If I can beat this rag, I am going to vanish— from everyone. No one, especially my parents, will ever know of my whereabouts, and I'll have another name. I pray to God (whatever he is) that you have not been nabbed for posses- sion; destroy this instantly after reading! Letters are more lethal than napalm.

Baby - you cannot return to S.F. If our current rela- tionship continues it will destroy us both—or me anyhow; my parents would readily clamp either of us behind bars to stop it. My mother implies that she has had my father notify your parents. I'm sorry.

You know how I laughed off the physical [SS] as if I had put something over on them. In truth, I didn't. I have been

ridden with guilt, drugs, booze, hang-ups and us for so long
that I really AM as I told the shrink.

My father had fucked himself up with LSD and alcohol the day he
went for the draft exam. This was one of the few ways to effectively resist
the draft in 1967. Otherwise, you'd have to be an undergraduate student
still in school, be on the police force or studying or serving in the
medical field, or be a married man with dependent children. Clearly, my
father was going for "Classification 4-F, Registrant not qualified for
military service." He must've panicked at the idea of those Selective
Service notes about his mental and physical state getting into the hands
of his father. He could see the whole crazy-ass world of it crashing
down, feeling—as indicated in the letter—as though he really was as
fucked up in real life as he'd made himself out to be for the draft board
in Oakland.

Incidentally, when I was about a year old, Richard Nixon signed an
amendment to the Military Selective Service Act of 1967, which began
the first-ever draft lottery from which young men's names were
randomly picked by birth date and year. My father's number could well
have come up and he'd have been selected for military service. So as
much as my birth in 1968 interrupted the flow of his young life, perhaps
it also helped save it.

Thirty years later I would voluntarily enter Vietnam, traveling overland from the border of Cambodia and catching a taxi into Saigon with
an American guy who sprinted for the same ride. We ended up traveling
around the Mekong Delta and throughout South Vietnam for 10 days,
being gawked and smiled at, treated kindly by the South Vietnamese,
and spending one unforgettable evening dancing in the streets of Chau
Doc to Santana tunes with a toothless Vietnamese grandmother and a
shirtless, big-bellied, happy Buddha dude. At the museum in Saigon, I
learned that in Vietnam they call it "the American War."

The Selective Service website indicates that all files, other than draft
registration cards and classification history, from prior to 1976 have
been destroyed. "Physical examination and test results, medical letters,
laboratory work and other medical documentation that may have been

included in these files no longer exist." Dang. What I wouldn't give to read my father's Selective Service files from 1967! I wonder what it was like when my grandfather received them in the mail. Oh man. I wish my grandmother was here right now. I'd have some things to ask her, and I know we'd be laughing our looney heads off.

It's still hard to imagine how real the stress and panic would have been for my father. Not just the draft-dodging, but the parents, the pot, the perceived danger to way of life. After all, marijuana is now medically legal in 33 states and recreationally legal in 12 as well as Washington, D.C. In 2020, most people surveyed seem to be in favor of recreational use in general. Let alone that LSD is making a comeback in psychedelic psychotherapy circles, and psilocybin (mushrooms) could well be on the verge of becoming mainstream mental health medicine.

But in 1968?

Back then, the Boggs Act of 1952 and the Narcotics Control Act of 1956 were still in place, making first-time possession of pot punishable by ten years in prison and up to $20,000 in fines. Let alone the atmosphere in our country was hyper-charged with protests, riots, and dissent. Across the bridge in Oakland, the newly formed Black Panther Party for Self Defense had amassed 2,000 members who were standing for their right to protect themselves against the police. That very February at South Carolina State, 33 activists were shot by local cops, and three of them were killed. Still at the helm of the FBI was the ever-paranoid and shit-swirling J. Edgar Hoover, going after any person or group he deemed the least bit subversive, using covert and often illegal tactics like wiretapping to expose everyone from Martin Luther King to Bobby Kennedy.

January 1968 had also seen the Tet Offensive, when the North Vietnamese and Viet Cong launched a series of devastating military attacks on South Vietnam. Although it ultimately helped turn the tide of American opinion about the war, at the time the mood was one of shock and horror. In my father's mind, and quite realistically, if he had been plucked out as a draft dodger, it could have meant being picked up by the U.S. Marshals or the FBI, being interrogated and investigated, and ultimately left with the abysmal option of jail time or going to Vietnam after all. Add to all of that, my grandparents—in their own "reefer madness"—could have had my father put in jail. That's how insane it all was.

Following fate

Daddy went on to say that he would never be able to work things out as long as my mother kept following him.

> You know that I wanted things to be different between us in the long run but there were too many obstacles for my mind to dispel. Too much of your life was behind you. I constantly changed in attitudes and preferences. Try as I might, I could never disregard your past. I loved you and wanted to make you my wife more than anything else in the world. At the same time, I knew I would never fully trust or respect you; petty arguments would always lead to my denunciation of your character and freewheeling affairs before I met you.
>
> Annie - you have tried so hard to be good to me. I know how much you love me. I know that I could search forever and never discover the joy I have found with you. This is not the important thing. What is necessary is that you not return to me. If you find you must, I will depart when you arrive. If I did differently, I would surely cast off the last remaining crumb of my sanity.

(Hint Number Two, loud and clear.)

> There is no more to say except maybe a few lines from the poem you quoted on the back of your picture when you left for Europe so long ago:
>
> For if the darkness and corruption leave/

A vestige of the thoughts that once I had/
Better by far you should forget and smile/
Than that you should remember and be sad.'

Forgive me. Love always, Ed

I recognize the familiar lines. I'd heard my mother recite them on one of those homemade cassette tapes but never knew the context until now. Nor had I known the import of the Christina Rosetti poetry books from the '60s with pages falling out at the seams, treasures that have been in my possession for years, which were once "theirs."

Despite my father's protests, my mother showed up some time in February 1968, and I was thus conceived.

But I notice something I never have before. I always perceived my mother as chasing my father and somehow holding him back—granted, a girl with a baby on the way could well do that—in this pivotal moment where my father was seriously on the verge of a nervous breakdown. I also see how much of a grip my father's parents had on his psyche and how much control they still exerted on his life at that time. He seemed so conflicted about all of it. To me, it's as though he's just trying to push my mom away along with the rest of it, regardless of what might have been there between them.

My grandmother and I did talk about these things in later years. We often laughed about so much family drama.

"Why did your mother have to follow him out there?" she would sometimes pose to me in her Virginia-accented, sing-songy way. "Gee!" she'd exhale, followed by a giggle.

I'd roll my eyes at her and shake my head, shrugging my shoulders, like how am I supposed to know? I would remind her of the absurdity of her question and answer something along the lines of without them (my father and mother) we wouldn't have me, and then we wouldn't have my stepmother Leia and the other kids and all of that. And then we'd both crack up because it was all water under a sorry-ass bridge by that time.

But through this particular lens, I see for the first time just how hell-bent my grandmother was on excising my mother from my father's life.

I'd heard it from my mother's point of view, but in Daddy's letters, it's potent.

Take another little piece

Even though she decided to stay in San Francisco and not return East, my mother saw that she would never be able to have my father.

"He was off philandering," she says, though with Daddy at barely 20 years old, and considering she'd shown up on his doorstep—twice—with what sounds like no particular agreements or allegiances between them, I'm not sure I'd even call it that. My mother brings up The 15-Year-Old Girl Who Shot Amphetamines in Her Legs, and of course there were others.

So, my mom—even though it was never her intention to entrap my father—quit taking her birth control pills. She found out she was pregnant in April when Daddy took her to the emergency room with stomach pain.

Now mind you, I've always known I wasn't quite in my father's plans, but for some reason this particular telling of the story hits me squarely, like "Holy Shit, Mother, you really abbreviated his whole life."

It's not something I internalize or feel guilty about, knowing how much my father loved me, but *damn*! It's like: *That was the fucking end of it right there.* My eyes start burning and I almost can't bring myself to ask her the question.

"So—" Tears are streaming down my face now, and the pit of my stomach grows rock hard from the outside in. "Did you ever feel responsible for having...you know...preventing him from becoming who he could have become?"

The great thing about my mom is that she's done a lot of work on herself, not to mention she's more than 35 years sober, so she's forthcoming about things. She seems eager to respond to my question.

"The influence I had on him was very much a denigration of him being able to express himself," she says, "with the caveat that the alcohol and the drug use was his choice and that colored what he chose to do with his life." She goes on to say that when she did her AA Ninth Step work with him—which involves making amends to people you've harmed not only by taking responsibility for past actions but by setting things right for the future by not doing or being that anymore—"I came really straight with him about my part in hijacking his life and I took responsibility for that, because I'm a little bit older and I was a little more clear-headed. That's when he laughed and said, 'Oh, I don't live in the past.'" My mother and I both roll our eyes and snort, even now. My father was always living in the past, especially when he'd been drinking.

My mother also points to her own emotional damage, partly because she'd had a brain injury from a car accident in 1962 when she was just 18 years old. She was in a coma for nine days.

"One of the ways it affected me was a real inability to make rational decisions for my own welfare, so I was pretty mixed up. I craved him, but I felt like we were drifting apart and there was nothing I could do. I didn't want to hold onto him, I just wanted a piece of him," she says, leaning in across the table and giving me a loving smile, "which was you."

In my mother's retelling of this story, I recognize my emotional stinginess. My mother during pregnancy was mostly alone, impoverished, homeless for a time even, and fending for herself, which is where my sympathy should lie, but somehow, I'm still unwilling to grant her that. I'm hung up on my father having no say in the matter of becoming a liable parent.

For a short time thereafter, Mom and Daddy moved in with two gay guys who were friends of theirs, but the living situation fell apart along with the relationship. My father pulled away and was just no longer around for my mom. Broke and homeless, she started living in her car at Ocean Beach.

"I'd wake up every morning to the grinning Chicanos in the windows." I've heard her share the story many times. She would use the public bathrooms to get cleaned up before going to work as a bartender at the Witches' Brew right there near the end of Golden Gate Park.

"I was a clean hippie," she used to tell me. "I shaved and took showers, and I had no interest in living with a bunch of other people. I was too freewheeling and freethinking." She also realized being pregnant on her own and living in her car, the only person she could trust at that point was herself.

But then a letter arrived at my mother's General Delivery mailbox in San Francisco from my father's address at 728 Cole Street in the Haight. It was dated July 22, 1968:

If I do not hear from you by Tuesday nite (July 23rd) I will assume you do not wish to contact me at all. If not, I plan to cut out of San Fran for good Wednesday. — Always, Ed

I can't help but wonder—had he expected her to make contact while she was expecting the same from him? By now it had been about three months without each other.

July 29, 1968
"If you wish to get together for dinner, talk or anything —I'll be at the intersection of Van Ness & Market (Bank of America) at 7 PM tonight (Thursday). I'll wait 15-20 minutes. Love, Ed"

Rereading this message, I'm reminded of how we used to make plans with people before the advent of cell phones. I'm amazed further still that a letter could indicate a meeting time the same day, but perhaps he had mailed it the day before or left it at the bar or something. Either way, this must've been the beginning of their reconciliation. But why didn't my mother ever express her concerns to him about the relationship? When they met up at Van Ness and Market and went walking and talking, didn't she say anything about how he had abandoned her and she was afraid he would never be reliable?

Nope.

She didn't. But back then, *people* didn't. There wasn't language for it. Psychology was a new field. People didn't openly talk about their internal state and emotions. There weren't talk shows and ways of working through things like we do nowadays. Yet at the same time, in my father's letters from that era, I sometimes see greater introspection, insightfulness and self-expression than my mother seems to have been capable of at the time.

Late summer, my father moved in with my mother, who by then lived in the Sunset District on 35th Avenue near Judah Street in the first-floor apartment of Jim Macfarlan, a good friend from the Witches' Brew. Jim had generously offered up his garage to my mom out of concern for her living situation, then invited her to move to the first floor to be better situated when I was born. Jim moved from the first floor up to the second with another roommate to give her and my father the space below.

Hippie crib in the hippie crib at Jim Macfarlan's place

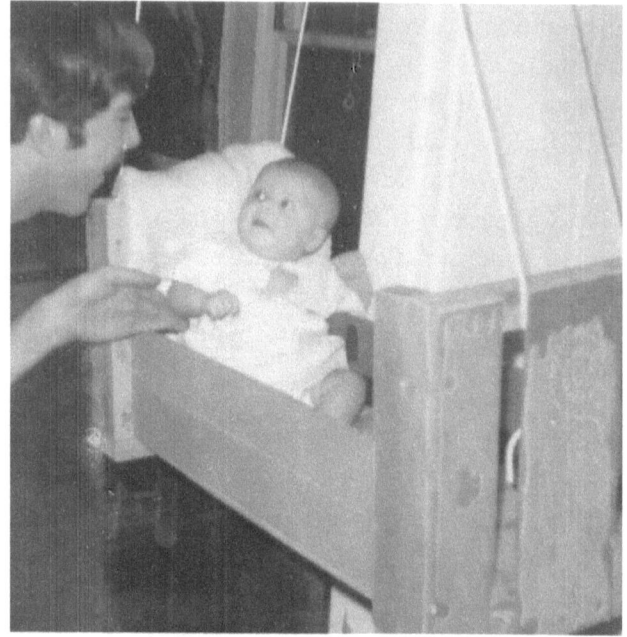

Hanging crate-turned-cradle

Letter addressed to my mother at 1327 35th Ave in San Francisco from Daddy, when he went home to Williamsburg for a visit:

August 19, 1968

Annie - the damned plane just would not crash. Bad scene here. Going to Salisbury Tuesday. Virginia is hot and people too much. Can't wait to get back. Hope all is well. Love, Ed

Once upon a family

In my baby book, an envelope held with triangular black tabs at each corner reads "Eve of Reproduction," my father's cursive playing on words from the popular '60s protest song about the Eastern world exploding on the eve of destruction.

My mother had already been in labor with me for 24 hours, having undergone an episiotomy and subsisting on a diet of ice chips, the only thing they would give her to eat. Men weren't allowed in the delivery room at the time, so my father waited it out at a bar somewhere, marinating himself in preparation for fatherhood.

Dearest Annie,

At present I can say little except that you fill every one of my thoughts. I suffer mentally whenever I dwell on your physical suffering. Christ! 24 hours of LABOR! I sat up all last night, smoked, and finished 'Been Down So Long It Looks Like Up to Me' and that perfectly describes my mental state.

He apologized for the pain she must endure, which he was—"partwise, at least"—responsible for. It would be another 16 hours before I was born at 9:53 p.m. on Monday, October 21, 1968, at San Francisco General Hospital. My mother was 25 years old and my father, just 21. *Twenty-one.* (Now that I'm in my 50s, it dawns on me that my parents are never that much older than I am at any given point.)

A few years back, I was getting energy work done with a practitioner who would tune into my body and my being to see where and when things like fear or concern had gotten stuck. Blocked energy, as it were. It may sound a bit voodoo, but if you believe in electricity, you can believe in the idea of energy in the body and how emotions and experiences get "trapped" in our cells.

Baby Me with Mama and Daddy in San Francisco

She would "read" me over the phone, muttering all the while to Spirit. Every once in a while, she'd go, "No, that's not it," and keep going. Then she'd land on something and declare, "That's it, there it is." It wasn't my two-year-old self or even the trauma of birth where things had gotten stuck. It was the moment of conception.

"You're holding onto some fear your mother had at that time," she said. "You carry 20 to 22 percent of your mother's regret energy from nine months (conception) to 12 hours after birth."

"She was afraid he was gonna leave," I confirmed. "Actually, she already expected he was gonna leave, based on what was happening."

"Alright, let's clear that."

And then she'd do her thing. If you imagine what it's like for a muscle to relax, like just melt and let go—that's the kind of work we did on an energetic level.

Big Sur

Six weeks after I was born, my mother took me back to San Francisco General to have my ears pierced. That's the way it was done back then. A baby gift list written in my mother's hand includes "gold stud earrings from Daddy."

Also in my mother's handwriting in my baby book, under the Travel Log section that reads: "Places I have been," she lists, in addition to a downtown San Francisco streetcar at 10 days, the Witches' Brew at 11 days, and Berkeley at two weeks, The Rolling Stones concert in Oakland on November 9, 1969, and Quicksilver Messenger Service with Daddy in August 1969.

Big Sur

When I was a baby, we three took camping trips to the Russian River and the Oregon Coast and down to Big Sur. We went to free concerts in Golden Gate Park, where Bay Area bands like the Grateful Dead, Quicksilver Messenger Service, Jefferson Airplane, and Big Brother and the Holding Company were often in the lineup. One time, my parents were seeing Janis Joplin and Big Brother and the Holding Company at Winterland or somewhere and Janis was just a few feet away from them during a break.

She holds her drink up and says, "Some bird shit in my drink!"

To which my father quipped, "Coulda' happened to anybody."

What was happening in San Francisco was permeating American youth culture, and my parents were right there in it. As Jill Katherine

Silos writes in *'Everybody get together': The sixties counterculture and public space, 1964-1967*:

> An equally important component of the content of the songs dealt with the experience of community in the Haight...The bands became acute observers and commentators on the world of the Haight and these songs chronicled the history and created the mythology of the community...

> These songs were political messages of a new kind. They spoke of a new way of envisioning daily life and privileged concerns about spiritual enlightenment and community over purely individual experiences. They traveled throughout the nation's hip communities to spread their messages, expanding the hippie presence in that way and contributing to the nation's public sphere.

Russian River

My first birthday

Love, peace, and marriage

The summer after I was born, my father landed in Tennessee for a job or to go back to school for something or other. The way my grandmother talked about it, you'd think he was on his way to something big and promising but was held back because of my mother and family life, as if he had no choice or he came back to us out of mere obligation.

Hardly, I say, when I read a letter dated July 25, 1969, from Knoxville:

> *My Dear Annie, Herein is the first letter I have penned in lunas multas that isn't a drug or booze-inspired collage of words spewed forth by a truly rotting imagination. Be out of here by Sunday, VA a day later, onto Fart (sic) Lauderdale and back to you and Kennerly. Busting out of the city, clearing the head, reading with an interest I never dreamed of, and shucking all past bullshit has allowed me to see past errors and the realities of the present, and finally, just what*

I am and can be, and what your life and mine and Kennerly's can be together if we put all we have into each other. I have developed, to me miraculously, in so brief a time and I know you will see the change. 'I threw it all away' - one of the deepest and most universal messages ever expressed by Dylan. I am so thankful you rejected the advances that were imminent and natural as soon as I left. For perhaps the first time, I see your goodness, your devotion, your intelligence, and we can make it together.

I want to hold you, kiss you, squeeze you, tease you and say all the things that have been unconsciously burning out my soul and guts for so long. Please be faithful because for you not to be now would destroy an awful big part of me. I am going to give you and Kennerly all I've got as long as I have it.

I should be there by the first week in August. Tell not a soul of our plans excepting Ma and Pa [my mother's parents]. I wrote Jim and Vicky and mentioned that I had proposed.

I miss you far more than you could possibly believe. I love you without equal.

Yours always, Ed

My parents got married in Golden Gate Park about a month later, on August 28, 1969. I heard many times of the drunken marital procession, "a total hippie scene trooping over to the park from our home in the Sunset," according to my mother, who was barefoot for most of her wedding day. A bunch of William & Mary friends who lived in California at the time were there, including Dick Losh of course, a couple named Chuck and Kathy Kilgore, and Bob and Lynne Davis, whom we often went down to visit in Monterey. Kathy and Lynne were sisters.

My parents' wedding in Golden Gate Park

In one of our email exchanges, Dick writes, "I don't know if your mother has told you, but in case she hasn't, I have to confess that I was the designated 'Bearer of the Wine Cup' at your parents' wedding in Golden Gate Park back in the 60s. It was a quite elegant and serious ceremony in an area of the park, which we revered and considered almost sacred back in the day."

Nobody came from back home, but my mother did invite Kitty and George, good friends of my mother's parents who lived across the Bay in Walnut Creek.

I was there, too, pushing 10 months old.

My mother's parents didn't know about me until spring of 1969, when my mother flew back to Maryland to privately tell my grandmother. My mom was certain my grandfather would have dragged her back home by her long, dark hair and forced her to give me up for adoption—had he known about me when my mother was pregnant—just like my paternal grandfather and my Aunt Sally and her baby. Though she was born just two months after I was, I wouldn't meet my first cousin, Kelly, until years later when she reconnected with us, her birth family. I tease her we were "womb mates" briefly when Aunt Sally was staying with my parents in San Francisco. I'm convinced that's why she feels a bit like a soul sister.

Instead of dragging my mother home, my grandfather kicked her out of the house. Against my mother's wishes, my grandmother had divulged the secret, that there was a baby. My grandfather put my mom on the next plane back to San Francisco.

Would it have mattered if my parents were married by then? Probably not. My mother imparted to me that even in later years, my grandfather would needle her with snide comments about having a bastard child in the family. This was never aimed at me, as I felt nothing but love from my grandfather. It was just his way of expressing his disapproval of her and the choices she had made.

Yet my mother heroically and unflinchingly forged her own way. She had no other choice than to be who she was.

When I ask her about getting married, insinuating that Daddy was "doing the right thing," according to Grandmother Clay, my mom is quick to correct me.

It was more like a good idea, she says. "We thought maybe it would be *easier*, if we were taking you home to meet the family back East."

As far as she and my father were concerned, appearances and doing the right thing were irrelevant. All of that was from a bygone era. It seems my father's mother had added to her own telling of the story to make it more palatable for herself. I could also hear her laughing out loud in retrospect because really, who the hell cared anymore? Besides, come to find out from my grandmother herself in the last decade of her life, she had been pregnant with my father before she and my grandfather married. They had a spring wedding, and he was born in October. Talk about taboo! Especially in their generation.

Over the years both my parents had shared fondly with me how they set off on their honeymoon to northern California only to realize how much they missed me. They ended up turning the car around and drove all the way back to San Francisco to pick me up from a friend who was babysitting, then set off again, heading north on Labor Day weekend, not having made reservations anywhere.

"I was driving all over northern California and we were both loaded as hell," says my mother unabashedly. "You were in the backseat, he was laid out drunk, and there was no room at the inn! We ended up driving back to San Francisco at five in the morning the next day."

Your mom and I went to Oakland Coliseum in October of 1969. Ike and Tina Revue opened for The Rolling Stones. You stayed at home with a babysitter, namely Gloria (G-L-O-R-I-A) Moganum. A wonderful girl about 19 at the time. Arabic and sexy. Her father owned the corner store. It was the only concert I ever went to without you. And I kept saying 'I wish she were here.'

[and in closing]

Thank you for loving a father who couldn't be there for you. And my very best to Steve Skinner. I'm only a friend for a lifetime.

Altamont, a low point

In December of 1969, we—along with 300,000 other people—descended on the Altamont Speedway for the giant outdoor free concert that was to be the West Coast's answer to Woodstock, featuring the Rolling Stones, the Grateful Dead, Jefferson Airplane, Santana, and others. The Dead hired a bunch of Bay Area Hell's Angels to run security at the event. In one photo of 14-month-old me, there's a giant wine jug in the foreground at my feet. Everybody at Altamont can be seen swilling from these massive jugs and passing them around. When I was growing up, my mother would sometimes tell the story of the woman who wanted to hold me at Altamont, and next thing my mother and father knew, the woman had wandered off with me.

Altamont promotional poster (public domain)

"There we were, stoned immaculate, when your father realized she was trying to take you." I have this image of my father sprinting after some woman, dodging all the drunk and stoned hippies sprawled on blankets.

On Daddy's shoulders at Altamont

We were way far back from the stage like most everyone else, unaware until the next day of the black teenager who had been stabbed to death by two Hell's Angels. Up by the stage, the Angels had been hostile and brutal. Not the kind of peace and love people were used to. Even Mick Jagger couldn't get things under control, as you can see in the Rolling Stones documentary *Gimme Shelter*, which chronicled the whole debacle. The footage also shows people completely tripped out of their minds in an excruciating display of debauchery. Bad acid trips. Bizarre physical antics. One clip shows a naked woman looking strung out on something, flanked on either side by two guys leading her by the hands. People were behaving like the freaks the previous generation thought them to be. Watching the film reel, it's like being the only sober person in the room witnessing everyone around you get embarrassingly drunk and stupid. You just wanna flee.

Me at Altamont

Ultimately, there would be four deaths at Altamont (not all related to the Angels) and a clear signal that something had shifted.

Rob Kirkpatrick, author of *1969: The Year Everything Changed,* writes:

> "Left on its own at the end of the decade and seemingly gathered at world's end, the Altamont congregation straddled the line between freedom and anarchy and experienced the ugly underside of a generation's collective dream."

I've never been sure if it was my own imagination and created memories of being out West at that time, but internally, soulfully, I have always felt the weight of it, a bygone disappointment weighing down on our little triad as though the end of the era signaled the end of *us,* and we were so unbearably entangled in music and hippie culture and a certain time and place that there was nothing left to do with the relationship. Like it had run its course.

revisionist history

"It is the function of art to renew our perception. What we are familiar with we cease to see. The writer shakes up the familiar scene, and, as if by magic, we see a new meaning in it."
— Anais Nin

Whenever I asked my mother why we left San Francisco, she would say, "Things were getting weird."

The drug scene in Haight-Ashbury was out of control, and the Altamont thing was such a downer. My parents decided it was time to go back East and be close to family. It was time to introduce me to everyone.

We drove cross-country with our two cats, Ulysses and Cassandra, our first stop on the East Coast being Newport News, Virginia, to see my paternal great-grandmother, whom we affectionately called Mammonk. My father knew she would welcome us with open arms. From there, we headed three hours north to the Eastern Shore of Maryland and soon settled into a house down the road from my mom's parents.

Daddy worked a bunch of odd jobs at that time. He drove a blue bread truck with a sliding door I can still remember climbing through. He worked with a guy named George Staples who cultivated oyster beds in the Chesapeake Bay, using oysters to clean the waters. "Brilliant guy, very progressive-minded," Mom says. "I find articles all the time now about using oysters as a cleaning mechanism."

Grandmother & Grandfather Clay, and Uncle Ray, visiting Daddy and me, Quantico Road house

Daddy also worked at the ice plant in Salisbury and did some construction work pouring concrete in Rehoboth, Delaware.

In April 1971 he wrote from Fort Smith, Arkansas, thumbing his way from east to west, stopping off and visiting with his friend Kilgore, and later Dick and his wife in New Mexico, where they jammed with guitars, congas, and harmonicas. Then Daddy got a temp job with Manpower to fuel the rest of his trip to California and back.

Sandia Mountains - snow began falling like inauguration confetti.

Sold blood for money. Only thing wrong is I miss you and the girl so much it hurts. As I told you when we talked before I left, I felt like I was arriving at the conclusion of my frustrating growth...I am mellowing some. Take care lil' darlin' I love you forever and always, Ed

P. S. Give Kennerly a kiss from Daddy

Mom and Daddy dressed up for mom's Wi-Hi high school reunion in 1971 at my grandparents' house on Crooked Oak Lane in Salisbury, Maryland

Daddy made it to Pacific Grove, California, where he stayed with friends, joined up with Bob and Lynne for dinner ("draft and Feds down on Bob's ass") and headed up to San Francisco to get drunk with Jim Macfarlan and stay in Jim's garage where my mother first lived when she was pregnant with me. He met up with Steve, their William & Mary friend and roommate, as well as old friends from the Witches' Brew bar, their gay roommate, Frank, plus an old work buddy, a Black guy named Willie Brigham I always heard about from my mother growing up.

Daddy had second thoughts about thumbing all the way to Oregon, he said.

California weird. I don't want to live here again. Everyone running amok and paranoia thick.

By May of 1971, Daddy was thumbing his way back home to us from San Bernardino, "trying to get me arse back to you and 'that girl.'"

Daddy and I blowing out my third birthday candle
(1971)

But just like their honeymoon—when my mom drove all night looking for a place to stay and my father was passed out drunk in the back seat—any sweetness to the phase didn't last long in Maryland. When my father landed back on the Eastern Shore, he wrecked my mom's car (drunk). My mother fell and broke her leg (drunk) and had to have a full cast for nine months. She found herself with a three-year-old kid, no car, living on welfare, and hitchhiking to work every day. It was time for my father to go.

Daddy left for Florida, where his parents lived, to look for work.

In this letter, Daddy recaps our return East in a letter written in the early 2000s:

You, your mum and I came from California in 1970 pulling a U-haul with two cats. Got to Mary and John's in Carolina with nada. Borrowed $10.00. Went to Mamonk's. Borrowed $10 more. Got to Salisbury and stayed at the Wythe house (my grandparents' house, a replica of the Williamsburg home of George Wythe) nearly a month. Your g-father found us Taylor's house on Quantico Rd. All this time I'm desperately pounding the pavement looking for steady work. Nothing but temping. Finally got a job with Osprey fishery. $80.00 a week. Ate white bread and raw oysters for lunch. (Our sex life was good.) That fell through. I wrecked our car. Took $20 and hitch-hiked to California, working here and there. In Albuquerque I teamed up with Richard Losh and sold carnations on the side of a highway. Made $50.00 one day and mailed yer mum $30.00. Went on to San Francisco, got home-sick and hitch-hiked back. Got locked up in Virginia and bailed out. Was gone for 29 days. Grabbed a 14-hour day unloading a barge of soybeans for Perdue at $2.00 an hour and then became an apprentice at Bay Steel - $2.00 an hour. Finally gave up and went to Florida to work.

The Florida years

That's when the letters really began to flow, sometimes weekly, it seemed, month after month. From Eddie Armadillo, Barry Dingle, Blind Boy Grunt—my father's pseudonyms and twisted alter egos.

"Outside of missing you and the Pooh, I'm happy down here," he wrote. "Bursting out of the Eastern Shore scene (bleaker than Poe's bleakest) has kept my brain from sliding down the drain," referring to life as it can sometimes be on Maryland's Eastern peninsula. He sent checks of $20 or $30 in each letter—even $60 one time—and he was adamant about an additional $50 payment each month to my mother's father for the Ford Falcon Daddy had wrecked. He mentioned "Heart of Gold" (Neil Young) and "Low Spark of High-Heeled Boys" (Steve Winwood) and asked my mom to send his eyeglasses left in the cubby hole in the living room. "Give your parents my love and say hello to Marsha, Bruce, Beth, Bob, Andy - anybody who gives a damn."

He then signed off with "Take care, baby" as though things were still in motion and he was coming back at some point.

"P.S. Tell your mother I didn't give you gonorrhea and that I've never had V.D."

Looking again at the dates of the letters during that time, I notice not just the frequency but the year.

March 12, 1972
March 22, 1972
March 27, 1972
April 4, 1972
April 7, 1972
April 11, 1972
April 18, 1972
April 27, 1972
May 1, 1972
May 8, 1972
May 10, 1972

Wait. What? Counting on my fingers. October 1968 I was born. October 1969. One. October 1970, two. October 1971, three. October 1972...I would've been four. I look ahead in the letters to see what's happening in the timeline...when does it really end? In the narrative of my life, the story I've always told people is that my parents were divorced "when I was like two" and they were only together for a couple of years.

All I've ever known is what it was like for my mom, hearing how she resolved to do everything on her own because it was clear that my father might not stick around. I never even knew my father had some intention of sticking around, at least from the way he wrote in these letters.

So in my mind they would've been long done by 1972. Yet here they are in this conversation that never really stopped. Of course, when there's a child to negotiate, parents have to communicate, but through these letters I am getting a glimpse into what might still have been possible—at least from my father's standpoint—and it is nothing I've ever had access to before. It's as though my whole being was never allowed to consider the possibility that my father was planning to or wanted to come back and be with us, be with *me*.

Emotion suddenly seizes my body, surging up into my throat. I can hardly breathe. Giant tears bulge out of my eyes, and I am stunned. It dawns on me that I have inherited only my *mother's* story, her version of events, her emotional state and experiences and memories. There was never an alternative point of view. I never considered or imagined my father's voice or view.

Letter to Maryland friend Andy Crockett from Florida

> April 11 1972
>
> Monday, Monday
> A: "Told you once and toldyatwison
> There will be no other Bison."
>
> Well my friend,
>
> Numerous hours have wasted away in time's continuous scorn since we last met. Florida has bequeathed me a healthy tan and a respectable beer-belly. The local library is well-stocked and I have consumed 9 volumes of Kerouac, 2 volumes of Henry Miller, and all available Lenny Bruce. Books, beer, music, and occasional liaisons with earthly

members of the female species have kept my tired brain from
dissolution.

"I took a trip down to L'Everglades to trade some beer
for an alligatoress..."

Have you continued on the road of collegiate wisdom or
have you slipped peacefully into bumdom? Whatever the case
I wish you well.

I have been assisting in the vital erection of swimming
pools and I make almost twice as much money as before. Jobs
are tight here at present so I can't get you any leads. I will
write if anything subtly irresistible arises.

Give me love to Rachel, a fiendish guffaw to Don, and a
stale fart to the Saddle Club. (Excepting me dear friend Flo
and me grandmother Gertude.)

By the way, my truck has gone 2500 miles since I left
Salisbury with a flat tire being the only casualty.

Take care me friend and send a weary epistle if it
behooves you. I will remain here at least a year. Unless sour
winds of sister Fate force me to elsewhere roam.

Buffalo Ed

"Your father could remember lyrics word for word. He had a really
sharp mind and a good memory," says Andy Crockett, an old friend of
both my parents. "I met Ed when I got out of the army in 1971, we met
down at the Saddle Club in Salisbury. Things like *Whole Earth Catalog*,
Ken Kesey, Kerouac—I'd never heard of any of that until I met Ed."

At the time, Andy was in the leather business. He had a store in
Salisbury and one down at Trader Lee's near Ocean City. They sold
belts and unique buckles designed by a guy named Duncan Lorry from
Pennsylvania.

"We bought all we could get because they were such a big hit," Andy
recalls. "We bought and resold a lot of them."

My father wore one of those buckles, a rounded brass one with little spokes coming out from the middle, for years. It's in just about every family photo where his belt buckle is showing.

"I was single and free and Ed had a family to worry about," Andy continues. "I didn't have anything like that. I was busy going to college when he was working in Salisbury. Then I dropped out of college to do the leather business, and when that finished later on, I got the farm. I didn't marry Sara until I was 27."

Some of my fondest memories from childhood are parties at Andy and Sara's house on the chicken farm. Sara had a daughter Deedee who was about my age, and we were good playmates for each other. We loved listening to the drunken adult banter and loud rock 'n roll on the stereo, and there was always good food (I remember having my first taco at their house). When things quieted down, we'd lie in our pajamas on the large warm vent in the living room or build forts with sheets up in her bedroom. We played "Wildfire" on the record player over and over again, imagining the pony that got lost in the blizzard and what "lost" really meant.

But those memories came later—after Daddy was already long gone.

"Breaking up with Anne and all that, you could tell it was trying on him," says Andy. "He had this Kerouac self-destructive seed in his mind, and he lived out that book."

Then Andy tells me a few things I never knew, things I'm not sure my mother knows.

"He met Leia through me, through my roommate. I got an apartment on Camden Avenue close to town that I shared with a couple other fellas. He wandered over to another small apartment building, and that's where he met Leia."

I always knew my father had met my stepmother in Salisbury when she was going to college there, but I never knew any backstory. I just assumed they ran into each other somehow, somewhere since he was working all over the place.

Andy answers the question for me. "He was working at the icehouse over where the Evo beer place is now."

And all those times Daddy was writing from Florida, apparently he was writing from a house full of people that included Andy as well as my stepmother-to-be Leia, my Uncle Ray, even Kevin, my mother and father's old buddy from San Francisco. I can hear the awkwardness in Andy's explanation. I doubt my mother knew any of that version of things, or that it even mattered, but Daddy certainly didn't advertise it in his letters.

My Uncle Ray later tells me that he and Daddy and Aunt Sally all lived together in "Fort Liquordale" when Daddy first started working on the truck and Uncle Ray was working for the phone company, so it must've been somewhere in between those years when friends from up north would come down and stay and live with them.

Hearing this as an adult, the same need to protect people comes up for me. I'm finding out information that my mother didn't know and my stepmother probably never wanted me to know or that my father didn't want my mother to know, and suddenly I'm the little kid caught in the middle, worried about people's feelings. It is exactly the *same* as it ever was.

"I have lots of Kevin stories," Andy reflects, conjuring a familiar humor whenever this name comes up. Daddy used to tell me stories about crazy shit he and Kevin would do, and my mother adored Kevin. He and Jim Macfarlan were the two guy friends from Witches' Brew in San Francisco who insisted she take refuge in Jim's garage for the duration of her pregnancy.

"He was a crazy Irishman. I've never forgotten him. He was a lot older than us, way into his 30s and we were still in our 20s. He was borderline emphysema and had severe alcoholism. He was psychologically beat, really down."

My mom and I visited Kevin in Colorado when I was seven and we took a cross-country Greyhound trip to San Francisco. He drove us up Pike's Peak and we visited with his mother, who bequeathed me an antique doll that I would later use for a Statue of Liberty school project. We visited him again one time in Long Island when I was first going to school in Manhattan. He was working as a security guard somewhere. He died at 45, I think, of complications related to alcoholism and obesity.

"There was another friend with a VW bus that had T-O-L-E-R-A-

N-T written on the back of it. He was traveling around with his wife, worked with the Boy Scouts or something."

That was Kilgore.

"Anyway, I stabilized, and he got on the truck. and it's hard to do that and be stable with family. He always said I did the right thing putting down roots, buying a farm."

Andy and his wife of later years drove his motorcycle to Greenville and dropped in to see my stepmother Leia a few years back. He remained friends with her throughout the years as well.

My father could also be pretty shitty sometimes. For some reason he got activated when it came to cars. Maybe because his father sold cars for a living. Maybe because Daddy had already wrecked a half dozen of them and figured why buy a new one if they're always gonna get wrecked? As long as I can remember, my father always drove shitty cars. And he let my mother know in no uncertain terms.

Your idea of a new VW is a fucking bomb; you buy it and I'll stop sending a single fucking penny. I'll not contribute to any new car in any way. If you want a $300 car my old man will find a good one and I'll buy the thing. If you get a shittin' new car with time payments you can shove it up yer ass. I'll have no part of that kind of stupidity. You bought the Ford and I'm gonna pay for that bitch altho' I shouldn't. Make another dumb move and you're totally on your own. $30 more mid-week. But if you don't want the slender thread holding us together to snap you'd best not buy anything on time. My love to your folks. Kennerly's writing is fantastic. Take care. Love, Ed

In his next missive, he apologized for the harshness while still reaming my mother for even considering buying a new vehicle. My

Grandfather Clay did come through and supply her with a car. I think it was the old Chevrolet we had with the turquoise vinyl interior and the "wings" on the back. Daddy told me once the reason they stopped making those cars back in the 60s was because of kids and skateboards. Kids were getting impaled on the wings.

If you wish to join me say at summer's end, or fall's leafy catastrophe, you'd best arrange to nab back $325 or what not from the school and cancel out. The girl has only 2 years before grade school. She should have one of those free— perhaps 6 months of traveling and experience.

In those early years, my father contributed gladly to my private school education, aligned with my mother on the decision to not send me through what she considered a horrible county school system at the time. He'd say things like, "If you owe any money to Salisbury School, send me the bill. I want to do it for the girl." Then he sounded so optimistic that she and I would be joining him in Florida, canceling school and our lives in Maryland to be with him. I do kinda like the idea of six months of traveling and experience—but I was three years old after all.

I hope Pooh isn't constantly unhappy. She should be able to adjust to my absence.

The letters continue into early summer, plans being made for Grandfather Clay to drive up to Maryland to pick me up and bring me down to Fort Lauderdale to stay with them for a month. (Precautions duly noted about the swimming pool that now had extra locks and doors so I couldn't get into the pool alone.)

Grandmother, Pappap (her father), Daddy and I

Daddy wrote, "I've been doing a lot of thinking since we talked, and I know that I do need you and want you and hopefully we can work something out in short time if you want to." He offered to buy her a round-trip ticket to come down for two weeks; she could have privacy at the place in Boca and I could stay with my grandparents. He listed a bunch of record albums and advised her not to buy duplicates unless she planned to remain separate.

I appreciate your allowing her to come for a visit.

But maybe the next sentence didn't exactly win my mother over.

Only thing new is my drinking has tapered off this week. Sunday Ray and I took truck to ocean; he two fifths of wine and I did in seven quarts of beer. He threw up magnificently in front of a liquor store and I annihilated myself internally—

system was lousy for three days. I've only had a 6-pack all week. Take care of yourself, Doll. Give the Pooh a kiss for me. I love you, Ed.

Through my summer visit to Florida, the letters continued, along with invitations to my mother to come down to Lauderdale to visit or perhaps even relocate. In Miami, Daddy went to see Blue Oyster Cult, John Hammond, Alex Taylor, Allman Brothers Band—a benefit for the World Dolphin Foundation.

In the early 70s, people were becoming more aware of the slaughter of dolphins and the inhumanity of captivity, thanks to Ric O'Barry, former trainer of *Flipper* from the TV show. His work on the set of *Flipper* prompted his awakening to the ills of captivity and he went on to start The Dolphin Project, receiving significant backing from musician Stephen Stills of Crosby, Stills, Nash & Young, who liked what Barry was up to. The Dolphin Project was the first to bring global attention to drive-hunting of dolphins in Taiji, Japan, and the organization continues to bring awareness to the cruelty of captivity.

Fort Lauderdale News and Sun-Sentinel, Sunday, June 25, 1972

Leas Campbell is planning a rock concert on July 8th to benefit the World Dolphin Foundation. The concert, to be held at the Miami Jai Alai fronton, will feature **Steven Stills, John Sebastian** and **Fred Neil** at this point. Word is that the other two-thirds of the original Crosby, Stills and Nash might show up for the occasion, as well as other rock entertainers of name caliber.

THE MIAMI NEWS

Thurs., July 13, 1972

. . . If some of you at last week's benefit for The Dolphin Foundation recognized a familiar face among the musicians participating in the jam it belonged to **Rick Danko** of The Band. . .

Stephen Stills and **Manassas** were recorded live at the Miami Jai Alai Fronton during the World Dolphin Foundation concert. **Ron and Howard Albert** handled the gig, using Criteria's remote equipment. Also featured were **John Sebastain** and **Fred Neil,** and proceeds were slated to go to the Foundation.

Jerry Regovoy has noted that

Ric O'Barry's best friend was a guy named Fred Neil, a folk singer-songwriter probably best known for "Everybody's Talkin'" from the movie *Midnight Cowboy*. A song he wrote that came out in 1966 called "The Dolphins" was later covered by Tim Buckley in a soulful version that's riveting and heart-aching. ("Listen to Tim Buckley's 'Goodbye and Hello,'" my father encouraged in one letter written to my brother Jeffrey in later years.)

From his earlier musings about dolphins, I wonder if they were something of a spirit animal for my father. Frolicking and free, exploring and adventuring—and trying to escape drag-fishing nets that would entrap them or kill them.

Years later, Daddy got a dolphin tattoo on his upper left bicep and Jeffrey remembers one old Pontiac where Daddy mounted two diving dolphins in place of the hood ornament. That's what Daddy would call "some real Clay class," akin to stuffing his sock with leftover steamed blue crabs at the all-you-can-eat restaurant or perhaps breaking wind at the dining room table.

I'll never try to tell this world how to get along. You know as I know that peace will come when all hate is gone. I had a dolphin carved on me arm. It looked like a positive way.

Aside from supporting dolphin rescue and rehab at the concert, my father wrote he'd been "zonked" on acid and had been doing a tab a week of Purple Haze while enjoying Tom Wolfe's *Electric Kool-Aid Acid Test*.

A letter dated July 3, 1972, has FUURTHER written across the top in Ken Kesey bus fashion.

Luscious o' Cassady in the school bus, Edward in his blue bus, gears churning like molten butter. Whee! My head and that book are two parallel movies. I think I shall get it all together through Cassady's inspiration. The girl and I both miss mommy.

Lest anyone think my father was tripping his ass off on acid while I was in his care, it's highly doubtful. I always stayed with my grandparents when I was down in Florida. Daddy would come and go, as I remember it, always having to leave for work. I don't even remember if he spent nights on the sofa while I was there. Most of my early Florida memories are of my grandmother and grandfather, not so much of time spent with him.

My mom has sometimes wondered if all that LSD affected his "swimmers," given some of the challenges my brother Jimmy (born a few years later) had. But it appears that science—even by today's standards and understanding of genetic influences—sees no long-term negative impact on offspring, regardless of the father's LSD usage.

Speaking of swimming, Daddy wrote that I was learning, albeit reluctantly, but by the end of my visit had jumped off a low diving board into the deep end and could swim my way over to the side of the pool. I was three. Daddy would be driving me up to Maryland at the end of July to bring me back home.

As you mentioned, she has picked up some half-assed habits at school and gets somewhat unmanageable at times, but all in all she is a happy delightful girl.

Daddy agreed with my mom's suggestion that if the both of them died, my Uncle Bob, my mom's brother, would become my legal guardian. My godmother Miriam, a friend of both my parents from William & Mary, was 3,000 miles away in British Columbia—a haven for extreme hippiedom (she had, in fact, defected to Canada)—possibly living in a tent or something. She had her hands full, being recently divorced and a single mom to her own child. My father may well have imagined she was living in a naked hippie commune with who knows who when he wrote, "Kennerly doesn't need rearing by freaks we've never known."

'Fatty' is certainly an eater; she's single-handedly upped the food bill here; her rotund little belly juts out in a mild maternity fashion; she asks for you often but is not perceptibly homesick.

But something must've happened when Daddy brought me back to Maryland. By the time he wrote from Brunswick, Maine, in October, there was talk of voluntary separation.

Daddy with dolphin pal

Breaking up

Daddy was staying with Dick Losh in Maine and started working at U.S. Gypsum, a drywall and joint compound-manufacturing factory job that Dick helped him get.

I am most certainly committed to work this new job for a year. To back out sooner is a breach of faith to Dick whose recommendation cinched my being hired.

In addition to medical insurance and beneficiary information, Daddy wrote to "delineate the reasons for my voluntary separation," saying that it hurt him as thoroughly as it hurt my mother that they had split up and that he loved her, he always would, and not being with me was like being minus a heart.

It's just that circumstances left me no other course. It seems that I am always taken for granted when I'm around and then missed or appreciated after I've gone away.

He wasn't able to endure any more of the strain or hassling and had become a personality that was shitty, he wrote. "Above all, a person that wasn't really me." He went on to observe that since they had married, my mother had acted as though she was "dubious" of her choice.

Staring at the words in the letter and rereading every line my father had written, I feel another surge flood my body. I try to distinguish the emotion. Is it sadness? Anger? Why couldn't my mother remember something so seemingly significant to their relationship?

I ask her and she shakes her head. "I was just trying to get by as a single mom, I guess, and like I said, I had already written him off somehow back in San Francisco, when he abandoned me when I was pregnant."

So none of what he was writing got through to her at the time!

She couldn't remember any of these letters having any impact at all.

At this point they had signed the separation agreement. He let her know in the letter she was free to go her separate way as if the two of them "had never been bound," he said, and encouraged her to be free of him for her own self-realization. "I believe that the less I write the more freedom of thought you will have to discover yourself."

I live on my own peculiar level and it works for me. If it didn't, I would have ended my life months ago.

I find these 25-year-old insights remarkable—given it took my mother 30 more years to figure out some of this on her own. Like why didn't she say to him before they got married, "Hey, I have concerns about getting married because I felt this lack of commitment from you when I was pregnant."

"I had zero capacity to communicate that to him at the time," she says, of not having the emotional communication skills she has today. But my mother's body and being must have somehow *known,* communicating without words her "dubiousness." My father had picked up on it and perfectly articulated it in a letter that Mom can't even remember reading in 1972.

I have one gripe. My mother wrote that she heard from you regarding our split. Perhaps she misconstrued your words as she has a tendency to do, but she mildly upbraided me for my 'Wanderlust' and self-centeredness. I am not so much in love with myself as you suppose and I am not so predisposed to wander as you or she presumes. If you must explain to anyone, don't fucking misrepresent the facts. Coming up here was to escape Salisbury which I have endeavored to do since we landed there 2-1/2 years ago.

And it's here I think my father might be lying through his teeth. I've never put two and two together, exactly—never needed to, wanted to, cared that much, and it's not of great import in the big scheme of things—but I know my father and eventually-to-be stepmother Leia spent time in Maine together. My mother may have been spot on with her accusations, in some respects, again not that it mattered at that point. She wasn't having him back, anyway. But Daddy's going to Maine with Dick may also have been the opportunity to be with Leia outside of familial scrutiny. Or the wanderlust could have referred to any number of previous wanderings, who knows.

Until I chatted with Andy and it happened to come up.

"Leia's dad went to Ed and begged him not to take her to Maine. Ed swore he wouldn't, but she followed him up there anyway. Maine was cold and difficult, and the two of them didn't get along well."

My father—always being followed by women. And always leaving again.

I am surprised to realize in the timeline as well that 1973—the year I always remembered going to Disney and remembering that Leia was there—it turns out my father was on the road at the time and wasn't even at Disney with us. So she was already a part of his Florida life, and I had already been introduced to her this early on, though I made no connection between his and her relationship.

I remember laughing about this very thing with my grandmother one time. I must've offhandedly asked how Leia ended up in Florida.

"Well, she followed your father," my grandmother said matter-of-factly, and then cracked up, realizing the inanity of it all, given we were in the same women-following-my-father conversation we were in before. Then she threw her head back and laughed even harder. "I guess she followed him to Maine, too!" We were both howling by that time. Anything to do with ex-wives—between my father and Uncle Ray, there were at least five—sent us into fits of laughter.

The letters continued steadily through the end of 1972, dated November 9, November 20, December 11, December 15, December 18

In the November 20 letter, I notice what may have been the first hint of that magical thinking showing up, what my brother Jeffrey was later to call "delusions of adequacy." Just after details of drinking a fifth of tequila every three days and how it kept my father warm and high, he wrote:

Pete, Chuck, Kathy, Marianne, Dick and Carol talked me into voting. Nixon's victory decided a nagging question within me. I have definitely decided to leave the country and to expatriate as soon as I'm established elsewhere. Canada (western), Spain, and Mexico are my only three considerations. Hope to work on Cousin Norris' tugboat Feb. 1st; on it—I'm going to study navigation, work, and write. In six months to a year, I'll save at least $5000, and then I'm cutting out of here.

I imagine my mother reading this letter to herself back then, probably with heavy sighs and eye-rolling. "Ed, you have a child. Have you thought this through at all? If you miss her so much, how do you think it's going to be when you're in another country?"

The names Pete, Chuck, et al, of course, mean nothing to my siblings, but these were my parents' college friends, so I grew up on these names. Marianne was a close friend of my mom's, kind of an auntie or second godmother to me, whom I was very fond of. Her first husband, Peter, was a bestie of my father's at James Blair High School in Williamsburg. When she attended my wedding, it was probably the first time she'd seen my father since the 1960s.

In the very next sentence, Daddy wrote:

Whenever you write, I would appreciate it if you would describe Kennerly's situation: scholarly, emotional, growthwise, etc. That girl keeps me awake a lot of nights.

Daddy finally commented on the fact my mother got her leg cast off, which, she makes note of, he didn't mention a single time during the entire nine months of epistles. Never asked her once how she was doing or how it was coming along. I would naturally stick up for him here, but I know what it feels like to wish somebody—especially your husband—actually gave a shit enough to ask.

Sorry for the delay in writing. I've been on the longest and deepest downer of my life. Don't feel like talking, much less writing letters.

And then December 30th, there it was for the first time. A letter written directly to me:

Dear Kennerly, How are you? Fine I hope. I heard you were given a big bicycle for Christmas. It must be lots of fun to ride. Happy New Year. I love you. Daddy.

I blink and read it again. My father is talking to me like a little girl. I am transported to that moment while feeling in the present every ounce of hurt and sadness that came in between then and now. Another letter is dated January 19, 1973, and after that there are more letters to me—documentation of our early life together that I have only a faint recollection of. A conversation between father and young child that was virtually erased from my memory, all here in writing. This was the time before he remarried and had other children. The time when I was still his only child. The time when everything I did was everything that mattered to him.

Before reading these letters, I never reflected much on that time. I couldn't remember it. The letters, Daddy's words, pierce my memory, and little by little, my early childhood begins to come back to me.

January 19, 1973: Dear Kennerly, How are you? I miss you very much. I thought the picture you sent me for Christmas was very good. I hope you are enjoying school and your new bicycle. I love you, Daddy.

January 26, 1973: Dear Kennerly, I hope you are happy and having fun in what you do. Mamado sent me a picture of you with Santa Claus. You are a very pretty girl. I am too busy to write any more now. Take care of yourself and your mama. Love, Daddy.

And to my mother:

I love you and I'm sorry that things fell apart. Take care, Ed.

What ifs

By February 23, 1973, Daddy had left the job at U.S. Gypsum in Maine, essentially breaking the agreement he previously felt so strongly about. When I mention this breach of faith to Dick, he is doubtful it contributed greatly to my father's loss of relationship with himself or any ability to keep his word.

"The job was awful anyway," Dick assures. "He had a tough time in that factory, it was hellacious! You had to stand at this machine with ear plugs and a face mask. It moved fast. These huge machines punching tiles out, stacking this and that. And your dad couldn't get it. He didn't catch on real quick, he just wasn't fast enough. I hated that place. It was likely a lot of stress more than anything related to how long he promised to be there."

Yet I can't help but refer back to what my father had written, and how seriously he took the recommendation and had intended to honor it. When you can't uphold your end of an agreement, whether or not it's serving you or whether it's all that important in the big scheme of things, doesn't really matter. There's a reckoning you have to do with yourself and others, and you can do it with honesty and integrity in a way that leaves nothing residual. No guilt, no regret, no excuses. Whether or not this happened for my father is purely speculative. It gives me pause only because I am on this quest to understand why my father ultimately spoke into a fictitious, wishful reality in which he saw himself showing up responsibly for things people might need him for.

Just when did he start pretending?

No doubt a sequence of minor failures and accumulated half-truths he told himself and others, further convoluted by drugs and alcohol, contributed to a way of thinking that just wasn't in touch with reality.

March 12, 1973

Dear Kennerly, I am visiting Grandmother and Grandfather Clay in Florida. It was nice to visit with you. I wish we could be together all the time. I might be coming through Salisbury some time in April. If so maybe we can get together. Take good care of yourself and your mama. I love you pumpkin. Xxxx Daddy P.S. I am starting work tomorrow. I will send a hunk of green within two weeks.

I scan the letter again, a vague memory making its way back from the recesses of my five-year-old mind, remembering what it was like trying to comprehend what he meant by hunk of green. "I wish we could be together all the time..." His words are now hanging around my heart, weighing it down with such heaviness I struggle to make sense of where the hurt is coming from.

I've already had to forgive myself for being born, for fucking up the trajectory of my father's young life. I've had to forgive my mother for going off birth control. Forgive her for entrapping him, even though that wasn't her intention. And forgive her for not forgiving him for his abandoning her during the pregnancy that he didn't sign up for.

From the very first letter in December 1965, a new story has unfolded for me, one that has never been told before because I never even knew it was there to tell. My father wanted to be with his wife and little girl and "loved us more than anything else on earth."

Letters like this continued right into 1975, in which he alluded to a big decision he would have to make once and for all. Within a year, he would be remarried and my baby brother would be on the way.

This leaves me a crying mess. Completely, utterly, without reason, without rationality, I am suddenly a 52-year-old child who wants her daddy. I armored up my whole life to be just fine without him, to be stellar in fact, to be exceptional and extraordinary and high-achieving and successful, in pure defiance of my father having walked out on us. My mother had a strong hand in this, of course, grooming me to be independent, to learn how to play by myself, to travel by plane at three years old, chaperoned by the pretty Delta stewardesses all the way to Fort Lauderdale, and later to see New York City and Europe and reach for a world much bigger than my small hometown.

While I never once allowed myself to even wish for my parents to be together again, I find myself in awe of the bond that was formed when they were young and why it continued throughout the years, in spite of the contentiousness of the child support era that was to come.

In reading Daddy's letters, I have also had to come to terms with complex emotions towards my mom—irrational feelings of blame and supposition that my 52-year-old intellect knows are unreasonable, but that a three-year-old is suddenly raging about.

Mother blaming. It happens even when the family is intact and fairly functional. It's just this inherently selfish, childish thing about expecting our mothers to take care of us and protect us and fix everything. If she's the only one left at the end of the day, she's gonna get it. I know my own children do it to me, and still I do it to mine.

How could she not have seen or heard how authentic he was being when he wrote to her, telling her how much he wanted to make a go of it? How he had transformed and was willing to put everything into the three of us?

Why couldn't she have given him a chance?

Why wasn't she willing to have that conversation?

How come he was so attuned and insightful, but she couldn't recognize some of these same things?

What if he could have been a completely different person if she had been present for him?

What if he could have been a completely different person if he could have been the father he wanted to be for ME?

Everything he wrote in all the early letters to me was so impassioned, so fascinated with me, so eager to know what I was doing, aching to be with me all the time.

What if I would have made the difference for him?

What if I could have saved their relationship?

I know. It's a childish response.

What's really true—and deep in my heart I know it—is that my mother did us all a big favor by protecting me from years of having a second parent's alcoholic indentations on my life on a regular basis.

But rather than counter this moment with all the reasons why things would never have worked and should never have been and it's better that it didn't happen that way because God knows what hell I'd have endured, just look at what the other kids had to go through when they had him at home all those years—

I'm just going to let it hang out there a little while. This possibility that was never allowed to exist. It fills me with dread and sadness and makes me feel like putting the lid back on quickly before it consumes me.

Not that it matters now and probably wouldn't have mattered then either. There was nothing that would have changed our living situation, especially with him in Florida and my mother having no plans to leave the Eastern Shore. Not to mention his drinking and her controlling. It was done. Done like the Summer of Love and concerts in Golden Gate Park and the Haight-Ashbury scene. Done like the voices of Martin Luther King and Bobby Kennedy, Janis Joplin, Jimi Hendrix and Jim Morrison. Done like when my pregnant mother realized my father was never going to be reliable for her.

But it now occurs to me there's something else to forgive everyone for that I never knew I missed out on: the love and devotion I would have gotten from my father if he had been around.

My mother sees the emotion on my face as I'm flipping through her notes garnered from the letters.

"You know," she says slowly, "you probably have some abandonment issues that have never been dealt with..."

It's something I'm willing to ponder, knowing that it's common for divorced children, especially girls, to end up with some kind of hang-up about being left behind by their father in favor of another family. It's not the first time I've considered this. I've been on this self-reflective track for a pretty long, sober time, but much as I look and delve, I cannot find one single pang of abandonment. It just isn't there for me. It was not my experience that my father abandoned me. Due to the nature of the long-distance truck-driving lifestyle, it was expected that he would be coming and going for long periods of time. It's as though he just gradually drifted away.

Soon after my father returned to Florida from Maine, my grandfather introduced him to the idea of driving a truck for a living. In many ways, it checked a lot of boxes for my gypsy-soul father. Freedom and autonomy. Travel. And for many years, drinking without scrutiny. Plus, Daddy could always walk out, leave it all behind. It was expected that he would. His job required it

"Truck drivers have a whole lot of freedom because they don't have to deal with the daily family things," says Al Miller, Daddy's old trucking buddy. "But it costs a lot to do that. I've been through two marriages because of it. I would assume your dad was like me in that respect. He was hard-headed and wanted to do what he wanted to do."

From my earliest memory, Daddy had always been out on the road. In my young mind, it didn't connect whether he was living in Florida or driving a truck or living with us—he was just "on the road." My sister has the actual certificate Daddy received for commercial driver training/semi-tractor trailer. It's dated June 15th, 1973, from Dade County Public School's Division of Recreational, Technical and Adult Education.

In the early years of truck driving, he drove big rigs across the country and back, so he'd be gone for weeks at a time. I have snapshot memories of postcards I received from places like Chicago and Texas. He once brought me a mini sombrero with sequins from Mexico that I fitted onto the head of one of my dolls. It's probably still there amidst the dusty relics in my mom's house.

A few times when he came to visit, he pulled up in an 18-wheeler in front of our house on Quantico Road. I must've been no more than four years old when he hoisted me up onto the seat and let me pretend drive. I remember hoping that people we knew would pass by and see me sitting there in that tractor trailer, and that they would see my daddy. Whenever my mom and I were in the car together, I imagined every big rig we passed on the road would have my father in the driver's seat. From the passing lane, we'd catch up to the truck, and I'd eagerly lean forward to see if the guy sitting up there was my father, but of course it never was. Still, I'd have my yank-your-horn gesture ready, and they always honked, usually with a smile and a wave. Even now I get an anticipatory feeling when matching speed with a tractor trailer.

Some time this summer I'll start looking for a school bus to make a home and camper of. Sometime when you are between 5 and 6 we will take a short trip in it.

When I first come across this promise of a school bus-converted-to-camper trip with my father, I remember nothing about it. After it bounces around in my head for a few days though, the vague recollection of an anticipated adventure that was sure to happen begins to creep back into my mind. Daddy talked about this a number of times, I'm sure of it. My five-year-old self remembers now how much I looked forward to going on the road in a makeshift camper, just me and my father. I had romanticized ideas of converted school buses and hippie road trips, having been on one such memorable adventure with a bunch of my mom's stoner friends to Ocean City, or maybe it was a fiddle festival somewhere. I remember sitting knees crisscrossed on a mattress on the floor in the back of a painted pale-blue bus amidst the thick, sweet reefer haze listening to the guys picking guitar and crooning "Black Water" by the Doobie Brothers.

I try to remember why the camper road trip promise had to be broken. Maybe life got in the way. We all make lofty promises, like "I'd love to do XYZ with you" to our kids—and we don't fulfill all of them. I don't begrudge my father that one. It just wasn't practical on some level.

The next several envelopes have the letters "GROK" above the return address. My mother has no idea what it refers to. In fact, Daddy wrote several cryptic, rebus-like postcards that neither of us could figure out. But when I look up the definition of grok and find this one, coined by Robert Heinlein in his 1960s sci-fi novel *Stranger in a Strange Land* —and its meaning—I'm pretty sure this is what Daddy was going for:

> "...from the word for 'to drink' and, figuratively, 'to drink in all available aspects of reality,' 'to become one with the observed' in Heinlein's fictitious Martian language."

There were other letters written to my mother and me, individually, during this time frame, but these are some of the highlights.

Daddy, still enthusiastic about paying for my private school education.

May 7, 1973

Dear Pumpkin - Sorry it took me so long to write. I am very busy these days. I enjoyed hearing you on the phone last Sunday. You are sounding more and more like a big girl. Everyone is dying to see you again. At present, it looks like Grandfather Clay will come to bring you down. Possibly though, I might be able to drive up around June 22.

Mommy says you are doing magnificently at your school. This is good news and good for your mind also. I am going to pay your way next year. I have got to sleep awhile now. I love you, Daddy

Daddy's work schedule ramped up, hardly ever around on weekends.

May 1973

Dear Pumpkin, Thank you for the drawings and work papers. I enjoy seeing your schoolwork and looking at the pictures you draw. It's the next best thing to seeing you. I'm sitting in Florida today soaking up some rays. This is the first time I've been here on a weekend in 6 weeks. I hope you had a good holiday. I love you, Daddy

Daddy working 18-hour days, trucking, and who knows what the buffalo reference was but probably a picture of some sort, or perhaps a buffalo nickel taped inside.

May 14, 1973

Dear Kennerly, Hi Doll! This has to be a short note because I am occupied 18 hours out of every day now. I also look like a huge lobster from being in the sun. I hope that the clothes you got for Easter fit you well. Your Uncle Ray, grandma and grampa all send their love. We are looking forward to having you down here. There's a buffalo in this letter. I love you, Daddy

Daddy trying to connect but sometimes I was already in bed. I remember this well into adolescence.

June 20, 1973

Dear Pooh, How are you? I just got back from Chicago. I called last Thursday nite but it was late and you were asleep. I think your grandaddy is going to fly up to get you at the end of the month. I hope you are having a fun vacation and I love you. Daddy

Evidence that Daddy wasn't even there for my one trip to Disney. I always thought I had gone there with Leia AND him.

June 1973

Dear Kennerly, I had to go out to Omaha. I hope you had fun at Disney World. I will call you from the Mid-West. I love you, Daddy

July 14, 1973 BBG 400 NW 29th St. Ft. Lauderdale, FL

After returning from North Dakota, I had only 2 days free before I had to trek off to Chicago and back. Then reached Florida last Sunday nite. I left Tuesday night for Lubbock, Texas. Presently, I am enduring a layover outside Abilene, Texas. I've had only limited time with Kennerly but she seems to be immensely enjoying her visit. Slightly home-sick at times but by and large happily occupied. She's quite a girl.

I am enclosing $20 in buffalo meat with witch you may enjoy as you choose. Instead of sending checks while Kennerly is here I am laying aside $25.00 a week for her schooling. When she returns home I'll send a check with her.

Perhaps you can can use this dough for your trip. If not, throw yourself a party or something. I hope today was a lucky one for you. Love, Ed

My mother left on a bus trip for California the very day, it seemed, that I returned from Florida, which was very upsetting for me. While she was gone for several weeks, I stayed with my maternal grandparents.

Every Tuesday my maternal grandmother would take me with her on the 40-minute drive to Eunice's beauty parlor in Berlin, Maryland. That's where she went, our family would joke, "to get her hairs done." It was always the same thing, a curler or two and that fluffing up of thinning hair that older ladies do, followed by 360-degree blasts of aerosol hair spray to make it hold until the next week.

I enjoyed the ritual. Usually, I got some Nekot crackers for 25 cents out of the machine or maybe a peppermint candy from the dish by the register. Certainly, I'd garner all kinds of attention from the ladies.

"Bettie, is this your granddaughter?" they'd say with enthusiastic approval, adding something complimentary about my behavior or adorableness.

Someone would shoot me a question, like, "You must enjoy coming here with your grandmother, isn't that so special?" And I would nod, because it certainly was.

When my grandmother asked if I'd like to get a haircut, it sounded new and exciting. I had no idea what a "shag" was—carpet or otherwise —but having a haircut with a name sounded like fun. The shampoo girl fussed with the snap at my neck, and I spread the plastic cape out over the sides of the riser they perched me on to make me taller. When I leaned back, my neck didn't quite reach the cradle, so I scooched myself a little but stayed still at the first sensation of warm water spraying against my skull.

When the lady with the scissors started cutting, I remember an uneasy feeling. I was thinking to myself, "Oh no, this isn't what I meant."

I don't think I really understood until that moment what a "haircut" would be. After all, my long tresses had never been trimmed. The next reflection was me looking back at myself with locks butchered in different directions. I immediately hated it but smiled politely and said nothing.

Back at my grandmother's house, I ran upstairs to her bedroom. As I came around the king-size bed, I stopped short in front of the full-length mirror at the sight of my light-brown, choppy hair.

Instinctively, my right hand went up to it. I didn't like it, not one bit. And neither did my mother when she came back from California. She was pissed that my grandmother did something so shady. My grandmother always hated long hair.

Daddy heard about my haircut.

August 27, 1973

Dear Kennerly, It was swell to talk with you tonight. I have been too busy to write for awhile now. You are sounding bigger all the time on the telephone. I am leaving in the morning for Boston. If time permits, I plan to come down through your way Thursday. I love you and miss you Pumpkin. I can't wait to see your haircut. Love, Daddy

I would have been confused by the mention of him forgetting what his address was in Florida, not understanding he was referring to having been away from home so long.

September 12, 1973

Dear Pumpkin, It was nice to hear from you. I am glad that you have friends nearby and a kitty to sleep with. I came home Sunday night for the first time in 2 weeks. Then I left Monday night again to go to Boston. I've forgotten what my address is in Florida. Wish your mama a happy birthday for me. I'll try to see you soon. Love, Daddy

It took me a while to understand the trucking business and what Daddy meant when he wasn't able to stop by when he was driving through Maryland. If he stopped at a weigh station and was carrying too heavy a load, he wouldn't be able to drive certain routes.

September 24, 1973

Dear Kennerly, It was swell to talk with you Thursday night. You sound more grown up every time I hear you. I'm glad you are still enjoying school. I just got back from Boston Tuesday morning. Tonite I am leaving Miami for Louisiana and then Texas. Sometime I will fix it so you can make a trip with me - if you would like to go.

I tried to see you last weekend but I was overloaded and couldn't get near the Eastern Shore.

Gotta run now. Take care Pumpkin and I think of you always and I love you, Daddy

———————⊛———————

December 10, 1973

Dear Pumpkin, Sorry I haven't writ in so long. I hope you are enjoying yourself. I will call when I'm sure we'll be coming by to pick you up. Love, Daddy

———————⊛———————

February 4, 1974

$25 enclosed If the strike ends by this weekend I will endeavor to send more. I hope your tests have had favorable results. I appreciate no end your sending Kennerly's printing and artwork. I love her and miss her unbearably at times and these things are all a delight. Especial thanks for a highly articulate story on me workspace with the exception of some misstatement of present-day trucking facts, he does paint a rather authentic picture. I enjoyed it immensely. He writes a lot of how I think on it all but never get to lay it down.

Well - this was wantonly scrawled as "Goat's Head Soup" raged. All seems like a hundred years ago. Take care. Love, Ed

P.S. Pleasantry exists only in the absence of pain.

Daddy expressed appreciation to my mom for keeping him involved in my life. This is something she made a decision about early on, to be amicable with him, to not use me as a pawn in their relationship, to keep me connected to his side of the family and to not speak ill of him to me, even though she must've wanted to many a time when I was little. Only when I was old enough to handle the truth and had the maturity to simply see things for what they were, did she tell me matter-of-factly when my father was not coming, and why.

Duvall was the Salisbury law firm handling tax-related stuff during their separation.

March 15, 1974
The Joker 400 NW 27th St

  Thanks for sending along the pictures. The pumpkin is developing a fine sketching hand. Sorry about Wednesday night's blow-up. I should have called Duvall instead of you.
  Gotta close. I ramble on now. Love, Ed

Completely loaded—referring to the truck, that is.

March 22, 1974
South Holland, IL
Written from stockyards, St. Paul, Minnesota

  Dear Pumpkin, How are you? I am sorry I haven't written in so long. I have been working almost non-stop for 5 weeks. Right now I am picking up 40,000 pounds of pork here at St. Paul. Your mother has been sending along some of your writings and drawings. The pictures are especially good. You seem to have a knack for art.
  I am very proud of your progression in school. It is good to love to learn and your excitement over your workbook tells me that you are enjoying what you are doing.
  I've got to close now as I am completely loaded. Be a good

girl. Even if I don't write I am still always thinking of you. Love, Daddy

    Mama - the 1st of every month I will send 2 checks: $100 payable to you and $50 payable to Salisbury School

Letter to my mother from Grandfather Clay in Florida

June 30, 1974

    Dear Anne, Am sending Kay $5.00 and I hope you and she are well. Anne I used to have severe nosebleeds until I was 16 or 17. So I don't believe you have any problems with Kay's nosebleed. We are sorry she has to have tonsils removed. As you know, it is a pretty serious operation. Of course the doctors know best. We will pray for her! How is the old car running? Let me know when it is about to play out.

    Anne, I don't guess there is any hope for you and Eddie however I believe he still loves you. He is not the same Eddie, very responsible and no one would believe the improvement being on the truck has been good for him, such long periods with no drinking. I am grateful and hopeful for more improvement.

    Hope to see you this summer.

    Love, Dad Clay

    Dearest Kay, Here is something for you special. I want to see you soon. Be a good girl and I will see you this summer. I saw your swimming instructor yesterday.

    Lots of love, Grandfather

July 10, 1974
Cassidy (sic)
Kenworth Place Cummins, USA
Chicago, IL postmark Fulton Market

*Dear Kennerly, It was certainly good to see you on the
4th, if only for a short time as it was. It's incredible that
you are so big and grown-up. I am very proud of you.*

*Right now I am dragging my rear-end around the
narrowest most congested regions of nasty inner Chicago city
peddling a load of not-so-fine pickles from North Carolina.*

*I suppose Grandmother Clay will have you down to
Carolina soon. If you are there between July 15th and July
22nd I will probably get by the Highlands to see you. The
next time we're together be sure to ask me about "the half-
dollars." I forgot this time. Gotta halt this letter now.*

I love you, Pumpkin Daddy

*P.S. I'm crazy about your vest. I wear it for days on end,
usually until it sticks to me back.*

I (and my mother) had given Daddy a suede fringed vest as a gift.

And then, came a letter I have read and reread to decipher its meaning,
seeking not to add my own meaning but now reading it within the
context of Daddy's other letters, the plainspoken truth.

My father made one final plea to my mother—reminiscent in a way,
of that long ago invitation to meet on Van Ness Street in San Francisco
if there were any hope left at all—to reconsider, or just consider, period,
their relationship, a potential future together, the three of us as a family.

Here's a final opportunity to give it a go before everything changes for once and for all. He saw it all coming and he told her in plain English.

And she never heard a fucking word.

August 17, 1974
Cassidy
5800 NE 20th Ave
Anywhere USA
NC postmark

My dear Anne, this will probably be the last lengthy serious letter I ever write; that is, in regard to our most curious ralationship (sic). I have reached a point where I am going to:

1) find a very young woman who suits me (and vice versa) and have 7-11 children, or

2) marry a divorcee (with 4 children) or

3) reach an agreement and arrive at a workable plan with my current wife and our daughter whom I love beyond anything on this earth

I have been beaten down; learned mucho; and risen up; and I am preparing to make a move of a lifetime. There is no bluff here. I am almost 27 and I feel that the time is ripe and necessary. And so I write to you, my long-lost wife and tell you of this - seeking sympathy or help none - but informing you because despite all, I love you and "that girl" more than anything in the world. Therefore, I say that, me time being naturally short, I am getting ready to make a HEAVY move, as it were, with far-reaching consequences.

All I ask on yer part is that ye think over what ye feel (if anything) and send a letter, note, etc. to me folks' address to ME.

If there is nothing to tell, an empty mailbox when I get

to Florida in 6 weeks will be sufficient communication. The "Empty Mailbox" sums up my expectations at this point. I merely write to express my feelings honestly and state me purpose.

If I hear nothing, I shall write nothing else regarding all this. I will continue sending what dough I did as before but if my new needs dictate I will send what I did before minus the school, as it has done all it can do for now.

There is no animosity here, just an honest effort to convey informative truth.

I will drive the truck I am buying for 14-18 months more; steadily; after which I will own it. Thereafter, I intend to buy a small farm and run the truck as needed - ca. 18-20 days a month.

Anyways, the time has arrived whereas things must be decided, so here it is.

Judge the heartless vagrant carefully, for all may lose.

I love ya anyway, Ed

September 3, 1974
The Gypsy
Waynesville, NC (postal service KY)

Dear Annie, My apologies for the late appearance of this installment but this last month as a rule is the slowest in trucking (especially my line which is produce) and I haven't been an exception.

I assume that Kennerly's upcoming school year is paid for so let me know how you want this month's balance made out.

I trust my letter arrived and I hope Kennerly got the

postcard with the bear on it.

I've been farting around quite a bit out here in the mountains. I pull stunts like driving 10 miles up a steep-assed narrow mountain road to pick up a quarter-load of tomatoes coupla' weeks back I damn near slid coupla' thousand feet down into the abyss when a shoulder collapsed under the trailer. I pulled clear, emptied the crap out of me britches, and spotted Lover's Land Leap. Certainly would've been a hell-of-a-funky way to make that jump.

Wanna hear some fine music? Pick up on Jesse Colin Young's solo albums; "Song for Julie" and "Lightshine."

By the way, here's wishin' you a happy birthday Friday the very 13th, nonetheless.

Enclosed is a remembrance worth a record or a bottle of wine or sumpin'.

Please remember me to the "Pumpkin."

Farewell, Ed

(10-cent stamp on envelope reads: "We hold these truths" - next to it Daddy wrote: GIMME SOME (truth, that is)

December 3, 1974

"From the eye of the December doldrums"

Dear Annie, Good to listen to ya last nite. I wasn't a talker at all, for a change. Going thru an overdose of mental aggravation these days, you understand.

Kennerly seemed brighter than ever. I was sounding her out on books, trying to figure an appropriate one to give her for Christmas. Incidentally, if there's something clothes-wise in particular she needs, pass the idea on to me or me mother.

*This promises to be an excessively vicious winter. My last
trip to middle Wisconsin showed 11 degrees temperature and
heavy snow at 10 am. Just the same, I can't wait to get back
up there. Anywhere beats this so-called "Sunshine State."
Must get on with some work now. I wish you a Merry Christmas. Love, Fixable*

When they were first courting, my mother's nickname for Daddy
was Huggable and his for her was Lovable. Fixable is suggestive, perhaps,
of that bygone time and still some potential.

*February 12, 1975
Cassidy
5800 NE 20th Ave
$875 check*

---

*April 10, 1975
E. Clay c/o Clay, Inc. P.O. Box 4003 Ft. Lauderdale, FL
Postmark Browerville, MN*

 *It appears I will be going west, probably for a powerful
spell. I don't know as of yet if I'll be able to come through
there but I'm sure things will be all the same whether I do or
don't. I think I am still regretful of the way things turned
out (Kilgore's occasional moods of dejection and rejection
abetting) but I guess there wasn't any solution and there
never would be.
 Anyways, I'm gonna miss you a little bit more. Kennerly
I'm going to try not to think about.
 I hope you find a good man who suits you and is good to*

the girl and hopefully one who says "stay away from the job today; we don't need the dough anyway."

Wanna hear a funny thing? Every woman I've come to know in the past 6 months has been 5 ft. to 6 ft. Four, 120 to 145 lbs, blue or green-eyed, and very well endowed cup-wise. Crazy! Love, Ed

My father is still rueful of their separation and speaks to the hopelessness of the situation, that things will always be the same or that there's nothing more to do, nowhere else to go with it. Worst of all he has to dismiss me from his mind to get over the pain of separation from both of us. In the end, the only assets they had to divide up was their joint record collection. My mom told me they went through them all one night, splitting up the albums like the years of their marriage. He took the heavy stuff like Jim Hendrix and weirder, edgier artists like Captain Beefheart. She held onto albums she'd purchased pre-him and maybe some Beatles, Dylan, and Stones they'd bought together.

July 3, 1975
146 NW 40th Ct., Ft. Lauderdale, FL

Dear Annie (and it's all I got) Here's fifty. Will try to have another to you by the fifteenth. Hope you're faring well. Tell Pooh I said hello. P.S. I might arrive before this does. Love, Ed

The next letter dated October 14, 1975, is a plea for "evidence" of divorce papers. "Gimme some truth!" he said.

Letters dated November 20, December 9, December 19, January 9, and March 2 say nothing of the fact that my father was remarried on November 29, 1975, to Leia, and that my baby brother Jimmy would be born end of March.

And then it was "them," not me.

they called him "dad"

"Desperation is the raw material of drastic change. Only those who can leave behind everything they have ever believed in can hope to escape."
— William F. Burroughs

No sooner had I returned home from the Highlands of North Carolina in summer of 1975—where I'd spent several weeks with my paternal grandparents, riding a horse, taking nature walks, going square dancing, and singing "Oh come, come, come, to the Church in the Wildwood" at the little country chapel—than my mother dropped a bombshell on me. My father's parents were getting divorced.

My grandmother had found my grandfather in bed with another woman. She then dumped a pot of spaghetti on their heads was how the story went. I was barely seven, so thinking about my grandmother rounding up a pot of spaghetti and dumping it on my *in flagrante delicto* grandfather and girlfriend was an odd thing to imagine. Was it still hot? Did it have sauce in it? I could see my grandfather and his soon-to-be wife sitting up under the sheets with strands of spaghetti hanging off their heads.

And I was dumbfounded. I had just spent all that time with my grandparents in North Carolina. How on earth could they be getting divorced? I drew the conclusion then and there that all marriages end up in divorce.

As my mom and I are reading through the letters from 1975, increasingly more urgent regarding the divorce papers, I'm suddenly disgusted with my father.

"How fucking disrespectful! Are you kidding me? At what point was he going to tell you he was getting married and having another kid?"

My mother and I try to remember if my grandmother may have leaked the news to my mom at some point. It's just as possible I found out on my own, maybe even before my mother, when I went down to Florida the following spring and met my baby brother. The reason I went to Florida at all was to be the flower girl at my Grandmother's rebound wedding. She would be divorced from him within a year or two because he turned out to be a total drunk.

"How fucking shitty can you get?" I gasp again. "Do you mean to tell me that he's expecting another child all those months and he never once mentions it to us in a letter? What the fuck?!"

Now I'm really pissed. If not for my mother, for myself as well. Outrageous.

I know I'd be much less forgiving today than I was back then. Of course, back then I thought my parents were *already* divorced, so none of this stuff was even registering with me.

I also think of my younger sister Shannah and the lingering resentment she has towards our dad. I wager this is partly because she was older when she had to go through all the stuff with our father—compared to any perceived trauma I might've gone through, years before —so she was better able to piece everything together and remember her own hell all too well. She bore a much bigger brunt than I ever did. My being much younger for some of these things may have served as a buffer, I suppose. Besides, I've always been more readily able to forgive.

There's a photo of me sitting between Daddy and Grandmother and holding my baby brother Jimmy, a bicentennial baby born in March 1976. I've got on my favorite turquoise T-shirt featuring The Who's Roger Daltrey as "Tommy," his wild, long, curly hair emblazoned on the front. Underneath it says "DALTREY" in big white letters. My hair is cropped short, revealing gold hoop earrings, and my smile says it all: proud, excited big sister.

I vaguely remember arriving at Daddy's house and being greeted at the door by the woman I had met before when we were at some other place I couldn't remember that time we went to Disney. It was my new stepmother, Leia. And I now had a baby brother. Sitting there on the sofa holding the baby, it hadn't quite occurred to me that my father was now remarried.

Family tied

Daddy and Leia and baby Jimmy moved up from Florida to Annapolis, Maryland, sometime in the fall of 1976. At least this way, Daddy would only be about two hours away from where we lived.

I visited sometimes and played with my new baby brother. Leia showed me how to change Jimmy's diapers, pulling the little sticky plastic tape tight towards the middle from each side. While the baby was napping, she taught me how to play Rummy 500 and Solitaire and how to shuffle cards, curving them just right so they fluttered into alternating layers—a skill I still wow my kids with to this day.

But almost immediately, money was tighter than ever with a new wife and baby and the shared cost of rearing me.

One time, Daddy apologized to Mom for the fact that our electricity got turned off and sent along what little money he had to spare. In another letter, he was making plans for me to come visit them in Annapolis. The letters were soon months apart. None to me or my mom. One was even from Leia, a check for child support because Daddy was so busy on the road that he didn't have time to send the check.

Kennerly, we sure did enjoy having you visit. Jimmy misses playing with you. Hope you come again soon. Leia

By March 13, 1977, in response to a letter from my mother which must have upbraided my father for lacking attentiveness to his first child, Daddy wrote back:

> I regret that my time is pinched at present and I'm unable to afford you a highly detailed reply to your letter. Enclosed is half of my present fortune.
>
> You need not endeavor to snap me into reality regarding either my age or economic failures. I am well aware of my shortcomings over the years. I am also doing my damndest to provide more.
>
> There is no one on God's earth equipped to loan me $400 except my father and for obvious reasons I don't intend to ask him for a fucking thing. I still owe my mother $500 and my grandmother $250. She's had to help Al and Nira since the year began and can't continually lend me money.
>
> So here's all I can do for now. It was forthcoming regardless of your letter. You are cordially invited to denigrate me at will. When I do my best and it isn't good enough my reaction, as you know, is simply 'fuck it.' This doesn't mean I don't care; it just means that I'm momentarily tired and discouraged. I expect better times in the months to come with this the case, things will consequently be better for you. Nothing is being withheld and nothing will be but there won't be any empty cupboard in this household on behalf of another.
>
> No one intends to pull any disappearing acts, etc. I don't recall throwing that one at you lately but I assure you I ceased running away from things long ago.
>
> I hope this helps. Love, Ed

Every letter after that—aside from inviting me to come visit after my baby sister Shannah was born—was laden with loss of work, out of work, odd jobs, late payments, no good union jobs available, can't even raise a down payment on a used car, had to borrow $200 to pay the rent, going to be poor for at least seven weeks, and utter frustration at all of this in spite of two raises inside of 50 days and an average of 70 hours a week on the road when he landed a new job. Then he suggested that both he and my mother needed jobs that were more lucrative.

But there just isn't enough money to go around...rather than badger me when I'm continually destitute, perhaps you might find a means to increase your own income. If I could sell my ass for a high premium, I'd probably do so and give it to that girl. Unfortunately, I'm a lousy prostitute. I hope ye are faring well. Love, Ed

By October of 1977, the courts got involved and would soon indicate what amount my father would have to pay every month. To which he replied, "I don't know what the courts will designate, but until my job becomes more lucrative, I can manage little more than $100.00 per month...The issue really is not what I'm supposed to pay but what I have in my possession to pay."

With inflation today, that $100 would be equivalent to $448 in 2021. If you've got a kid, you know how much it costs just to get groceries. Then start throwing in all the other expenses that come up, from sports activities to school fees to needing a new pair of shoes to going on a school field trip, let alone health, dental and vision care, clothing, recreation and vacation opportunities. Now imagine that $448 sometimes cut in half. Or just not coming at all. And all there is to get by on is one person's meager wages.

And so it went, on and on. These were the conversations I remember. The back and forth on the phone, my mom being stern with Daddy on the line, never yelling but deservedly patronizing, and me feeling the unbearable hopelessness of the situation, knowing that he couldn't afford to support all of us.

In the summer of 1978, he did pay for me to go to a day camp near where he lived in Annapolis. My stepmother had her hands full—"the

strain is already immense with two in diapers and soon both walking"—
so it worked better for me to be occupied during the day. There's still a
wretched JC Penney photo taken of the four of us that summer, my
stepmother and I and the two babies. My face was round and puffy and
bright red as a tomato from sunburn.

By end of summer I was down in Florida visiting my grandfather
and his new wife. My grandmother knew I would be down there, and I
ended up being part of an uncomfortable tug-of-war between my grandparents involving a go-between who picked me up at one grandparent's
home and dropped me at the other.

Around that time, my father started sending my mother money
orders on the sly, instead of checks. He was trying to supplement our
household without my stepmother knowing and he did this on and off
for some years, though it's not like it was ever a reliable flow of funds.

Letter from Daddy to Grandmother, June 1977:

> As difficult it is for me to sit down and write anymore,
> I've resolved to write this note to you, irregardless of how
> much screaming (Shannah), whining (Jimmy), and interro-
> gation (Kennerly) occurs in the process...
>
> Kennerly has been here nearly two weeks and has
> enjoyed herself, it seems. I've been wondering lately how you
> can possibly raise three children at once, and, I might add,
> I've come to appreciate you as never before your motherly
> devotion and sacrifice in my behalf. I regret I've so far been
> a sorry return but fear not, I'm destined to be a late bloomer
> (at least I believe it!)
>
> Kennerly is at least four-and-a-half feet tall and wears
> the same shoe size as her mother. To have a young lady of
> her size and maturity call me Daddy is baffling and very
> nearly incredible at times.
>
> Jimmy is the largest kid for his age I've ever seen. He is
> as big at 14-1/2 months as Kennerly was at two years. He's

so darned huge I often find myself over demanding towards him - he must be seen to be believed.

Shannah is cute and active and COLICHY (can't spell). Last night Leia was ill - I sat up with Shannah from 3-till-dawn - slept 2-1/2 hours in all. Wish there was something to ease COLIC!

I finally had my wisdom teeth yanked - PAIN as a life-style I'll describe it, after 8 days I'm still taking occasional codeine pills and not eating in comfort. Glad that they aren't baby and permanent as well. Trying to rustle up work this week. America no doubt has the most jobs in the world and the dullest! If I had no one but me I wouldn't turn a lick. A day spent in meditation is more worthwhile than 90% of the jobs I look into.

It was splendid to hear from you the other night. Everett sounded far above normal. We hope you're able to make it up in July. Gotta go now. Another diaper detail.

Love always,

Eddie

A home where the buffalo roam

I remember my grandmother once asked me why I still called my father Daddy as an adult. I reasoned that because I didn't grow up with him, it never had a chance of evolving into "Dad," as it often does around adolescence. And in my relationship to him as a child, it never became that chummy because he remarried and had other children. Our visits became fewer and further between, and rarely just the two of us.

There were occasional trips to the Salisbury Zoo, Daddy and I leaning over the fence together, peering at the capybara.

"Uh-uh, I-I say"—stuttered and intoned like the cartoon character Foghorn Leghorn—"he looks like a pug-nose revolvahhh!"

I giggled, imagining the flat-faced profile of the South American creature resembling a handgun.

Then down the wooden planks we walked to the bison, with Daddy narrating about the stink and enormity of the turds yet with a certain reverence that still has me associating my father with buffalo.

Daddy with buffalo at the Salisbury Zoo

Other than that, Daddy doing a lot of Dad-like things with me just wasn't part of my experience.

But in family photo albums with my brother Jimmy and sister Shannah as babies and toddlers, and later on when my brothers TJ and Jeffrey came along, my father is being Dad all the way. Giving them rides on his back (I was too big for this by the time Jimmy and Shannah came along), Easter egg hunts, Christmas trees, birthday cakes, fishing trips, days at the beach, vacations, family events, the tree house he built them in the backyard.

TJ remembers something about a buffalo and plodding around, riding on Daddy's back. "We'd run out to see him when he'd come home from driving the truck. He'd bring us Dunkin Donuts. Usually, his arrival was a happy change of pace." Here, TJ pauses. "Whether that played out and continued to be a happy change of pace is debatable, but initially him being there always seemed to be a good time."

He was always aware of Daddy's drinking.

"The little disclaimers here and there: 'I only drink for the taste,'" TJ remembers. "And we could sip little foams off the top of his beer at a young age. I remember him letting me have a glass of wine when I was young. Mom didn't like any of that, but she didn't have much of a say."

There were fishing trips to the local pond, mostly Daddy and Jeffrey, although the rest of the family went along a few times.

"Potentially, I saved Dad's life one time," Jeffrey recalls.

All the ponds were frozen over, too cold for fishing, but Daddy asked Jeffrey if he wanted to go for a drive.

"We picked up these super big rocks to see if we could break up the ice and went walking out on one sheet that was close to the size of a football field. We got all the way out to the middle and started heading back in. We were 15 to 20 feet from shore and the ice started cracking. First thing Dad says, 'Son, get off the ice!' So I scooted off the ice and he went completely through."

Daddy was able to get his arms up onto the ice and told Jeffrey to get something long to reach out to him. Jeffrey found a six-foot PVC pipe, and Daddy kept telling him not to come out on the ice, just slide it out to him so he could reach it. As he started to pull himself up on to the ice, the pipe fell through the ice and took him under again. When he came back up, he was able to pull himself up and told Jeffrey to get him a big branch like the one he'd been playing with earlier.

"He had started to break through the ice with his elbows a little bit at a time so he wasn't out quite as far as before, but still pretty far out," says Jeffrey. "I put the branch out to him and he was able to use that to pull himself out and slither off the ice. And then—

"He was just amazingly calm through the whole thing, came out with one shoe. I remember him shaking and shivering and driving the van back. He gets home and hops in the shower and Mom asked me what happened, then starts yelling at him while he's in the shower. We never talked about it much. Years later Dad told me Mom had said I was kind of down and needed to spend some quality time with my dad, and that was that day, probably before I was ten years old."

OBLIVION

We wait with dead certainty
Belleview in the Mist
Rose in the fist
Out of Time.
Once took a Romp with Jesus;
Water black an glaring
Fell in to the chin
Came out shiver and Grin.
Few know the pain of total release
Need thesaurus I b'lieve
Currents of time.
Wade 'em
Worry be want.
Let us love.

At night the boys, as TJ and Jeffrey were referred to since they were so close in age, would wind down listening to music or dance around the house.

"We'd sit on his lap and he did this, 'Little piggies, this little river don' run to 'aintree. God, now that I know that was from *Deliverance*!" TJ cringes.

I can picture my father cracking himself up with that half-laugh every time he said "little piggies." He wrote me once in a letter, when I told him I'd never seen the classic movie with Ned Beatty and Burt Reynolds, I must have been among the few people on the planet who'd never seen *Deliverance*. I then made a point of watching it and reporting back to my father. "Hideous!" Daddy said, tossing his head back with that half-laugh.

"You got the feeling he was always having a good time," says TJ, "not exactly considerate of everybody that he had obligation to, but he was having a good time himself most of the time."

I asked my grandmother once what my father was like as a child, and after reflecting for a moment, she had a ready answer. "He was always cracking himself up. I could hear him laughing and laughing through the house. He just liked to have fun and laugh."

Sometimes the boys would lie in bed and listen to stories my father would tell them of life on the road.

"There was always a sense that he was out there having adventures," says TJ, or he'd tell tales about characters like Andy Armadillo. "We'd picture it in our heads because we knew he had this friend named Andy, 'and the bullet ricocheted off a fridge and hit Andy, and one day I'm gonna tell you about the time Andy Armadillo went to Disney World.' It was all a bit anticlimactic when he told the one about Shannah and Jimmy going onto Space Mountain with Andy Armadillo."

Without knowing the back story to any of this, you'd think the other kids got the better deal. They had *him*. Even though he was gone a lot from their lives as well, he lived in their home, he returned there, he was known to all as their dad, whereas no one in my community just under two hours away even knew who my father was. In fact, when I got married, an elderly family member asked in a hushed tone, "Is that your *real* father?"—which made me realize, half my mother's family may not have known my father was even in the picture all those years. Certainly, none of my friends had ever met him.

So—my siblings got to call him Dad, got to have *him*. All of him. And as it turns out, they got the very worst of him, too.

Because in between the happy moments were many of disappointment and loss. Like the infamous Dutch Wonderland trip. They were driving up to Pennsylvania one time in the old Dodge Ram van. The boys were elementary school age, and Jimmy and Shannah were teenagers by then. Jimmy kept farting and smelling up the van.

"Dad made Mom pull over and stop the van, and he got out and just started walking," TJ tells the story. "He wouldn't get back in the van because of Jimmy's gas. It was supposed to be a family trip and a good day for me and Jeffrey. We just ended up leaving him on the side of the road."

In Jeffrey's rendition, he says it seems like Daddy already had a plan. "He had a bag and his guitar and just got out and left. I don't think we ever went to Dutch Wonderland."

Looking back, TJ adds, "For us it was like, is he gonna be okay? It was pretty fucking selfish on his part. Time spent with him always seemed unpredictable. Things never felt exactly safe or held together. Even though I was always excited to see him, I was never completely comfortable when he was around."

There were some good times playing baseball in the backyard, catching pop flies, but then the occasions when he'd want his father to be there and be the most proud—and "present"—like Little League or soccer games or having friends over, TJ almost wishes he hadn't been there at all.

"There was always an embarrassing sense of his volatility. I was always worried he was going to act out in some way. Like he'd be out there drinking a beer, yelling things that were not funny or interesting, just embarrassing."

One of those times was at the end of fourth grade at the Little League all-star game. "One of the only times he saw me play baseball," adds TJ. "He was hanging right behind the umpire with a Miller Life tallboy in his hand, slurring, 'Knock the hide off that puppy, son!' I was embarrassed in front of the other kids. And after the game, one of my coaches was walking with his girlfriend and Dad pulls out the old 'Don't I know you from somewhere?'—the oldest pickup line ever. At one point, the coach took a walk with him and told him how his behavior might not be appropriate for Little League."

It didn't help that the entire neighborhood already knew their older brother Jimmy's reputation by then. "Jimmy getting into trouble, and our parents being on and off definitely separated us from friends and houses we were allowed to go to," says TJ.

One time Daddy was driving TJ over to his grandmother's place, my stepmother's mom's, on the other side of the Chesapeake Bay. "I was aware he was drinking and driving, and I was not feeling safe. He was farting and opening the driver side door in highway traffic to let the fart out. He thought it was hilarious. I was terrified."

There were also the familiar disappointments and minimal expectations, like the time Daddy was supposed to show up at Jeffrey's school and have lunch with him and how excited Jeffrey was for that to happen.

"I asked Mom if he was going to make it and it wasn't looking like he was going to, so Mom showed up," he chokes, "probably took off work to come be there for that one. I don't ever remember an apology from Dad or anything like that."

The embarrassment and conflicted feelings of love mixed with pity and revulsion my brothers must have felt as children makes me sad for them. I feel a pang of guilt even saying I'm lucky I didn't have to experience what they went through. That was not my burden to bear.

This Life (written to Jeffrey)
1-20-02

Take her and run her
Down
The road less taken
Is the sweetest
Live by no man's terms.

God gave this to you.
No yesterday.
No tomorrow.
Partly sorrow.
Forgive him.

In the right space
and time we would
all die for one another.

everything out the window

"The sway of alcohol over mankind is unquestionably due to its power to stimulate the mystical faculties of human nature, usually crushed to earth by the cold facts and dry criticisms of the sober hour."
— William James

By the time she was a teenager, my sister Shannah was practically rearing the younger boys, while Jimmy was getting into teenage trouble, dropping out of school, and eventually leaving home. Jimmy's thing was huffing gas—often to the point of passing out and probably close to dying a couple of times—along with the death metal scene, raging irreverence, and general hooliganism in a low-rent town where nothing happens and kids have nothing to do but fuck themselves up and get into trouble. It must've been agonizing for my stepmother.

To see him now, towering and bearded like a Viking, a swollen belly way too big from decades of slamming beer and junk food, with an endearingly negative attitude and something to say about just about everything in the world—you'd think he'd be the last person to have a balanced perspective on his childhood and how things went down.

Within a few minutes of our conversation though, I'm finding an easy way about him I hadn't recognized before. Between the occasional murderous rants about pedophiles, his pseudo-Satanism, and general disgust for life, Jimmy is kind-hearted to the core. He loves family. He's articulate and ridiculously intelligent. He conveys a certain wisdom that cuts through drama and bullshit, be it within our own family or out in the world, that leaves me nodding in agreement. Some days I even find myself thinking how right he's been all along about how fucked the world is and I'm the deluded one trying to paint it positive.

I'm proud of him for having such a mature outlook on life and an ability to reflect on childhood that comes across as thoroughly self-examined, responsible, and accepting.

"I never blamed anyone for any of the bad shit. I was a shithead kid, always in trouble. Blame it on my ADD or whatever," he says. "I didn't pay attention in school. I read the whole book while everyone else was on chapter one. I got the whole test right and I didn't have to study."

Jimmy dropped out of high school and started playing music. Later he went on to get his GED. "I had already been across the country and lived in another city by the time my dumbass classmates graduated."

As a little kid, Jimmy thought it was perfectly normal to only see his dad a couple of hours on the weekend. Daddy was still doing long-haul trucking, so he was gone all the time. I can see now how we were all so conditioned to be comfortable with a father who wouldn't be around and that it didn't really bother us much. It was the truck-driving life.

In those days, Jimmy says, "When Dad came home, his first job was to whoop my ass for all the bad stuff I did all week. My mom stood there with the chart."

When I used to visit them in Greenville when I was younger, I saw Jimmy getting walloped on the backside many times. There'd be a slight delayed reaction as the sting of my father's hand came over him, then Jimmy would start wailing while doing a little dance of rage and frustration at the humiliation of being whooped. Sometimes it seemed swift and just, coming at exactly the right time while we'd all be sitting there at the dinner table, aghast at some behavior of Jimmy's. I'm sure I rooted for it to happen a few times. Other times it was out of proportion with whatever the transgression, but I could tell the last thing my father wanted to deal with after those long hours and days on the road was rotten behavior from kids and bullshit to deal with at home. That extra edge often landed on Jimmy's butt.

But Jimmy gives him pardon. "He wasn't abusive—I heard how Granddaddy was abusive. Dad was just doing what he thought was right."

One time in fifth or sixth grade, Jimmy recalls he had shoved his mom because she slapped him. For that one, he was dragged out of bed at two in the morning.

"Had the hell beaten out of me. But I didn't blame that on the drinking. I was a shithead, I was impulsive, I hit my mom. Of course, I made my mom out to be the asshole. I liked my dad a lot better."

There were fun times, too. "He had a big bicep when we were younger and he could do armpit farts. I thought that was great. I became our generation's champion for a while."

Weekends when Daddy was home, he'd get Jimmy and Shannah all wound up before bed, running around screaming and laughing, playing something about Niagara Falls and the Three Stooges and they'd run and hide. There were trips down to Andy's place, the chicken farm near Crisfield on the Eastern Shore of Maryland, and many road trips down to see Mammonk, our great-grandmother, in Newport News.

Jimmy recalls "stopping at that store just past Pocomoke called T's, I think, on the border between Maryland and Virginia. It had all different colors and flavors, candy fucking heaven!"

On the ride down to Virginia, they'd roll through one-horse towns like Accomack, Onley, and Exmore, past farms and fields and chicken houses in Perdue country, and old abandoned houses with bleak, gray, shabby clapboard siding that had lost whatever color they wore long ago.

"Funny thing about Dad," says Jimmy, referring to the dilapidated houses with broken windows and vines that overtook the old beat-up structures like they would eventually swallow the whole darn house into the earth in one gulp. "He'd tell us, 'Yup, the old homestead ain't looking so good these days.' He had me and Shannah convinced we had lived in every abandoned house on the Eastern Shore. When he and Mom were talking about moving and we were all out looking at houses,

Dad would point to a derelict farmhouse, the kind with toilets fallen through broken windows and half-ass white-trash Indiana Jones shit, and say, 'We're gonna be moving in next week.' Shannah and I would wail 'Noooooo!'"

Jimmy was still wearing Underoos when Daddy started giving him sips of piss-warm Schaefer at backyard BBQ parties at their house just about every weekend. "I did perceive pretty young what 'drunk' was. I knew Dad always had a beer or a mixed drink in his hand."

Jimmy was seven or eight when he and a friend were playing near some abandoned factory across the field, lighting matches and throwing them into clusters of dried grass. "The fire got out of control. Dad walked up and asked what the hell's wrong with you two? We had soot all over our faces and I'm thinking, 'I'm dead, I'm dead.' But Dad and his friend hauled ass and put the fire out. I think he just wanted to get back to partying. He yelled at me, 'Don't do that stupid shit' but no ass whooping, and then he said some 'food's ready' kinda thing."

Steamed Maryland Blue Crabs seasoned with spicy Old Bay would spill out onto a picnic table with a bunch of *Star Democrat* newspapers spread around as a tablecloth.

"Everybody'd pick up guitars and be playing and singing. Those were good times. People who had kids, we'd be running around doing our kid shit, it seemed normal." Jimmy rattles off names of truck-driving buddies he remembers being there: Al Miller, Bill Haddaway, a guy named Glenn who had a piano.

Al would be a best friend to my father for many years. They met in 1977 when they both went to work for TRP Transport in Wye Mills, Maryland.

"Ed was a very likable guy, outgoing as he could be, and we just kind of hit it off," Al reminisces. "He had more hair than I did, that's for sure. He had a strong jaw and was actually a pretty good-lookin' guy, I would think. We'd go partying a little bit, stop on the way home and get a snootful. Like myself, he liked music and we got along well. Say if I needed help with something, he'd come help me or I'd help him. I put on a roof one time and asked him to come down and he did. We all were drinking pretty hard, all had sore butts and none of us had ever done it before. Of course I was worried he was gonna fall off the roof. A couple years later I had to go up and renail it because we had done it all wrong. And I knew back then—I could smell it on him—he was drinking when he was driving a truck, too. I was afraid he was going to get locked up."

Music and alcohol were the constants in life with my father. "Dad was kind of adequate on piano," Jimmy concedes. "He played Greensleeves rip-roaring drunk, banging and howling like Tom Waits with Down syndrome. Played the dulcimer, always had an acoustic guitar sitting around. I think he knew a G chord and an E chord." Jimmy does that amused half-laugh like something else really funny is about to fall out of his mouth. It sounds so much like Daddy, you'd think you're hearing the same person.

"I wouldn't go so far as to say he was talented, but he tried and he was supportive. I wouldn't be playing music if it wasn't for him. And I wasn't being ironic about how much I love Fleetwood Mac, it's embedded in my brain. He told me he was proud of me, he was proud of the fact I was talented, and I thank him for music."

Jimmy's always had an ear for it, some hereditary musical aptitude like my paternal grandmother who was a trained pianist and could also play by ear. My grandfather could also play, having taught himself piano with a little book he ordered out of a magazine when he was a child. TJ has the gift as well, plays drums and guitar, and my older son has taught himself keyboards and some guitar. The rest of us got skipped over, although love of music is something we all share.

The trucker parties were fun, but they caused "turmoil in the house," Jimmy says. "Dad would get hammered, then get in the fucking car. It was the after-effects. He'd fuck up all weekend."

Among Daddy's flaws was a stubborn Clay streak. "You couldn't tell him anything," Jimmy says. "He'd get mad. But still, considering his free ways, how many men go off to get a pack of Marlboros and never come back? At least he took some responsibility and helped out as much as he could."

In those days, Jimmy says he and Shannah were "like guerrilla warfare trying to kill each other. One time we were on our bikes with training wheels, and I was spinning in the mud, kicking mud all over. Shannah was right behind me, and I kept spinning and spinning, it looked like she'd been riding down the road when Mount Vesuvius exploded." Jimmy still relishes the moment. "I didn't care what the punishment was, they could've sent me to reform school and it still would've been worth it."

But the best feeling was coming home from school and seeing their Pop-pop's truck in the driveway. A visit from my stepmother's parents was always a welcome reprieve. "We'd put on our best behavior, like if we pretended to get along, maybe they'd take both of us for the day."

Dreams and visions

When he was just four or five years old, Jimmy had a memorable dream one night that turned out to be a premonition.

"Whenever there was a huge thunderstorm, the whole house would shake," he says. "Either that or it was Dad had come home and was cranking Pink Floyd in the middle of the night and the part in 'Time' where the alarm clocks are going off, Mom's yelling, 'The kids gotta go to school!' Dad's naked, hunched over, drunk as shit, eating something."

Jimmy's bedroom was downstairs across the hall from Shannah's, so the two of them woke up from the storm and came upstairs to the living room with their sleeping bags and laid down in front of the big front window.

"Then I woke up out of this vivid dream in the same place—like you know you *were* just dreaming, right? But now you're *really* awake, but still in the dream. Then suddenly the window explodes outwards, BOOM!, like that storm outside, and this werewolf with a magician's cape floats up in the window and reaches out and beckons to me. He grabs my foot and is sliding me towards the window, and then I wake up kicking, trying to keep myself from going there. And I start crying."

About a month later Jimmy remembers coming upstairs and finding the couch by the railing no longer there. In fact, the entire front bay window was gone.

"Dad was sitting in the chair with a bottle. He had thrown the majority of the furniture out of the front room and it was all out on the lawn. This was pre-him-cheating-argument days. This was a direct result of the two-family situation."

The rare weekends that I visited Daddy, Leia, and the kids, I remember how it would often transition from that feeling of rosy, warm optimism that comes with the first sip of coffee or beer, the first track on the record, or the first drag on a cigarette. Daddy would get up on a Sunday morning and maybe put on some Gordon Lightfoot. "Sundown" would start booming through the house as the coffee aroma mixed with the smokey sizzle of bacon and scrambled eggs with diced peppers and onions. Daddy knew his way around the kitchen, and his charisma at those times drew us like moths to a flame, basking in his presence when everything felt momentarily happy and easy.

As my father became increasingly inebriated, the glowiness would dissipate as tension mounted between him and Leia. There would be minor disagreements at first, or she would correct him for whatever missteps he had taken, or if Jimmy did something to set my father off and got walloped, the ensuing argument over the punishment being out of proportion with the crime. Jimmy's face would go long and mournful so my stepmother couldn't help but pick him up, which would then set off more yelling and arguing. If Gordon Lightfoot was still playing, nobody was listening anymore.

As time went on, Jimmy savored the moments when he could just disappear from everybody's radar. "Like when my mom found out Dad was banging some truck stop ho', my room was downstairs and I could hear them fighting with each other. They didn't give a fuck about me, but in a fucked up, selfish way I loved it when they fought. In all the animosity, they left me alone."

Then Daddy would leave to get back on the road, and all that anger and frustration had nowhere else to go.

"Mom would take it out on me," says Jimmy. "In later years I'd call her a fucking bitch—treated my mom like she was the bad guy—when *he* was the drunk, and drunks by nature are selfish."

Even in Jimmy's acknowledgement, I can hear a certain commiseration with Daddy and the nature of being selfish. Maybe not letting him off the hook per se, but rightly identifying with the experience.

As I got older, the stretches between visits got even longer. I started babysitting on weekends at twelve years old for a family up the road from my house, and I'd often spend the entire weekend at their home.

This went on for years, helped me with spending money for things like preppy clothes and my Europe trip in 10th grade, among other things. When I did visit Greenville to see my father and family, it was like swapping one dismal environment for another. As a teenager, I thought my own hometown was shitty, a little town of 100 people with zero going on. Then I'd get to their town, which felt only slightly bigger and shittier. Run down. Low rent. Bleak and troubled. I always thought, damn, why'd they choose this place? Why couldn't they have stayed in Annapolis? Or why not over where my stepmother's parents lived? But Greenville, where desolation crept in as soon as you turned onto the road that led into town. As the car slowed down and everything got closer, you could see the taint of worn-out, unhappy life on the adults, on the town itself. The kids looked like the ones you only played with when there was no one left around. I judged harshly. But mostly I was concerned about my siblings, wondering about the effects of living in that town and praying like hell into their adulthood they'd all get out of there. Thankfully, they did, but growing up there did have some side effects.

I always spent Christmas Day at my maternal grandparents' house. My mom wasn't much into the holiday, so we went to their house for Christmas morning and all the fanfare. Then a day or two later I would go see Daddy and Leia and the kids, and then I'd usually go down to Newport News or Florida, seeing my great-grandmother or my grandmother on Daddy's side. I always saw it like I got to have three Christmases, because as far as gifts went, there were three separate exchanges and flurries of openings and everybody's homes were still decked out. I never had a feeling of missing out on anything.

My youngest brother Jeffrey and I talk about this one day. "Man, we had every single Christmas and you weren't there," he says. "You were only like an hour away from us and you coulda been there. Why wasn't Kennerly there? You never had him, not even once..."

I'm impressed by his keen observation. Jeffrey is inquisitive about my experiences as a child and the effects of our family life on me. In fact, he was the first sibling to ever ask about this when we were all together at Nags Head to spread Daddy's ashes back in 2012. It felt a bit awkward, as everyone else was drinking and I didn't feel like self-reflecting on childhood. But he and I have enjoyed many conversations since. He picks up the phone for no reason and calls to say hi, and through his constant encouragement, this book has been spurred along.

Not that there was anything wrong with being with my grandparents for Christmas and visiting Daddy and everybody a few days later, but that missing out on being with Daddy for Christmas was symbolic of just about everything of consequence in my childhood. Not that he didn't show up for some important things here and there, but for the most part I was not a part of his world.

I didn't *have* him.

Yet if I had been there with the kids for those Christmases, I know I would've been disappointed. I am fundamentally constituted as an only child, so having to compete with the other kids for a glimmer of my father's attention would have bummed me out.

A Christmas to remember

One Christmas when I was about 12 years old, I *did* spend Christmas with Daddy, Leia and the kids. My grandmother was coming up to spend the holiday in Greenville. This was years before TJ and Jeffrey were even born. It was a big, exciting deal and I was invited (anything with my grandmother was special). I remember baking cookies with Jimmy and Shannah, hanging stockings, and having one of the most hilarious memories with my grandmother late at night watching *It's a Wonderful Life* on the foldout sofa in the basement. With hot chocolate and fists full of goodies we had squirreled away, we'd settled in to stuff our faces, when suddenly the foot of the bed went flying up and shit went everywhere. We were both wedged into the crack, laughing our asses off, trying to decide whether to save ourselves or our late-night snacks. Grandmother half-peed herself. Then we remembered the kids sleeping across the hall, and the more we shushed each other, the more we sniggered and sputtered and laughed.

We cracked ourselves up for years over that one. Whenever we'd wander down Memory Lane, Grandmother would get that faraway look in her eye and grow quiet, tiptoeing around the rest of what happened. "And then there were some not so happy times," she'd say, almost whispering. "'member that?"

It may have been Christmas Eve, that night my grandmother went to the church service. I don't know why I didn't just go with her, as if staying behind to hear Daddy and Leia arguing would somehow have been more fun for me. As the yelling escalated at their house, the voice in my own head got louder.

"This is ridiculous. Why should I come here and be subjected to this crap? Especially at Christmas."

I decided I would leave and go find Grandmother. Without anyone noticing, I slipped out the front door into the chill and damp and strolled down the dark, empty streets of Greenville with only an occasional lamp post to guide the way until I reached the only church I knew of. I was thinking the whole time, maybe I'd get there just as the doors were opening and out would pour the joyful families and the familiar face of my grandmother, who would certainly be surprised but happy to see me.

Instead, the doors remained closed. I stood on the opposite side of the street waiting expectantly. I didn't have the courage to go marching up the steps and hauling open one of those big doors only to have everyone turn around and stare at me. Plus, how would I find my grandmother without going up and down every row? Outside on the street, I don't remember anybody going by, not even a car, and after a while—a long church while—it started to rain. Heavily. Even though by now I was convinced this was the church my grandmother was in, the longer the service went on, the longer it seemed like it could still go and the more worried I got about having been away so long. When I had slipped out of the house earlier, I had definitely intended on "running away"— even if it was just down the street to the church—but at the same time, I kinda figured nobody would notice I had left. It would be just as easy to get back to the house and slip back in unnoticed.

I made my way back to the house, drenched by the time I swung open the exterior front door and stepped inside. I could hear the frenzy above in the split-level living room. Leia peered over the railing and gasped, "Where have you been, we've been so worried about you?" in a way that took me by surprise. I could tell she was genuinely concerned.

I could hear Daddy's voice in the hallway, asking if that was me, returned. Next thing I remember I was sitting on their bed explaining myself. I don't think I was straight with them, about the arguing. Too embarrassing for me; for them, too confronting. We pussyfoot around people's feelings, don't we, when we don't live with them or spend much time together? At least I did. Always sparing others' discomfort. I probably played a little bit dumb, like what's the big deal, I just went looking for my grandmother, sorry-to-worry-you kind of thing.

When my grandmother came back from church, I was still sitting on Daddy and Leia's bed with the door cracked open.

"I couldn't stand the arguing anymore," I whispered, as my grandmother sat down on the bed next to me. "I should've gone to church with you."

"You should've," she said, and we had a quiet laugh.

When the kids were younger, I couldn't relate to them so well, but when Jimmy became a teenager, we started to connect more. That's when my stepmother Leia asked me one time when I was visiting if I would have a talk with him.

"Because he listens to you," she said.

Jimmy was getting into trouble at school and around the neighborhood, and the gas-huffing was bad news—scary stuff even for me, who used to sniff poppers in the bathroom at lunchtime in high school. I offered him a cigarette, an insider gesture and rough camaraderie, as we took a walk across that desolate back field behind their house.

"So what's all this trouble you're getting yourself into?" I bumbled around, trying not to sound preachy while still fulfilling my sisterly mission to impart some kind of wisdom.

Years later in telling my brother Jeffrey about this early intervention, he laughs. "Yeah, obviously he didn't listen."

Even so, I felt more big-sisterly after that. If my stepmother considered me a role model for my siblings, then I should see myself more as a big sister, not some older relative who came to visit sometimes.

Mind you, things were never particularly warm and fuzzy between me and my stepmother. As time went on and money got tighter and mouths got wider to feed, I can imagine the resentment brewing. She never treated me disrespectfully or unkindly when I was around, but whenever I arrived at their house, I made myself as inconspicuous as possible knowing that in the background there was already agitation and burden. I didn't want to create any direct conflict or personally add any weight to it.

So I cleared my dishes and helped with the kids and offered to help with dinner and giving baths and I was usually roped into bedtime rituals because the kids wanted my attention, which I didn't mind after all. At least when I left each time, no one could say I had been a pain in the ass or a freeloader.

Once when I was about nine or 10 years old, I opened a letter in the mail. It was from Leia. By the time I had finished reading it, my mother had snatched it out of my hands, and I was just standing there bewildered, asking, "Why is Daddy going to jail?"

That was one of those times where we had to meet at a neutral location for a sort of intervention. Some mutual friends were having a party that weekend and we happened to be going, as were Daddy and Leia. I remember ambling around the back garden to the right of my father, who carried his lit Camel in his left hand. I mostly looked straight ahead or at the ground in silence while he alluded to something about lack of maturity and he wasn't really going to jail.

He asked me if I was okay. I told him I was. Come to think of it, I was probably doing a lot better than my mom thought I was doing, but I guess it was the principle of the matter. The child support thing was heating up, and to get at my mother, my stepmother had tried to get at me—which didn't actually feel all that hurtful, but clearly it was hurtful to my mom.

Years later, Leia was one of the first people I talked to when I got sober. I wanted to let her know that any tensions between us were forgiven and I knew that she was doing the best she could under the circumstances. I was also grateful for my half-siblings. She did excuse her own behavior a bit, given that she was constantly dealing with my father, otherwise she would not have acted in some of the ways she did. I gave that to her because I couldn't imagine being in that kind of environment all the time, a bit like torture—constant fight or flight, total survival mode as a mother and wife. And the complication of codependency, of loving an alcoholic. Especially, I might add, someone as handsome and good-humored as my father. I'm sure she knew she should have left him many times over, but she just couldn't, financially or emotionally.

At my wedding, she tearfully came up to me and shared a memory of when she first met me as a little girl visiting down in Florida. I had asked her to give me a bath and she said it was the sweetest thing. She knew she wanted to have kids, and I was an example of the kid-ness she was after.

When my own first child was born, we took him as a newborn that Christmas to see her and the kids. This was before my father had even met the baby yet. When my son was a toddler, Leia sat and read to him. My boys call her Grandma Leia, and we've shared many memories since, including being among the very few people who were there together in Florida to honor my grandmother after she passed.

Imbalance of power

One day everything changed between Daddy and Jimmy. I'd heard tale of the legendary scuffle before, variations from TJ and Jeffrey, who were both still pretty young at the time, and Shannah's occasional mentioning it whenever I naively suggested that my father wasn't physically abusive.

"I came home fucking beyond high, smoking weed all day," says Jimmy, "probably huffing gas, too, had a big bowl of Grape Nuts cereal with a scoop of ice cream and Wheat Thins topped high as the table, and was eating out of a big salad bowl. Everybody was arguing and Dad yells, 'More rotten stuff in that bowl than anything in this goddamn beer!' Shannah came to my defense and called him a goddamn drunk, and he told her to shut up or get the fuck out of here or something and shoved her. I jumped up so quick—it was weird—I punched him upside his head and knocked him on his ass."

By that time, Leia had gotten in between Daddy and Jimmy, who was already taller than my father's six feet. Even though Daddy raised his hand to fight back, he must've realized there was no more disciplining of this kid. Jimmy backed out of the house, walked out the back door, and sat in the back field until Daddy left.

"After that, Shannah and I became friends," Jimmy adds.

Although Shannah doesn't want to talk about any of this and declined to talk to me, I know some of her bitterness comes from a childhood in which she was too embarrassed to have friends over, let alone the ins and outs and unpredictability of having an alcoholic father in the house.

There were other times when Jimmy and Daddy landed on the same page. "Like when I was younger, getting high and all that, I'd say, 'Who gives a shit? We're all gonna die anyway,' and Dad would raise an eyebrow and say, 'Can't argue with that logic.'"

"I never really considered myself an alcoholic," Jimmy continues, explaining his drinking has tapered because he hated how he kept turning into an asshole. I listen politely, wondering if he's feeding me a load of crap, given his habits over the years. But he's 44 now, has a good place to live, is playing music professionally in a death metal band, had a decent job up until the pandemic, is living a pretty good life, and is as happy as it gets—for Jimmy. If he says he doesn't drink so much anymore, I'm taking his word for it.

"Now I just do acid," he interrupts my reverie. "It's much better for me, plus you can't really get addicted to it." This makes all kinds of Clay sense, and I immediately get where he's coming from.

We are soon reminiscing about Jimmy's cross-country death metal tour as a guitarist for The Cop Killers back in the early 1990s and the van that never quite made it past the Arizona desert to California. I was living in San Francisco at the time, and I remember breathing a sigh of relief that the boys in the band weren't going to be crashing on my floor after all.

"I appreciated that about Dad when I got older," Jimmy says. "I still don't know how he did it," referring to the vagabond life our father seemed to be so at ease with. "I need a little security. I need a fucking place to sleep, shower, and shit—a place to do all those comfortably."

In Charlotte, Jimmy has always been comfortable, he says, working on and off for decades as a cook at Red Lobster.

"I've got some of Dad's work ethic, for sure. He worked all the time, brought in $1600 a month in the Eighties. I remember he worked a lot because mom didn't."

Jimmy's still talking, but my mind has taken a detour at the mention of Daddy's income in the 1980s.

I remember my mom dropping me off at their house in Greenville one time. Jimmy was probably about six or seven years old and came to the door, abruptly asking my mother if she was the woman who was stealing from their family. Those words have stayed with me all these years as I imagine the conversations my father and stepmother must've had, all those arguments overheard by kids, the stories that developed through young eyes and minds.

During the more difficult years between my parents, when child support issues colored their friendship and strained relations between our households, of course I lived in the house where there was a single mom receiving little and sometimes no support—financial, emotional, or otherwise—so my mother's frustrations were my own.

I was a teenager by then, and none of the kids were old enough to have conversations with about such things, so I had to live with whatever perception they might have—of my mother, of me, of us. I sometimes wondered what they had been told or what they believed, but I stifled it like anything else that would challenge things or make anyone uncomfortable. Wouldn't want to talk too much about my own mother in the presence of my stepmother, because surely she wouldn't want to hear about her. Wouldn't want to bring up all the times Daddy didn't come to see me when he said he would. Wouldn't dare mention how lame it was that I came to their house for the weekend and Daddy was always sleeping until Sunday morning breakfast. Wouldn't dare get into an explanation with an eight-year-old kid about how child support works, and that it's not "stealing."

Born with a silver spoon

My mother struggled to give me the gift of experience instead of things. After being on welfare and the broken leg slash hitchhiking era, we moved to a little town called Quantico, about eight miles west of Salisbury, Maryland, where we rented an old country house for $40 a month. From the time I was about four to the age of nine, we lived in that house, where there was no running water. Occasionally—like some great miracle—water would spit and sputter out of the pump house faucet in back of the house, but mostly I remember stopping off at the barn at my grandparents' house every week and filling up a five-gallon jug to bring home for cooking and bathing.

To take a bath, we boiled water on the stove and poured it into the tub, over and over again until it was full enough to feel like a bath. (Did I mention the tub was smack-dab in the middle of the kitchen, right next to the fridge and stove?) There was no indoor bathroom, so instead we had to use the outhouse in the back field. Keep in mind this was the 1970s; having to use an outhouse was unusual by any standard in the United States. I would make my way, usually in bare feet, across chunky mounds of dirt to get there. The outhouse leaned precariously back towards the ditch at a good 25-degree angle, enough to make your knees come up when you sat down. I was always afraid my body weight leaned back too far would make the whole thing tip over.

It stank like an outhouse, too, a hundred-year-old one, fetid and rotting there all those years. Worse still were the bitter winter nights when I had to poop. Bundling up. Flashlight beam bouncing across the field. Cold as all hell. A wad of toilet paper in hand in case there was none left on the rusty nail in the outhouse. And then trying to manage my coat and clothing and exposing my ass to the frigid, stinking world below. At some point, my mother must've gotten tired of it, too. We started using this little stool with a bed pan-type thing underneath for those rough nights when you just didn't want to go outside. But then I had to carry the pail with my turd, stinking in my face, across that same field the very next morning to dispose of it. Eventually, my mother got this eco-friendly thing called a Destroilet. It was mounted on a couple of blocks of wood in an upstairs closet. After you did your business and closed the lid, it would incinerate everything with a roar of flame. Except it left a lingering burnt poop odor you could smell for a while after the flush. Whenever my next-door neighbor friend came to our house to play, she'd always go back home to go to the bathroom. She was scared the Destroilet would singe her butt.

Imagine my glee when we moved to a different house up the street and saw that there was an indoor bathroom and running water!

So yeah, we weren't exactly living high on the hog all those years.

Admittedly, some of it was by my mother's choice. Mine was not a conventional upbringing, that's for sure. For one, we had no television.

"My mother doesn't believe in it," I'd say, haughtily, to friends who came over, as if they were the uninformed ones who had fallen for that TV crap. "She says it'll poison my mind."

On my bedroom wall growing up was a caricature of me as a young child, sketched by an artist friend of my mom's. A thought bubble over my head has a television in it. The sub-text reads: "Anne's worst fears come true."

A friend came to sleep over once and couldn't stop laughing at the notion that we had no TV. She thought it was the most bizarrely hysterical thing ever.

And since we had no running water, of course we had no washing machine. We'd gather up all the dirty clothes in a couple of round yellow baskets that were cracking at the rim—you had to keep switching the position of your hands so you wouldn't get pinched. Then we'd drive into Salisbury where there was a Norgetown laundromat. I could spot the big, globe-shaped sign high on its post as the car peaked on the overpass. At Norgetown, once we got all the clothes into the wash cycle, there'd be a vending machine and I always got those little Lance chocolate cookies with creme centers. I can still remember the steamy smell of that place with its industrial-sized dryers, where I learned to put my hand in and give it one last spin so any rogue socks or underwear could be removed.

Although we didn't have a dishwasher or a TV or a washing machine, by God, my mother was not going to send her child to one of those god-awful public schools. The whole district was run by some good ol' boy she couldn't stand, and she did not approve of the direction public education was going in Salisbury, Maryland, in the early Seventies. From the time I was two years old, I attended a small, fledgling private school whose education philosophy jibed with hers.

My quirky mom was into organic gardening long before it was a thing, and I remember conversations about the environment through consciousness-raising publications she subscribed to, like *Coevolution Quarterly* and *Whole Earth Catalog*. Our house was heated entirely by an old upright Warm Morning wood stove that my mother had bought from somebody down the road for like $25 so our carbon footprint would be minimal. She also had all the recycling separated out in paper bags in the kitchen. Once a week we put it all in the trunk of the car and drove it to the recycling center in town. I knew how to tell aluminum from steel cans and which barrels they were supposed to go in. I learned how to separate the different colored bottles. White ones over here, brown ones go together. I liked hearing them clink and sometimes shatter.

I went to school with cottage cheese and fruit, and an apple, maybe some tomato soup in a Thermos. My liverwurst and cheese sandwiches were on whole wheat bread. How I longed for a bologna and cheese sandwich on two slices of Sunbeam! Just to feel normal and fit in with what everybody else was eating. Sometimes I intentionally left my lunchbox in the station wagon of the mom who carpooled with us, so I could get donations from the other kids' lunches.

My mother was a San Francisco hippie living on the Eastern Shore of Maryland—a bastion of backwardness that lingers still—imbuing the place with her progressive-minded West Coast values. She was raising her little country-hippie kid as a single woman in the 1970s, long before divorce was so trendy, all the while receiving $20 here or $50 there from my father, sometimes with rhythm and consistency, but mostly sporadically throughout the years. I wouldn't be surprised if she still has records of every single contribution he made, all filed away somewhere in chronological order with paper clips and handwritten notes.

And while outwardly it would have appeared that my mother's parents—my grandfather being a prominent dentist in town—would have been generous with us, that was not how they operated. My grandparents functioned like a bank—very fiscally responsibly. Any one of their children who came to them for money had to sign a loan agreement with interest and a repayment plan. I remember my mother rattling off her debt repayments to my grandmother for Salisbury School, Camp Farwell, gymnastics. By the time I reached adulthood and was in need of a loan for our wedding, I knew I would need a payment plan in hand when I went to my grandmother if I wanted any financial support.

"When you were born, we had nothing," Mom would say, telling me the story of humble beginnings in San Francisco. So she went out with the money they had collected at the Witches' Brew (where everyone bet on what day I would be born) and she bought me a little silver spoon.

"I was determined that you would be born with a silver spoon in your mouth," she beams. Hence the opportunities. Private school, sleep-away camp in New England, piano lessons, horseback riding, a decade of gymnastics, sophomore Europe trip, and all of the things that kids of privilege would have the opportunity to engage in.

So I could only imagine what was going on in everyone's minds when my father was arrested on his front lawn, in front of his kids, during my senior year of high school for not paying child support. I would soon find out, surely, as my father's mother would get wind of it from one side or another and drop a hint here and there until finally I had to lay it all out in the open and tell her everything that was really going on.

"They say it's your mother having Eddie put in jail," she said with her sing-songy accent. "How's he going to pay child support if he can't work?"

"It's not my mother," I explained. "It's these new child support laws they're enforcing. It's done through the courts. She has nothing to do with it. If he's in arrears, they come after him."

"Well," she sighed. "I don' know anything about that."

Up until that time, child support payments were loosey-goosey arrangements. (Remember, we were divorce pioneers.) Child support back then was determined by judges based on the needs of the child and what the non-custodial parent could afford. Earlier laws enacted at the state level had failed to effectively enforce consistent follow-through on child support collection. There were more and more single-women households, many of them living sub-standardly with little to no support at all. Because of this, the federal government became increasingly involved to ensure that women and children received the support awarded to them and that more consistent award standards were applied in the courtroom.

I find myself a bit more fascinated by this topic than I expected. Pursuing my research further, I discover that we were part of a considerable problem facing low- to middle-income women with children at that time, reflecting a disturbing national trend that required the federal government to step in.

"The inadequacy of most states' discretionary standards in setting the amount of child support took on crisis proportions by the early 1980s. Insufficient child support had become a major cause of the spiraling poverty rate among women and children. Of the 9.4 million custodial parents in 1987, 41 percent had no child support award. When courts did award child support, award levels usually were inadequate, thrusting many children and custodial parents into poverty or a seriously diminished standard of living. In 1979 the average awards comprised only 37 percent of the estimated average monthly expenditure for children in a middle-income household and only 55 percent in a low-income household."

—Cahn, N, Murphy, J. Collecting Child Support: A History of Federal and State Initiatives. The George Washington University Law School. 2000.

I'd say we fell squarely in the low-income household category and those statistics are about right, times 15 years. This was also about the time they started garnishing wages and making tax refunds go towards child support if a parent (mostly dads, let's face it) was in arrears. There were a lot of pissed off men, I'm sure. But it was time to pay the piper.

"He's also been told that this was going to happen, so obviously he chose to ignore it," I defended further, getting annoyed. "If he had such a hard time paying child support for me, then why the hell did he have two more children in the last few years?"

"Well..." my grandmother bleated, defeated on that one.

I trod lightly, knowing that anything I said was going to be broadcast, probably to my father if not my stepmother, and somehow to my grandfather even though he was married to someone else and he and my grandmother didn't even speak to each other, so perhaps it went down the line by way of Aunt Sally or even my great-grandmother. Hell, Uncle Ray probably even heard about it, much as he tried to stay out of everything. Either way, I wanted to make sure it got translated perfectly and that nary a grudging tone was interpreted. At 17 years old, I had become masterful at this.

Clay kids with Daddy (TJ, Jeffrey, Shannah, Jimmy, me)

Jeffrey shares with me a conversation in which TJ divulged that when he was a kid, probably around eight or nine years old, Daddy said to him, "The only reason we had you was so your mother could keep me around."

The boys were doing LSD together that evening and it was a bro-bonding moment.

"Well shit," said Jeffrey, bringing levity to the perceived solemnity. "I guess the only reason they had me was so you would have someone to play with."

showing up

"The heart will break, but broken live on."
— **Lord George Gordon Byron**

When I moved to San Francisco to finish up my academic education, it coincided with the Rodney King verdict and riots in Los Angeles. In San Francisco, I was marching around the blocks with a group of social justice student activists, chanting, "The world is listening, no justice, no peace!"

I wrote my father often about the California Jesuit education I was getting, not to mention how I was walking in my parents' footsteps at free concerts in Golden Gate Park, like the Ben & Jerry's festival with Jefferson Starship, or going to see Big Brother and The Holding Company along with Commander Cody playing at the I-BEAM on Haight Street. Daddy got a real kick out of my meanderings.

Big Brother and Commander Cody. Wow! Hope they didn't stand up there looking ancient and distinguished breaking wind at 140 decibels. Thanks so much for the flyer. Be sure and send your mom one.

———————⬦———————

You and I are totally in step in reflections on the King verdict. I was very dismayed—I've been on his end of the stick more than once. If we don't become truly just we will ALL LOSE. Sad to say, I have NEVER received anything but injustice at the hands of police.

While I lived in San Francisco with my boyfriend, Daddy sent cassettes and CDs of what was speaking to him and what he thought would speak to me. Van Morrison's *Hymns to the Silence*. We played those tapes over and over. Neil Young's *Harvest Moon* had just come out, every track as good as the next. He sent probably five different Velvet Underground mix-tape compilations, which we devoured, especially on Sunday mornings. Then there was James McMurtry's *Too Long in the Wasteland* and Richard Thompson's album *You? Me? Us?* and U2's *Achtung Baby*.

In between, he'd send me random stuff like a Dexter Gordon tape with Boz Scaggs on the flip side. I ended falling in love with that smokey, melancholy Dexter Gordon saxophone.

"Courtesy of your Uncle Ray," he said.

Daddy and Uncle Ray had different taste in music but occasionally they'd strike a similar chord. Uncle Ray told me they also found common ground with Burton Cummings, lead singer of the Guess Who.

When Daddy came out for my graduation from University of San Francisco in 1995, we had some time together in my apartment at Stanyan and Oak. One quiet afternoon when everyone else was out, we sat in my living room with the bowed windows facing out over Golden Gate Park, listening to Quicksilver Messenger Service at top decibel.

"I took you with me to see Quicksilver in concert in 1969, had you up on my shoulders." Daddy's voice was low, a little slurry from the wine he kept hidden in a jug in his duffel in our extra bedroom. He was sitting on the floor in front of me, leaning back against the futon sofa frame. I was fully extended, kind of half-asleep or pretending to be. I must've draped my right arm over his shoulder at some point.

"You know who Dino Valente, the lead singer is, don't you?" he asked.

"Mmm-nnnh," I mustered.

"Dino Valente's real name is Chet Powers, 'fact he just died last year. Guy's a brilliant musician, also went by Jesse Oris Farrow. He wrote a song you probably know, 'Get Together' by the Youngbloods."

I always felt completely inadequate when it came to such knowledge of music, while Daddy was this living, breathing historical reference. My Aunt Sally later told me he could also rattle off the full names and birth and death dates of my grandfather's ten siblings, not to mention remember phone numbers from just about any time and place. Through the haze of booze, there was still this powerful repository of information in there.

"Yeah, you up on my shoulders at that concert; everybody thought you were al-right, kid." I tried to imagine my one-year-old self with my father squeezed into a packed indoor concert hall in San Francisco in 1969. Or maybe it was outdoors at Golden Gate Park. Without any other details, the vision faded. But as I was lying there—together with my father in the city of my birth for the first time since we both left—I was profoundly aware of why the music, particularly the Sounds of San Francisco like Quicksilver, Jefferson Airplane, Janis Joplin and Big Brother and the Holding Company, the Grateful Dead, not to mention the music I had discovered on those vintage cassettes of Daddy's: Dylan, the Doors, Buffalo Springfield, had always felt familiar, like it was way down in my bones and deep in my soul.

Daddy got quiet as we took in the music and lyrics, probably the first time we'd ever listened to Quicksilver together like that, ever. In the past, it would've come up in conversation, but it's not like it would play on the radio all that much.

Quicksilver crooned "Light Your Windows," the song we both knew was speaking to us, and Daddy took my right hand over his shoulder. Patting it, he said, "Aww doll."

It took effort for him to say those two words, as if the weight of it all —my whole lifetime, mostly without him—was there in that moment, in the music. And the music was a reminder of that youthful time in his life when so much more was possible. Where did it all go?

Some years later, the first seven words of that song would be how Daddy communicated with me from Beyond. During an energy work session, when I had asked for a sign—anything that would signal to me that my father was still around—the lyrics "Hold on girl, now don't be blue, dry those tears for me and you..." suddenly bleeped across my forehead like a radio station momentarily tuning in, then gone again when the dial moved just a bit to the left or right.

Santana girl
Independence Day 1998
Somewhere in Mayhem, USA
[letter excerpt]

I'm mighty glad you're coming home gal. You are more part of me than you'll ever know, Santana girl. Took you once '69 diaper to Matrix San Francisco. Mom at post office working. Was changing yer poopy on chair adjacent flirting with brunette Annette by name listening Taj Mahal and in popped Carlos heself. Simply joined in. 'Cept for Tom Waits best show, ever saw. (Sorry you don't 'member.)

An envelope postmarked June 16, 1995, has John W. Ritter Trucking, Inc. as the return address, C/O ED CLAY. Scratched off in the "To" part of the envelope are the words: "Ed Clay 5 Years." Within a few years, my father would completely lose his right to drive a truck—the envelope was a telling reminder of just how much there was to lose, a good job with a reputable company and a long career on the road. The letter is his follow-up to my graduation and also his having seen his old friend and college roommate Steve Skinner for the first time in 25 years at my graduation party in San Francisco.

Saturday, June 10th 5:00 A.M.
1995
TWO YEARS AfTER

You must understand that I'm not a lonesome ol' man. To put all in a nutshell, read Henry Miller. I wonder if people under forty know of him.

This epistle has been brewing since your graduation; not your 2-year old letter.

It moved me incredibly.

Also, "Yesterday's Wine." Great, painful writing.

As we concluded on that Quicksilver night in San Francisco, we could talk for a hundred years. Thank you.

Steve and I had very deep conversations and he asked that question. "Do you have any regrets?" I initially said "none." Then I said I had one. "I wasn't around for Kennerly."

I beg no excuses. You've grown up far more balanced than either of your parents with far greater pain. I took your letter (1993) as forgiveness. I also have alligator skin when it comes to me. I've done dozens of things wrong.

(BREAK)

How do ya like Ken Kesey stationery? ORANGE NEXT!

I'm so glad the video worked. Don't worry about "The Mountains of Madness." I remember playing that as myself, H.P. Lovecraft, and Rod McKuen all at once. Horrible, I'm sure. (But it healed.)

Footnote: After reading "Yesterday's Wine," I reacted: "Honesty will have a beautiful revenge! And hurt only the weak."

Friday—16th

Let's drop me for a bit. I want to know EVERY dEtail

about your tEaching stiNt in JapaN; also, if you so choosE; youR status with loaNs and dEbt. WritE this to mE.

JEffREy callEd mE and toldmE how much thEy EnjoyEd OCEAN City with you. That makEs my wEEk! Which lEAds to aN ExplaNatioN of "No 'grEts'. With fivE childREN likE I havE, I could NEVER RUE A thing that happENED. (I'VE maNagEd to livE two lifEtimEs whEN most mEN would havE bEEN misErablE foR 20 odd yEaRs.)

YouR grandmothER, during ViEtNam, told mE, "I livE through my childrEn." I Now do that as wEll as musicAl, artistic, and somE litErary pursuits.

Let mE boRE you ONCE moRE: You aRE thE 2nd Clay through college (and summa cum laude.) I am so proud of you.

Two footNotEs:

1 YouR mothER and LEIA stoppEd taking the pill w/o me knowlEdgE. (and I'm glad!)

2 I wasN't stoNEd at AltamoNt. On anything! I watchEd the womaN's EvERy move. You wERE bEing takEN. Easy moVE.

I hope this is good.

Love, Daddy

Delusions of adequacy

My father had good intentions, even if he couldn't always fulfill on his promises. He would say things like, "Well, I'm going to help pay for the wedding" when he was just getting out of jail and had no source of income. Or when he got such-and-such he was going to do such-and-such. He was always creating this expectation of future possibility and accountability, something we could rely on. In letters he wrote to my Grandmother, he'd say she could count on him for being there for her, but there was no way in hell she could have counted on him for much of anything. It's not like he never did anything for her. When he was occasionally sober enough to cook or shop or get things repaired around the house, he was certainly a help to her. But he was so inebriated most of the last 20 years of his life there's just no way he could deliver. In his heart he wanted to be depended upon, and she *wanted to believe she could* depend upon him, but that was probably her polite, pretend understanding, along the lines of, "Yes, I believe that's what you want to do or wish you could do, but we both know you will never be able to do that."

It was a polite little game we all played with him. We were accustomed to these assertions that he couldn't possibly come through on, yet we rarely called him out on the bullshit. No one said, "Hey Dad, you know that's not possible. You're never gonna do that. Who are you kidding?" I guess we spared his feelings, especially when he was trying to redeem himself after some failure.

"I'll be running trucks from Walmart going from here to here and we'll spend time together this summer," he'd say to the boys, hopeful of getting his license back after the DWIs and jail time.

Jeffrey says he knew Daddy would never get his license back and he would never be doing that.

"I had small expectations, like I'd be looking forward to getting to hang out with my dad this weekend and Shannah goes over to his girl-friend Jean's house and sees he's completely shit-faced—'so you're not going over there'—and that would be the end of it."

Jeffrey sometimes overheard conversations between Daddy and Leia about the whole drinking and driving and losing his license thing.

"Son, your dad's an outlaw," Daddy asserted.

"Don't talk like that with him in the car," my stepmother scolded.

"He doesn't know what that is."

"Do you know what an outlaw is?" she asked over the backseat.

"A bad guy?" said Jeffrey.

Exasperated, my stepmother said, "See, Ed?!"

Years after I'd finished my associate degree in New York and completed my undergraduate degree at University of San Francisco, I must've been thinking out loud in a letter to Daddy about how much debt I was in: nearly $50,000 by the time I left San Francisco in 1995. From Japan I had been paying nearly $400 a month on my student loan debt, diligently sent via international money order every month and hopelessly making no difference in paying it down. I had been locked into a horrible nine percent rate in the late '80s when I consolidated my first set of loans. It felt like I would be buried with that shit forever.

In his typically and so completely-disconnected-from-reality way— and quite presumptuously I might add (in such a way that made me wonder what the hell *he himself* may have been telling his own family all along about our presumed financial condition)—he wrote:

Far as I know you're a lone grand-child.

(referring to my mother's side)

Just do your thing. Your loans are covered. If not by ye mom's parents then by me. Money ain't life insurance. Do your whatever [writing].

Clarification: $50,000 in loans in my name were never going to be covered by anybody but me. Certainly not by my grandparents. Like I said, one might *assume* that they would have offered such, but that's not how they rolled. (Coincidentally, years later my mother insisted on paying off my student loan debt with some inheritance money from my grandparents.) Reading this letter, I get annoyed all over again 20 years later at how clueless my father was. The delusions of adequacy screaming, as if my father could ever have covered my student loan debt. I'm sure it did bum him out that he was unable to significantly contribute to my education, hence the grandiosity and magical thinking and promises he would never be able to keep.

Like the agreement he made to work at U.S. Gypsum in Maine for a year—a near solemn oath it seemed in that letter, such was his relationship with Dick. He didn't want to let him down. I still wonder about that "breach of faith," as my father put it, when he pulled out of Maine after just a few months on the job. Up until that time, the letters—though rife with booze and drug experiences—still had a vein of responsibility for life in its entirety. One hundred percent in-touchedness with reality. I sure saw glimmers of it slipping away in those letters from Maine and thereafter. Those delusions of adequacy that crept in and hung on in embarrassing silence.

Drinking conversations + my drinking story

I remember distinctly when Daddy and I first started having alcohol conversations, long about the time he had gotten those DWIs and had lost his trucking license and the whole descent had begun. Early 90s. Back then, it was "I can take this stuff or leave it, I have no problem with alcohol," followed by various examples of why he had no problems with alcohol.

Initially, he would say things like, "Oh, I can stop at any time," using that faulty defense of alcoholics everywhere who insist that because they once went to a bar without drinking or they only drank one and left, they couldn't possibly be alcoholics.

I was in my early 20s getting sober—and I was calling him out on all of it.

Just like my siblings, I grew up around partying. Pretty much everywhere my mother went, I went as well, including the pot parties, where we sat around at people's houses in the smokey haze of sweet pungent weed from joints being passed around. Guys taking too big of a hit and hack-laughing as the smoke came bursting out of their nostrils. Somebody would start singing, "Don't Bogart that joint...my friend..." and everybody would join in the chorus, cracking up as the rolled paper cigarette went from one person to the next.

"You might not want to share about the marijuana with your grandparents," my mother would occasionally point out when I was barely six or seven years old. "They wouldn't approve."

And that's all I needed to never utter a word about any of it.

As the singed orange joint would go around again, someone would round up a roach clip to make it easier to toke on the dwindling joint. I'd sit there and play with these little wooden toys that all the guys were making back then, these small square blocks of wood with a plus sign carved out on one side and a little handle you could crank that guided a little piece of wood in and out, up and down the grooves of the plus sign. It all felt quite normal.

"Everybody says what a neat kid you are," my mother would lean over and say in a hushed tone. I was always commended for being mature for my age and for being able to hang out, presumably without being a nuisance.

Back then my mom was seeing a guy who lived down the road from us in Quantico in a dilapidated farm house, which also had no running water. Morgan was a student at Salisbury State College at the time, a bit younger than my mother. He had a gaggle of friends who were always in and out, playing guitars and partying. He taught me how to belch loudly, on command, and how to burp-and-talk at the same time. I'm still good at it. He had an old upright piano out on his side porch and sometimes he'd sit me down on the round wooden spinny stool and teach me to play the refrain from "Evil Woman," the hit song from Electric Light Orchestra, along with "Heart and Soul," the only thing kids who don't know how to play piano ever learn how to play.

Morgan played softball catch with me in his dusty driveway, me with my little blue, left-handed catcher's mitt my mom gave me one Easter, which never worked correctly given that I'm right-handed. His nickname for my mother was Queenie. Mine was Runt. We did a lot together for a couple years there when I was pretty young. Steamed crabs, BB guns and glass bottles, camping trips, stuff like that. Maybe that's why my mother didn't notice my father's imploring. She was wrapped up in Morgan at the time.

At home my mother spent evenings in her reading chair in the living room, her bare feet propped on the stool in front of her as she read the *New Yorker*. Between drags on Merit 100s and sips from a can of Miller Lite, she'd start hooting over some George Booth cartoon of some wackadoodle older couple living in a house with too many cats. Under the light of a single-string lightbulb from one room to the next, the husband would yell something utterly inane to the wife as a cat looked on, perplexed, or perhaps constipated. I laughed just to watch my mother as it usually started as an outburst that revved up to wheezing, knee-slapping, and tears pouring out of her eyes.

Aside from my mother's occasional boyfriends, it was just the two of us throughout my growing up years. But every male interest left some kind of impression. There was Robert, the dude who turned us on to Pink Floyd. There was my piano teacher for a while. There was Merrill, the guy from Rehoboth who'd been bitten by a bat one night and had to get rabies shots in his stomach for 30 days straight. Of course, we had Mick come live with us. A platonic relationship, he was a friend of Mary Renfro from Mom and Daddy's William & Mary days. He got busted and put in jail for growing pot on his land in Arkansas. After being in jail for nearly a year, he wanted to get out of Arkansas for a bit. Naturally, my mother invited him to come stay with us. He lived with us for about six months when I was going on 13 and he became a friend and confidante to me. Then there was Dave, the guy my mother met up at College Park when she was getting her paralegal certificate. I remember him falling down drunk in our front hallway one night. He ended up getting sober, even before she did.

We used to go to a bar down on West Side, which was just about everything west of where we lived, as you drove further towards the Nanticoke River through all the little country towns like Wetipquin, Bivalve, and Tyaskin. In the 70s and even early 80s, kids could still hang out with a parent at a bar like Ty's Tavern (later Whiskers 'n Wife, now Boonies). Back then, my mom would even send me into the market to get a six-pack of beer and a pack of cigarettes. The cashier would ask if I needed matches and they'd plop a blank white pack down on top of the aluminum beer cans. That's just how things were.

Oftentimes I begged to go to the bar, just to get the heck out of Quantico, tired of being bored at home by myself. Then we'd get down there and soon after I'd inhaled a grilled cheese with fries and enough Shirley Temples to make me feel slightly queasy, my mother would slip me quarters to keep me occupied. I could play three songs at a pop on the jukebox. I would drop my quarter into the slot and hear it clink against the other coins. Then I'd peruse the songs and artists on the little pastel pink song cards, flipping through until I spotted something that was sure to get everybody going. The regulars shooting pool would belt out the chorus from Kenny Rogers' "Lucille" or a favorite from the Outlaws "Wanted" album, like "Put Another Log on the Fire," with the entire barroom erupting into song and laughter, "*And come and tell me why you're leavin' me!*"

My mom tells me I even used to do my homework at the bar, and I sure played some mean pinball. When Pac-Man came along later, I played that in between to break things up.

We had favorites at the bar, too. I would tell my mother *sotto voce* that "Wink Dink" had just arrived. After he had a couple beers in him, he'd start bellowing, "Buhh-huuhhh!" which unfailingly cracked everybody up. Then there was Gail, who always treated me like somebody who could hold a conversation, along with Art and Elaine, who were larger than life and had the most fabulous parties at their house. I crashed in their living room many times as a kid, right there along with the snoring drunks.

"Heyyy Annie Clay!" another patron would come in and give my mom a big hug. She always sat down at the far right end of the bar where she enjoyed a full view of the entrance and the rest of the length of the bar and pool room.

They'd size me up. "Is this 'The Kid'?"

"This is The Kid," she'd beam.

One night after the bar had closed up, the owner allowed some people to stay afterwards and party on. Somebody offered me a glass of wine and at first my mother said no, but I guess with some coaxing she was persuaded. It wasn't my first taste, but it was the first time I was offered enough, throughout the night, to get good and drunk. I was nearing 12 years old.

I remember Buddy Fields was there. He always flirted with me, even though I was ridiculously underage. He'd come in and sidle up next to me, leaning over the bar on both elbows and loud enough for my mother to hear so she knew he wasn't being too creepy.

"When's your momma gonna let me take you out?" he'd say.

"I don't knowwwwww!" I giggled with embarrassment.

Sadly, he died in a motorcycle accident a few years later, but that night we slow-danced, one of my arms draped around his neck. I also remember doing handstands on the barroom floor (I was a gymnast, after all) and later thinking how foolish that must've looked, if anyone even noticed. When my mom and I returned home, we ended up talking in the living room into the wee hours as I sobered up. We talked about alcohol and its effects, and my mother was mildly surprised that I never puked. Never even had a headache. No hangover, nothing. They say that having that kind of experience, of not having a hangover or being sick or anything, isn't necessarily a good sign when it comes to the disease of alcoholism. It's kinda like my body and genetic makeup welcomed it all in.

Mind you, this was before the human genome was mapped and ultimately declared complete in 2003. We were not in a conversation as a family—or a country—about the ills of alcohol addiction and its effects on the next generation. Now we know that our genetic make-up has a lot to do with our propensity towards addiction.

> "Genetics are 50 percent of the underlying reason for alcohol use disorder. If a person is predisposed to metabolize alcohol in such a way that the pleasurable effects are more prominent than feeling nauseous, overheating, or experiencing mood swings, the person may be more likely to develop alcohol use disorder." — American Addiction Centers

Of course we also know that environment plays a role. Not only was I a product of divorce, but specifically, a girl growing up without a father in the house. So that, plus carrying a good genetic load since I had two alcoholic parents and myriad family members who tolerated booze pretty well.

> "Children who have one parent who struggles with alcohol use disorder have a 3-4 times increased risk of becoming an alcoholic themselves. Having more extended relatives, such as aunts, uncles, grandparents, and other family members, who struggle with alcohol abuse does not have the same strong association. While this relation can influence whether or not a person inherits genetic mutations that predispose them to alcohol use disorder, growing up in an environment influenced by addiction can also predispose a person to the condition."

Now plop me down in a boring-ass town with nothing for young people to do except get drunk on weekends. In high school we were like characters out of the movie "Dazed and Confused." Drunk girls stumbling around at keg parties in the woods, falling on our faces, laughing (sometimes crying and sloppy, too), everybody looking for somebody to hook up with.

My BFF and I would sneak into her grandparents' liquor cabinet and swill from whatever we could, or sneak out and down the lane to a carful of boys waiting to drive us to wherever the party was (usually out in the middle of nowhere, deep in the woods, a long line of headlights revealing staggering forms). Thankfully, I was never accosted. Although I do remember one party in ninth grade where somebody invited me to the back of a van. Even through the bleariness of eight or nine Solo cups full of beer from the keg, I somehow realized that was not a good idea, and I didn't go.

Whenever I reflect on reasons for drinking, I can't think of any. It was just fun. It was our school culture, and I took to it very well. It never felt like pressure; it just felt like "Let's party! Woo-hoo!"

In my fifteenth summer, I went to Europe for a month with my high school Latin teacher along with two of my best friends, and a handful of kids from our school as well as from the other two high schools in Salisbury. In London we met up with another dozen or so kids from different parts of the U.S. and their chaperones, all of us traveling together overland by bus, ferried across the English Channel into France, then on to Switzerland, Italy, Greece, and a culminating cruise on the Mediterranean. From the very first chalice of beer we could order in London without getting carded, we drank ourselves silly all through Europe. It was fun, tons of fun.

By the time I came back home, I had become a veteran drinker and smoker. (The cigarettes started in Paris where we practiced about the only French we'd come to learn: "*Je ne comprends pas Francais.*") I would have no more of my mother's rules and restrictions. I'd already been granted permission to drink and smoke all over Europe. Whaddya mean, curfew? I had tasted freedom and there was no putting the cat back in that bag.

I soon had a boyfriend who was on the football team. He had a party reputation and I'd overhear him say to his friends, "She's cool," referring to the fact that (most of the time) I was not being drunk and stupid like the girls who were just getting drunk for the first time. I was cool. I could hang.

I was never a puker, always a party girl. On a side note, I have always felt like my drinking persona also became my sober persona. Drinking—I believe—established my personality or reaffirmed something in me that made me want to be more adventurous, more outgoing, more outrageous, whatever. By this age, that's who I knew myself to be, whether I was drinking or not.

Still, crazy shit would happen. Like the night I got separated from my boyfriend on some back country road where we'd gone to sit and drink with two other friends. I went off to pee somewhere and decided I was suddenly mad at my boyfriend, so I hid in a ditch—perfectly logical—while they all called out and looked for me. I had in my mind that I would just casually show up at my girlfriend's house later on. We couldn't have been too far from there. After I could tell they had given up trying to find me and they had pulled back out of the lane, I went staggering around, knocking on farmhouse doors in the middle of the night. Somebody called the cops and when the patrol car arrived, I slid into the backseat, somewhat relieved until I found out they weren't going to drop me at the housing development where my friend lived. Instead they drove me all the way to the station in Salisbury, during which time I wracked my brain, trying to think of somebody over 18 that I could call (anybody but my mother). When my neighbor picked up the phone, I was practically whispering, as if my mom might hear my voice coming through our neighbor's phone. He put his older sister on.

"I'm on my way," she said.

At 16 after my junior year, I went and lived down at the beach in Ocean City, Maryland, in a two-bedroom house with seven other girls. By senior year, my friends and I were going out every weekend to party, often hitchhiking home in the middle of the night (none of us had cars, which was just as well). Back then, we didn't have heads filled with creepy shows about serial killers either. We just had places to get to and no means to get there. Staying home was not an option.

Ultimately, my mother relented. It was her own mother who advised her, "You'd better .... or you'll never...." (give me some rein or we'd never have a relationship or something like that). My mom finally made a deal with me that she would come get me on Sunday mornings, wherever I was. She couldn't stand the idea of my hitching anymore.

After getting picked up in town on a Sunday morning at whosever floor I had crashed on, I usually asked her to drop me off at church down the street from our house in Quantico. I'd be thoroughly polluted from the night before, same clothes and all, and still make it to church with my friends just about every Sunday.

But of all my friends, I was the one who blacked out regularly.

On Monday at school my girlfriends would do a play-by-play of everything that happened when we went out that weekend. We got a ride from this house to that one. We saw so-and-so looking super hot. We had a hilarious conversation with somebody else. Half the time, they'd have to stop and rewind until we got to the part I could still remember.

They'd look at me in exasperation. "What?! You don't remember any of that?"

So by 16, 17 years old, with the regular blackouts and all, I had also decided that beer was something I could manage. Liquor was something I couldn't.

The last weekend of spring break in senior year I got arrested. This was just after the infamous Florida road trip with Daddy and my stepmom and the kids, in which all four children—two of them toddlers—and I, plus my father and Leia, took off in the blue van and drove down to see my grandmother for a week, stopping off at my Uncle Ray's along the way. Jimmy and I slept under a coffee table at Uncle Ray's one night, both of us still awake listening to Daddy getting drunker and drunker, and Leia getting more upset, and the argument they were in about some woman, presumably the to-become girlfriend, Jean. I was 17, my brother Jimmy about 10. Another time we were somewhere in South Carolina or Georgia and we pulled into a bank parking lot and all of us kids were ordered out of the car. We sat on a curb, waiting and listening to the muted arguing going on inside the van.

I came home super tan, looking good, partying that final weekend before school started again. But then the cops busted up the party at our friend's house in Fruitland where we spent every single weekend. So we left with no ride, as usual, my girlfriend and I and these two guys we were friends with, staggering along the road that led to the highway. As another car went by, I waved a bottle of Mad Dog 20/20 in the air, thinking it might be one of the partygoers and a potential ride. The flashing blue and red lights of the siren flipped on, and a cop car pulled over in front of us. As the two cops got out of the vehicle, the boys took off terrified because they were both in trouble already. One hightailed it away on his bike. The other ran into the field, not without first stealing a heavy-duty police jacket from the back of the cop car while I was being mouthy and resistant. I ended up across the trunk of the car in hand-cuffs. My girlfriend kept getting out of the backseat so many times one of the officers had to stand guard at the back door so she wouldn't keep popping out. At the police station, I gave them a fake name ("Kimberly Johnson," the one I used for all my interactions with police that busted underage drinking parties) until my friend's mom showed up.

"I called your mother," she said, apologetically.

When my mom arrived at the station about four a.m., the first thing she said when we got in the car was, "Of all places to get arrested, Fruit-land?" We both laughed. I had to do some kind of community service and there would be no blemish on my record.

By that time, my mother had already been sober for about a year. Part of her own awakening was seeing the kind of trouble I was getting myself into and taking note of herself as the example. Although it was my unfettered behavior and drinking that first prompted her to get sober, she had also discovered that sober living was a completely different way of life—grounded in reality and based on spiritual princi-ples and a foundation of integrity with herself and the world. I went along with her to a couple of AA meetings, just to check things out. I could see that AA was working in her life and that it was a good thing for a lot of people. Yet it made no difference at the time because I didn't want it.

My mother continued to give me space, but she did advise me more than once.

"Just know that you have this genetic predisposition towards alco-holism on both sides of your family. If you ever want to do anything about it, I'm here for you—and so is AA."

During senior year I got accepted to Tobe-Coburn School for Fashion Careers in New York. My mom's mother had cut the school's ad out from the back of a magazine for me and handed it to me, observing my interest in fashion and beauty as a teenager, and I had applied. It was one of those schools for young ladies that had been around since the turn of the 20th century. I was promised an Associate Degree of Fashion Merchandising, Marketing and Management after two years and earnings of $30,000 before my friends graduated from college. It sounded good. And I needed to get the fuck outta Dodge.

I received a $1,000 scholarship, which they must've given pretty freely since I was an average student in high school, although I probably had higher SAT scores than some of the other incoming students. Nonetheless, I had someplace to go. My long-sought escape route from the Eastern Shore of Maryland lay before me. I was still 17 when my mom dropped me off in New York City.

I was finally *free*!

"If you hadn't left, I would've kicked you out," she later told me.

My first year in Manhattan I lived at the 92nd Street Y (Young Men's Hebrew Association) at Lexington Avenue on the Upper East Side, a co-ed residence where I shared a room with another girl. There was a communal bathroom and kitchen down the hall. Rent was $400 a month, paid for by my mom. The rest of my living costs, from food and leisure to transportation, was on me, as was most of my $8,000/year tuition, although I remember my mother stepping in to help numerous times with tuition deposits and payments while I was waiting for financial aid to kick in. I subsisted mostly on a diet of Oodles of Noodles (three packs for a dollar) and Saltines with peanut butter. If Daddy ever contributed at this point, it was twenty bucks cash here and there in a letter.

I arrived in New York City late August 1986 and by October had landed a job working at the gloves and sunglasses counter at B. Altman's, the famous Fifth Avenue department store, right across from the Empire State Building. (I thought I was pretty badass—for a Quantico girl.) Sadly, B. Altman's went the way of the other old original Fifth Avenue stores like Bonwit Teller, Barneys, and Lord & Taylor, but to my delight, it's made a dazzling return in *The Marvelous Mrs. Maisel* on Amazon Prime. It's where the main character "Midge" works for a time and it looks just like I remember it.

Mornings I took the subway down to 4th and Broadway where I

went to school. Afternoons I worked at the department store, while evenings I would go to my second job as a receptionist at a hair salon at 70th and Broadway on the Upper West Side. That's where I met Lue, who would become my lifelong friend.

The following year I went to London for a semester abroad, arriving with about $300 to my name at the hostel in Pembridge Square where I'd be living with college kids from all over the world for the next three months. I had earned it working on the boardwalk in Ocean City for about a month that summer. I figured I'd wing it as a waitress or something once I got to England.

Every morning during breakfast in the cafeteria was the exact time that Princess Diana would be dropping off the little princes next door at the Wetherby School. The car with the tinted windows would pull up and out she would emerge with all her poise and help these two little boys in their little gray uniforms out of the back of the car. She'd take their little hands and up the steps they'd all go right next door. We'd all have our faces pressed to the windows, watching the whole procession every day, as if we'd never seen it before. I think at one point we might've been told to respect their privacy, because we really did ogle.

Soon I was typing papers for my friends (one British pound per page) and writing them for others. I even sold a bunch of my clothes to one girl, so I'd have enough for beer money. The lunch vouchers or LVs we were provided for meals were also good for beer at the local 7-Eleven. What I couldn't afford myself was made up for by people buying me pints of "snakebite black"—lager with blackcurrant juice, my beverage of choice—and invitations to keep the party going.

During that semester, I noticed that I drank every single day for three and a half months, except for that one incident from drinking gin. I got all puffy and threw up for a whole day. I thought I would die from alcohol poisoning. While living abroad, I also lost bladder control from all the alcohol. I was peeing my bed almost every night and even when I was passed out on the floor of the TV room.

When I came back to the States, I was so polluted from alcohol you could see the difference in the photo taken in front of the airport before I left and after I came back. I left looking clear-eyed, vibrant, and tan from living at the beach. I came back with my face all pasty and puffy from imbibing. I was not a healthy-looking 19-year-old.

But I wasn't done yet.

Back in New York, I could barely make it to graduation, what with the multiple hits of Ecstasy and all-night clubbing several nights a week with my BFF and my roommate. She and I met in London and landed ourselves a little one-bedroom apartment on 51st Street between Eighth and Ninth Avenue, back when it really was still Hell's Kitchen. There were no delis or markets or people clamoring to move into the neighborhood, and Ninth Avenue hadn't yet turned gay-chic.

Our place was right next to the neon cross that flashes Sin Will Find You Out on one side and Get Right With God on the other, that shows in the previews on the Late Show. We'd come home every day and a homeless woman would be occupying half our front step, urine dribbling all the way down the steps and sidewalk in front of our building. The homeless and the hapless, junkies and all, would be mingling for a free something or other at the church basement next door.

"Piss and pizza!" my roommate Sarah would announce the smells of summertime in New York.

We three were now part of the whole underground club scene and gay nightlife. We'd go to Scrap Bar down on MacDougal Street to buy drugs from the bartender, then time it just right so we'd already be in a cab halfway to our next destination, King Tut's Wah Wah Hut in Alphabet City, before the Ecstasy kicked in. At some point, we'd bounce over to Alcatraz, another bar up the street, then hit Save the Robots, an after-hours club that was just getting started around four a.m. After a while, we'd leave there and catch a cab all the way across town to the Meatpacking District, where we'd go dancing at the Sound Factory until seven in the morning. I had become the ultimate fag hag—an overweight party chick doted on by gay boys.

And we did this...multiple...times...a...week.

All that while I was also working as an advertising assistant at *Town & Country* magazine. My office at 1700 Broadway was just a five-minute walk from home, so I usually came home for lunch. (Hour-long lunch breaks were the norm!) I remember when my paternal grandmother came for my graduation and stayed with us a few days afterwards. She observed that I was sipping wine before going back to work.

"Somebody left it here," I dismissed her concern. "It's just a little bit left in the bottle."

Although in the meantime, I would show up to my job on no sleep, coming down from a three-day, drug-infused weekend, and trying to navigate the moods and whims of a high-maintenance, high-powered ad exec (think *The Devil Wears Prada*) who had gone through seven assistants in seven months. It was my great misfortune—and hers—to become the eighth. It was rough. After a few months, she and I agreed on a "lateral promotion" to another department.

At Lue's insistence, we also chilled out on the party scene.

In fact, two years later he was the one who brought me home an AA brochure. A lot had happened in between. By then, Sarah had moved back to Seattle and he had moved in with me. One night I returned home from a Connecticut wedding. I woke up on a train, alone in the dark in Grand Central Station at 2:30 in the morning. My shoes were kicked off and my feet propped up on the seat across from me. Compared to some other nights, this wasn't all that bad of a scenario to find myself in.

A train conductor happened to be walking by the open doors and said, "Miss, it's time to get up. Last stop."

Funny. I never thought of that metaphorically until now. Last stop indeed. I had recently gotten into drinking a six-pack of Budweiser every day. Sometimes I'd get drunk off of one. Sometimes I'd drink six and nothing happened. In the evenings when I walked the 20 blocks home from the hair salon, I'd carry in a paper bag a Budweiser tall boy with a straw, sipping my way down Ninth Avenue.

That morning after getting back from Connecticut and waking up in the dark train station, I tried to laugh it off a bit. I told Lue about dancing with the best man and how I lost my contact lenses and somehow insisted that I be put on a train in the wee hours of the morning.

I'll never forget the look he gave me. "You know Ken, it's really not that funny anymore."

I think I experienced shame about drinking for the first time ever right then. I hated the idea of him being disappointed in me. I may have had a beer or two that day (a Sunday) and that Monday is when Lue came home with the pamphlet. I went to a meeting the next night and I haven't had a drink since, although I always consider that Saturday, September 24, 1990, as my last drink/drunk. I wrote about that time in a story called "Yesterday's Wine" for English writing class at University of San Francisco, which would appear in the school's literary magazine, *The Ignatian*. Daddy referred to it in one of his letters to me when I was living in San Francisco.

There's no rhyme or reason to why somebody suddenly decides to get sober because oftentimes it's like, how far down the scale do you have to go? How bad does it have to get? How many blackouts do you need to have? How many poor choices—not to mention lost earrings and pocketbooks and rent money spent on drugs and alcohol—do you need to have before you decide it's time to do something?

But of course the real work of getting sober is when you make changes within yourself.

Putting down the drink is just an access to self-development and healing and making of amends. The younger you are, the fewer amends there are to make, generally. I hadn't ruined anybody's life or treated them (too) badly or lied and cheated and stolen or embarrassed anyone other than myself. I didn't have children. My friends were all good friends, not just party friends, even though that was a strong common denominator.

It sounds a bit glamorous now when I think of my early sobriety in New York City. I was just about to turn 21 (seven years of hardcore drinking and enough damage to last a lifetime). I was working at Tony Roma's rib joint on Broadway and 48th Street—the late-night restaurant and bar scene had me staying up odd hours like a vampire—and I started going to midnight AA meetings down around 44th Street. I'd schlep up to this little room on the third floor that was so hazy with cigarette smoke you could hardly make out the giant Twelve Steps and Twelve Traditions banners hanging from the ceiling at the front of the room. But the place was packed with people whose eyes and voices were clear. I decided I wanted what they had and was willing to do whatever it took.

I even created a new context for myself, like wow, what kind of adventure would it be to discover the person I'm meant to be, free of alcohol? Who would I get to become as a result of getting sober? Someone I'd never known before, I concluded, and that it would be a worthwhile endeavor.

I was also motivated by fear.

Fear of becoming a tired old hag, hanging around the local bar, drinking, and hitting on young boys. And I guess you would call it the grace of God—which I had no understanding of or personal relationship with until I got into AA, despite all those Sundays I went to church —because the desire to drink alcohol was truly lifted from me. I started to pray about it, constantly, and I went to those meetings, as many as I could every week, until I heard what I needed to hear.

I also met my first sponsor at that midnight meeting. She was a well-known, stand-up comic who later went on to have a successful television show. I had no idea who she was at the time, but I liked what she had to say.

"You're probably like me, Kenner-lee," she'd drawl. "Dancing the waltz with the first three steps. One, two, three."

I did the whole fake-it-till-you-make-it thing with believing in a Higher Power and all that. I read every book I could read. I worked the steps. I listened with an open mind, even though there were so many things that "didn't apply to me." I certainly never lost it all, or lost a family or destroyed friendships or anything like that. I could have distanced or excused myself on a lot of factors, but I liked the analogy my mom had shared from the AA literature I later became familiar with.

"Some people don't have to hit bottom," she said. "They see the bottom coming up to meet them and they decide to get off the elevator before it goes all the way down."

That was me. I was choosing to get off the elevator at a higher floor.

There were some things I didn't do as I was told. I didn't change people, places, things. I liked my people. I liked my places. I took my chances because I felt like I could get away with still hanging out with friends in bars without drinking, because the urge to drink was truly lifted. So I drank a lot of Coca-Cola and smoked cigarettes whenever I went out. *I was 21, after all.*

I dealt with some challenges and pressures. Old friends that couldn't believe I wasn't drinking anymore. Or—to this day—would probably offer me a beer in a heartbeat if I told them I was gonna party with them. I don't begrudge them. Some people just don't get it. I also noticed that most of the time, nobody notices whether you're drinking or not. It just becomes no big deal.

I saw changes in myself. And I know others were noticing, too. One friend of mine told me what it was like before and what it was like after I quit drinking.

"You just make sense," she said. "You're clear and you make sense."

I saw clarity as something to strive for, especially since I wanted to get out of New York and start anew in San Francisco. I was planning to go back to school and major in English literature and writing.

"Good writing is clear thinking made visible." – Bill Wheeler, author and journalist

In sobriety, I saw that there were things I needed to say to my father that hadn't been said if ever he and I were to have an authentic relationship.

One time when I was home from New York and visiting at his house, we went for a drive so I could talk to him privately. We parked in some field nearby. Daddy popped a beer as I proceeded to tell him about my long history of drinking, from adolescence and high school into college years—and about getting sober. I also told him what it was like to have been his kid. To live with all the disappointments and unmet expectations. The missed visits. The promises not kept. The sitting around all day waiting for him to show.

We both just sat staring straight ahead at the field, never making eye contact, as I talked and he listened.

"I just wanted you to know I forgive you," I said, turning to him this time. "I just never had the courage to say anything before."

Daddy took a swill of beer and puffed out his chest a bit.

"If I had known it was that bad," he said, lamely, "I would have..."

All I heard after that was blah-blah-blah. Daddy making some suggestion that if he had been involved in my upbringing, none of that would've happened—an immediate signal that he wasn't getting me at all. There was nothing he could've done about anything. I chose to drink. And that wasn't the point of this conversation anyway. In his deflection, there was no apology, nor any excuse.

I let his response wash over me like an ocean wave. That's what the ninth step was like sometimes, I'd been told. The people you make amends with either don't get it or won't accept your amends, or in some cases they're just not around or alive to make amends to.

What did happen from that conversation, however, is that the burden of suppression and lack of self-expression with my father was lifted. From that time on, I felt like I had the courage to be straight with him and say whatever was on my mind. I also knew that to have any kind of relationship, I'd have to take him as he was.

When I later moved out to San Francisco, a whole new life opened up for me. It was as if the Bay Area greeted my sober self and said, "Here —here you can be, do, create, become anything and everything you've ever wanted to be. You've never been drunk here. No one here knows you in the past. Oh, and by the way, we have the best fucking AA meetings on the planet!"

My home group became the Haight-Ashbury Sunday morning meeting. Some of the most extraordinary people I had ever met were my source of weekly wisdom and ongoing examples of sobriety. Although I'm no longer in touch with most of them, they will remain in my heart forever for the warmth and connectedness, light and laughter, that came out of my time in San Francisco.

I got a really good sponsor who often helped me deal with my father stuff. In those days, I still believed that sobriety was a possibility for everybody, even my father, and that his downward spiral with the DWIs didn't have to keep going down.

By the time I went to teach English in Japan, I was nearly five years sober. Life in 1995 looked so different than it had before. I had graduated from University of San Francisco *summa cum laude*. I had started clubs, joined clubs, led groups, and worked, studied, lived, expanding myself in so many ways. Now I was living in Japan, another dream coming true. Eventually, I found an AA meeting not far from where I lived. I met some great sober people. Four to be exact. The other girl in the group asked me to be her sponsor (she didn't have many to choose from) and I remained loosely connected to AA while in Japan. My mother and I found a meeting in Bangkok on our way to Nepal, where we also attended a small ex-pat meeting in Kathmandu.

Beyond that, I never really re-engaged with AA.

I've been sober now for 30+ years and can't imagine my life with alcohol. When you can see your disease and recovery as the best thing that could've happened, by embracing it, using it as a "touchstone to progress"—well then, that's a life worth living.

Over the years I learned a lot about alcohol and the brain and how it affects personality. At first, when I was looking at myself and the drinking persona I had developed from a young age, my mother helped me understand the abbreviation of my emotional growth from the time I started to drink. For every year that I was drinking, I would need one sober year to grow and transform and develop myself into someone who was emotionally mature. That's what getting sober does. It allows us to grow up and be the geeks we always wanted to be. Plus, I wander around in a low-level asshole state most of the time anyway. No need for alcohol to make that worse.

As I observed my own behavior, I also became more conscious of alcoholism and its effects at play in my father. Some others in the family didn't recognize it so readily because they weren't alcoholics themselves. My stepmother and grandmother, for example, couldn't immediately grasp that alcoholism was a disease, and drinking to excess merely a symptom of myriad sicknesses of mind and spirit.

"Well Eddie says he's gonna get his truck driving license back," my grandmother would say with wishful optimism that sounded like a question, as though she was waiting for me to either confirm it or deny it.

"He's never going to get his license back," I said sternly, my frustration mounting as I continued. "Daddy cannot drink responsibly, because he's an alcoholic. He has no way of controlling his drinking. It's just how he's wired and how he's become over the years because of it. He doesn't want to stop drinking, and there's nothing you can do about it. He has to want it for himself—and he doesn't, and probably won't ever."

"Well, what am I supposed to do?" would come my grandmother's sing-songy response, a bit defensive. "He's my son and I love him. And he has a problem and he's made bad decisions in life. But when he's not drinking so much, he's alright. He helps me out."

The word "out" came drawling out in two syllables and she intoned it as though I was supposed to see all the things Daddy could possibly do for her outweighing everything he had done to make her life hell in later years.

Within a few years of losing his trucking license, it seemed as though Daddy went ahead and embraced his will to drink. He must have seen that it was easier to overtly go for it versus defend it. Easier for him to just say, "I drink and that's what I want to do." Because I seriously doubt he believed his own denial of being able to stop any time. Nobody else believed it, for sure.

So then he was just full-on drinking.

There was one long phase where he'd look around at life's inanity or some family drama and circumstances with feigned wonderment. "And they ask me why I drink?!" he'd say, dramatizing the word "drink" with a toss of the head and a half-laugh.

At times he was spot on and funny (usually when something absurd was happening or my grandmother was riding his ass), but eventually it became a sorry-ass excuse for stepping out into the garage for a nip. He could go obliterate himself without having to be responsible for any fallout.

"Why *do* you drink?" His cousin Nancy actually broached the subject. To my knowledge she got the straightest answer he ever gave anyone.

"He would quietly talk about his failings," she says of their intimate conversations, sometimes by phone, other times when he passed through and stayed with her and Jim, hitchhiking his way between Maryland and Florida.

Nancy and my father grew closer throughout the years, in spite of his drinking.

"I just loved him. He had a quiet wit," she says. "And do you know, when my son Barry had a brain aneurysm and stroke and was in shock trauma in Baltimore—you can imagine the state we were in—the first person I saw there was your father standing right in front of me. I looked up and there he was. I have never been so happy in all my life. He didn't have to say anything. He just hugged me."

When they talked in later years, Nancy said Daddy would admit to her, "I have awful habits. I drink, I smoke. I just do it because I like it."

"I know it changes a person," Nancy continues. "It was sad to see. Even though he adored and loved all of you, he did not fulfill on being a father and didn't live up to his obligations. I know he didn't contribute a lot to your mother and Leia. Of course he didn't have a lot, but he just didn't live up to his responsibility as a father because he was so addicted to alcohol, and it ruled his life. I did ask him sometimes, 'You think you ever might hurt somebody doing whatever you want to do?' And he said he just couldn't stop. He said he just knew it and he lived with it."

Incidentally, a man was apprehended in West Virginia on December 23rd having coitus with a sheep in a 'live' nativity scene. And they arsk (sic) me why I drink. To kill the pain of the sheep, of course.

Nowadays, living with often unbearable depression, I think of this statement differently. Knowing my father was a sensitive person who felt things very deeply from a young age, I know he was probably a depressive like me and that everything hurt. A lot. Life is painful for everyone, and then there are people who feel pain more deeply than others. There are also those of us who have a higher threshold for pain because we endured a lot of it growing up.

So when I hear Daddy's bold, defiant voice in my head now, "They ask me why I drink," I can say, *Shit man, I can totally see why you drank.* Why anybody drinks—to create that buffer between them and pain. I think that kind of drinking is for people who feel things a bit too much.

But I have no buffer. So I feel that pain, often and a lot. Sometimes I wish I still drank. But I can't—and I won't. Hell, sometimes I wish I had a fucking heroin habit. It's all just too fucking painful.

anytime the Sun is there 'tis a new start. You gotta feel it. You must have hope. I know you do, I wish you well,

---

I never knew this before, but Daddy wrote in TJ's little dad-tell-me-about-your-life book that when he was between 15 and 16 years old, he had a mysterious illness.

"Hospitalized twice in 4-5 months." Daddy wrote. "Excruciating back pains. No clear diagnosis. "Virus" (MDs)."

Daddy continued, regarding the incident, "I determined cause was stress (peer pressure). I removed that, got drunk and cured myself, after a solid year of codeine addiction. NEVER CAME BACK."

Nowadays, when young people have surgery or any kind of medical issue, if there are painkillers involved, there's much greater oversight and short-term prescribing restrictions (especially since the opioid crisis and problems with young people getting hooked on pain medications). It's also pretty common knowledge that if a young person gets addicted to pain medication, they have a much greater chance of becoming addicted to alcohol or drugs. Not that my father wasn't already on that path, but it kinda makes me wonder how much that codeine addiction kicked off his affinity for alcohol.

Be patient with life, You have no other choice, Desperation breeds despair, and mistakes.

dad in detention

"The vilest deeds like poison weeds Bloom well in prison air; It
is only what is good in man That wastes and withers there."
— Oscar Wilde

After graduating from University of San Francisco in 1995, I was
accepted on the Japan Exchange Teaching (JET) Programme, sponsored
by the Japanese Ministry of Education, an international citizen diplo-
macy program that brought native English speakers from around the
globe to teach English to Japanese junior high school students and
essentially serve as cultural ambassadors from our respective countries. I
requested to live near Kobe, as one of my best friends from university
was a Japanese girl who lived there with her husband.

As anyone who received my missives from that era can attest, I wrote
prolifically, pages and pages of typewritten letters about my experiences
and observations of Japanese culture and my own insights, challenges
and frustrations as I adjusted to living in a country where, for the first
time in my life, I lived by myself in a little *danshi* (apartment) out in the
country and was gawked at as a *gaijin* (foreigner) amidst a sea of people

amongst whom I was a minority. For many, I was the first foreigner they'd ever encountered.

I went with the intention of staying for one year and ended up staying for three, teaching not only junior high but being selected to teach at a local elementary school as well.

A letter written to me when I first arrived in Kobe, dated August 11, 1995, from my father goes:

My Kennerly,

I thank you for a wonderful and inspiring letter. Especially details about Japan. Also, you may as well forgive everyone. Otherwise, you can't get to where you wanna go. (I don't mind ye holding a grudge against me. I HAVE SEVENTEEN.) Back in '67 I was set to work on an Indian reservation in Southern California (Hopis) and I chose the motorcycle and fighting draft. Your Kobe sounds like paying dues. I wish I could be there with you (and help).

I can't imagine your capability to mingle these languages and translate, relate; incomprehensible to me! I know you're gonna be fine. God - what a challenge!

You are possibly the only person I ever envied. You managed to chart your own course; what's extra special, you're my daughter. I'm proud!

Another:

First day of Spring USA 1996
Hello Doll,

I've been unable to write in a positive way for months

and I won't go into any of that except to say that Leia and I are finished. These things take time and obvious trauma.

Your thoughtful Christmas gifts were wonderful. I took your cigarette lighter case from Bangkok and hid it for me old age.

I trust all is well and your illnesses are stabilized. Same thing happened to me when I spent time over the Mexican border. (Ignore my lightness)

I have no idea what you have written or sent to your mom or Greenville in terms of your letters or journals. Leia is mum and forwards no mail to me.

[Clay Inc. 1480 Lowell Ct. Crofton, MD 21114]

About me: I stopped driving last November 22 when I slipped from a trailer and broke me foot. I took five weeks of Workman's Comp and attended and graduated the Maryland Bartending Academy. I've been bartending part-time and working with a friend establishing a business in home alarm systems. Ain't you feeling horrible living in a country where you probably could sell only 500?

I mean to say I wish the hell I knew the Japanese language so I could get out of here for a long while or as a steppingstone to forever. I'll probably brush up on mi espanol and finish life in Mexico.

As you know me so well I'll make no explanation 'cept to say I'm sorry.

I love you very much.

Clay

P.S. Do you want a tape of the 1st Quicksilver? I just bought the CD.

Daddy at Ocean Beach March 1999

After my last year in Japan, I passed back through San Francisco to see old friends and also see Daddy, who was there at the time. I visited him in the Sunset District at the home of old Anna Li, the Chinese lady he was helping out with errands and housekeeping, and we walked and talked and drank coffee at Ocean Beach. I was just back from traveling in Asia for six and a half months, and the world was my oyster.

Coffee at the ocean

April 1999 (San Francisco)

Right now life is very lonely. I give and don't get much.
Don't need much. Man-o'-man, your father is a great depres-
sive. Perhaps Burroughs and I have abused and used and he,
Keith Richards and I marvel people's addictions in all forms.

It's everywhere and every day. I understand your island but even there you were drinking marijuana (kava).

> "Nocturne"   10/2/98
> I heard you crying through the wall,
> A midnight inconsolable wail,
> I heard you groaning in the hall,
> Then singing thru' an Asian tongue
>   I could never tell,
> Salty tears in San Francisco Rain,
>   Maria (Korea) now,
> Sad to say nothing can stave your pain,
> Waly waly native American glass,
> Lo siempre sweet Oriental lass,
>   You've only just begun
>   the pain of America,

On the previous page, Daddy had written about Anna Li. She was fond of my father and grateful for the help. He wrote that he had just vacuumed her place before Easter but had also found her tripping up the hill towards her house with what he diagnosed as a "cracked rib I'm sure," but she refused to let him take her to the hospital. He tried to call her all week but got no reply, and when he went by again and rang the doorbell, the curtains were closed and there was no answer.

After that, he stopped at my old place on Stanyan and Oak overlooking the Golden Gate Park panhandle and top of the park. My former boyfriend Gary still lived there. To ring anybody in that building meant yelling up to the third-floor windows because there were no doorbells. Our kitchen window was almost always open a good six inches, so usually you could hear people yelling up. Gary didn't answer the door or the phone call. I remember he mentioned some years later my father had stopped by one time, but Daddy was inebriated and Gary pretended he wasn't home.

I know he felt bad for my father, he'd even gone out to dinner with him a time or two previously, which I thought was absolutely noble of him, but he also knew exactly what was in store if he were to get into a sloppy evening with him. The hours of slurred conversation and repeated revelations, the bro-bonding that weirdly shouldn't be happening at that point, the feigned politeness and pretending to have a good time with Kennerly's old man—I didn't blame him. I could imagine Gary turning out all the lights and music and TV and just lying in bed, barely breathing, until he could hear Daddy grunt and amble away, or maybe even stage-whispering up and down Oak Street, loud enough for the homeless, shopping-cart drunks across the street in the park to hear: "I guess eez not 'ome. I'was just gonna stop by and see if he wanted a beer." And then half-laugh to himself on his merry way back to the Tenderloin to write me this letter, aptly:

I think my description tonight is wistful. Surely lost in age and memory.

He then referenced my grandmother (my mother's mother) having finally accepted him after 30 years (who knows when and how that happened; he talked like he had struck up a correspondence with her or something), and a sort of nostalgic sending of his regards to my grandparents—that gap in generation having never been filled.

"I believe that life is mind. Whatever else happens. Reason for statement is, as I am there be no reason to cling (not this one anyway)."
—Ed Clay

Spring Fool

My dear Daughter,
I'm sending and unloading my baggage only because there's no one else who'd understand or truly be innarested. I believe in you. I know you believe in me. Receive my crap minus distraction. Just unloading to write some more. Stick to your guns. I'm so glad you have this chance. 'Member 98% of all is temporal with writing and else. I love you, Pancho

Daddy in front of Jim Macfarlan's old place in the Sunset

Like the rest of us, Jeffrey—who was the last to come along—was conditioned to Daddy leaving. By the time he reached adolescence, he was used to just seeing Daddy on weekends when he was living over at his girlfriend Jean's house.

Other times Daddy would show up unannounced at the house in Greenville.

"Impeccable timing, when Mom wasn't there," Jeffrey adds. "I think he always enjoyed being home with his boys."

Like Jimmy, Jeffrey laughs a lot like Daddy, and he shrugs with an oh-wellness when it comes to stories about our father. He's 6'3", even taller than Daddy, so when he's sitting across from me on the sofa in his basement hangout room in Maine, he still seems way taller than I am.

Of my three brothers, Jeffrey is the only one married with children.

From the time his two boys were born, he's been a devoted stay-at-home dad. Whenever I see or talk to him, he seems in the moment with his sons, having fun with them and experiencing their wonder. He's also acutely aware of having broken a long and vicious cycle of poor relations between sons and fathers.

Jeffrey's got some of that mettle that kept my father going all those years (I reckon we all do). In fact, in just about every one of Daddy's letters to the boys, he wrote something about attitude. In one letter it was 95 percent of everything; in another it was 200. Jeffrey's favorite was: "Attitude is always 90 percent of everything; take the other 10 percent and run like hell."

For Jeffrey, it gradually went from seeing Daddy here and there to not seeing him at all, kind of like how he just faded away from me when I was little. But in the early years, Daddy had been there for the boys.

Jeffrey remembers Daddy as funny and smart, brash, too—"full of himself a bit, and stuck in his ways. There was always a sense that something different was going to happen when he was around because he and Mom were so different. With Pops, all bets were off, like there was gonna be some kind of adventure and you never knew what to expect, but you knew it was gonna be a good time."

Daddy was there for birthdays and Christmases and family trips and events.

"One Christmas morning he got me a BB gun, kinda like *A Christmas Story*, the Red Rider BB gun. It was Dad and Jimmy and I, and Dad put a full beer bottle out there and said, 'Go ahead, son.' My first shot exploded the whole thing. I'm sure Dad was thinking he shoulda put an empty out there."

Through the family grapevine back then, my grandmother would tell me all the goings-ons. I distinctly remembered her conveying my father's words about leaving his boys behind, around the time they were reaching adolescence.

"Agghh, they don't need a father at this age," was how it supposedly went. I could imagine my father's dismissiveness, a certain bravado about boys coming of age and being independent while also letting himself off the hook for not being there.

I found it appalling. I couldn't think of a better age for boys to need their father.

"Yeah man, this cold weather's not good for me, my hands are crackin'," Daddy said to Jeffrey when he was first blowing out of town for the West Coast. "Gotta get out to San Francisco where it's warmer."

"How am I gonna see you if you're out in California?" Jeffrey asked. No answer.

Daddy had complained of the cold for some years. He had worked his ass off in freezing temperatures with his hands exposed while loading and unloading tractor trailer hauls. He was getting older and Maryland winters had a way of settling into the bones. San Francisco wasn't all that warm either, but it sure wasn't finger-splittin' weather. Still, the conversation he probably wasn't up for with Jeffrey at the time was that if he didn't get outta there, he'd be picked up and put in jail. He hadn't served his time for the multiple DWIs, and it may have been the start of several bench warrants for his arrest in Maryland.

> I'm sitting and writing at Sutro Heights Park in SAN Francisco, mid-morning fog Rolling over my corn-bread ass. You gotta be old to love all this. The fog is like US 301 in the spring (MD.) Sea-lions are wallowing on the rocks perhaps 200 feet below. It's a new day.

Daddy left Maryland altogether, pinballing his way to Florida, Texas, and California, then eventually back to Maryland.

"Pops had been gone for two years and this was his grand return," says Jeffrey of my father showing up at the house out of the blue one day when Jeffrey was about 14. "He was a goddamn mess, but I was happy to see him nonetheless."

As the day wore on, they stopped over to visit Al Miller, who by now had been sober a long while.

"Al had his truck there," says Jeffrey. "Dad was walking around it, asking questions. He seemed in awe to be that close to one again. Dad was going, 'Hmmm,' rubbing his chin, 'Humm, I think I could teach'—it was like he was meeting one of his idols, the truck itself. I said to Al, 'Yeah, I don't think he'll ever be behind the wheel of one of those again,' and Al shook his head in agreement."

By the end of the day, Daddy told the boys he was going to the graveyard to visit old friends, living and dead. Al had even picked him up there at the cemetery a few times.

"I found out later that Mom and Shannah called the cops on him. Maybe they thought it would do him some good and straighten him up, but no such luck."

My father landed in the Caroline County Detention Center (CCDC), where he would sit until the following spring.

A letter to me from "Caroline County Detention Center Animal Farm and Nervous Hospital, Denton, Maryland," December 16, 1999:

> If one is young jail can be a valuable learning experience, i.e. soul-searching, self-examination. When you're old, it's sheer punishment. (You're too old to spank.) They control you and put your life on hold. I do not recommend it for anyone. Mostly it is wasted time. Perhaps the real trick (in either of our present quandaries) is to bury our negatives and get to work. 'Damn the torpedoes' as it were. An irony of life is whenever you have time to dive into your interests, you're usually too balled-up to produce. I'm characteristic of this!

Letter from CCDC:

> Hope you guys are enjoying school and doing well. As I pore over this miniscule library, I imagine you delving into American history (9th grade for me) or modern European (10th grade). I hope you're still liking the subject. When I watch

the History Channel, I observe how effortlessly I'd be able to narrate many episodes.

"Dad had terrific penmanship and cognition throughout the letter," says Jeffrey, "but man, the boastful tone, as if he's trying to compensate for where he's writing from. I think he was embarrassed that he couldn't do much to help his kids once he left. Maybe saying those things, he didn't want us to hate him, or forget about him, maybe why he wrote letters, always optimistic and hopeful, or maybe he always thought at some point he would get it together."

"Floyd" (hurricane) made my waterfront view innaresting and knocked out cable for 3 days here. Never heard so much protracted obscenity in my life. I pity folks with tunnel-vision and an absence of imagination. I also have a tendency to despise same.

Daddy asked Jeffrey for help with a few favors, to keep an eye out for any court summons, to get him a postal money order, to remove the tension on his guitar strings (unless TJ was playing it) and thanked him heartily for bringing him his reading glasses. "16 novels and 10 letters in 30 days."

A second page front and back was titled "Licks (from County Jail)", a delightful collection of all-original, dirty limericks, the cleanest of the batch being:

> "Now hear of a cook named Davey
> whose dangle was talk of the Navy
> As long as an arm
> It raised much alarm
> Dragging its way through the gravy."

Just to be sure, I Google it and it looks to be an Ed Clay Original. February 25, 2000, in response to a letter from Jeffrey:

I only wish I had a tale or so about me to give back. Nothing except that I'm working on a novel.

(This would be the unfinished-and-ultimately-stolen-in-a-duffel-bag-somewhere-between-Texas-and-San-Francisco-"East of Nowhere.")

"You've gotten mathematical aptitude from your mom. I got D's in Alg II even with tutoring," he writes. He closes, wishing he could watch *Braveheart* with Jeffrey but "looks like my legal shit's gonna run into summer."

I never knew Daddy had Ds in algebra, even with tutoring. I did, too, tutor and all. We excelled with words—not numbers.

I'm concurred with Pop's theory that men be born devoid of penises and grow them at thirty. (I recommend at rate of one inch per year.) Just think - starvation and poverty could be eliminae (sic).

"And so I'll sign off with one more unspeakable display of rhyme," he writes later in a letter from jail to me, dated December 16, 1999:

> A damsel from Sandusky
> With a scent so coarse and musky
> At the local pound
> While selecting a hound
> Was buggered by a husky.

> 'Twas a paratrooper named Adair
> Who loved to jerk off in mid-air
> While savoring a stroke
> The parachute broke
> And jissom speckled a bear.

My Aunt Sally shared another story from high school days with my father. Back in the early '60s when they were both enrolled at James Blair High School in Williamsburg, they had the same biology teacher but at different grade levels. One day when my Aunt Sally arrived home at 3:30 in the afternoon, the principal of the school was sitting there in the den. My father was being grilled by my grandfather. Sally was told to go to her room.

It turned out Daddy had been expelled from school, brought home by the principal, and told he couldn't speak this way. What way?

"Eddie Boy, because he was an editor and writer for the James Blair High School monthly paper, covering school sports and activities and such, had simply drawn a picture of a large toad with a gig in his rear."

It was pretty common to "gig a toad" back then, especially out in the country on a farm. "In the caption, for the upcoming football game, my father had written 'Let's gig 'em!'"

Copies of it circulated around school. "That's how I found out," Sally continues. "And because I was having to dissect frogs that we caught and had to bring into school for science stuff, I thought it was funny. Everyone laughed—except our parents and the school. He ended up getting kicked off the paper."

My Aunt Sally chalks it up to my father's "different intelligence" and being "ahead of the game," whereas I hear him being in trouble, misunderstood, cut off at the pass, and never getting where he wanted to go—starting way back.

While some girls have jitters about the fairy tale wedding ceremony, mine involved wondering if my father would get out of jail in time to walk me up the aisle in October 2000. Amid whispers that my step-mother might have him arrested on the church steps in front of God and everybody, I was a bit freaked.

Jeffrey says he saw Daddy once when he got out of jail around mid-March of that year but doesn't know where he went from there. If I had to speculate, it would be Jean's house. To the kids, she was known as "the other woman" he'd been seeing for years.

"I'd never met anybody that was so much like him," TJ said one time when he was younger. I think he was alluding to the fact that Jean was just so accepting of everything when it came to my father. The loud music. The huge jugs of wine. The chain-smoking and the acoustic strumming on the patio all night. They just kind of got each other.

"She was a heavy drinker and heavy smoker," says Jeffrey. "I can understand the attraction. She was a lovely lady. She knew who our dad was. One time we went out on the river and caught a bunch of fish, had a great time. It was supposed to happen again, but Pops was in a drunken stupor, passed out. She said, 'Hey, want some breakfast? He just needs to sleep it off.' She was nice—and very nice to me. I'm sorry if she broke up the marriage, but at some point Dad was the one who would have done it anyway."

Jeffrey and I both wanted to reach out to Jean for her memories of our father and that time in life. I was able to find her daughter whom she was now living with, but Jean declined to talk to me. I suppose this was all so painful for everyone, including her, and I always had the sense that things ended badly between her and my father. Like he did something to wear out his final welcome with her—it must've been pretty bad if even Jean wouldn't have him back.

In August 2000, just a few months before my wedding, I received what Daddy called the "strangest letter you'll ever get." I never appreciated just how much heartbreak he was experiencing at the time--he loved her so much, but it was over and he was a bit like a ship without a moor, while recognizing he still had a daughter's wedding to show up for.

Aug 2000

Me Pooh Doll,

Strangest letter you'll ever get is in your hands.

(CHOWAN USUAL)

You give 16 years of your life and it's gone. You broke yer back to stand at weddings. You pulled fools from drunken blazing cars and walked frozen children up Nyack roads to spare them the idiocy of their elders.

Bethany Jean hand-in-hand jumped upstate New York
brook to no avail. (I'm LOST)
Kennerly - I really wish to check out.
I'm not sad
" " bitter
" " hating life
I am sick of stupidity and I'm no big deal.
I'm just a Daddy who loves you. If I go
Before Halloween
I died of loneliness.
That is my fault.

P.S. 'Member - Things change in a heartbeat.

Crofton
8/14/00
Shorline Blues (song)

I knew it was over
Yeah
When the raven turned blue
Yes - I knew it was over
Till I thought of you
Guess I'll tough it till October
And head for skies of blue.

Carlo Rossi has got me
I've got cheeks of ruddy hue
Yessch - Carlo's got me
There's nothing really new
Our time is summer Indian
And I'll be there for you.

You're the firstborn of mine
I now know what to do
Yes, darling one; I shure know
What to do
I'll dance at that der wedding
And moon everyone but you.

8/15/00

Quicksilver Blues

God bought me a Mercury
She rolled jest like wagon wheel
Yeah she bought me a Mercury
To watch the tires I peel
She got canary paint
Lord I'm sweating at the wheel

The top is lily white
And she throws my old head back
Flathead belching heat
Down the railroad track
Baby moons flying
We'll never go back

Well I know it now
Quicksilver is my soul
Cool sweet irony

"Mom knew we'd be fine if we went over to Jean's," says Jeffrey. "But if she knew what he was doing over there. A couple times TJ and I would breathe into his breathalyzer to get the car started. We didn't really know what was going on. Once we must've mentioned it to Mom and that's when she brought Shannah in. That's probably when TJ felt like he could get out of going anymore.

I met Jean several times, once when she and Daddy came to Ocean City and took Kirk and me out for a crab feast. This was a few years before we were married. She had short, thin, wispy blonde hair cropped close to her head. She may have smoked even more than Daddy did. She was easy to talk to, with a ready laugh that sometimes turned wheezy. She didn't strike me as the type for my father, but then again, my step-mother—compared to my mother—didn't seem like the type either. As life went on, Daddy's type was probably any woman who could tolerate him.

I once visited Daddy at her house that summer before I was married. They had a lop-eared bunny named Liberty Valance, named after the 1962 western starring Jimmy Stewart and John Wayne.

The 'Valance' is hideous. I believe we should marry him to Kirk's cat.

"You've never seen the *The Man Who Shot Liberty Valance?*" Daddy asked incredulously, with a faraway look and knowing smile spreading over his face. He leaned back in a kitchen chair with one elbow behind his head, the bottom half of a Chesterfield slow-burning between his fingers.

"Ohh man!" Daddy was clearly delighted to fill me in. "Liberty Valance is an old western, you've got Lee Marvin playing the outlaw Liberty Valance and Jimmy Stewart as the good guy. You've never seen that?"

As with many things my father said, I took it in but didn't go right out and watch the movie. In recent years though, I continued to find unfamiliar references in his letters that compelled me to research on the internet, digging into whatever was in his head and trying to better understand what he meant at the time. I did eventually watch the movie a few years back, which was considered to be the last great western ever directed by John Ford and in fact was symbolic of the end of that era. It was 1962 after all, and things were changing. Out with the old, in with the new. Just like in the movie, the old, pre-railroad town and lawless ways of settling things giving way to the inevitable new ways of the world. I might have been adding all kinds of meaning to the lop-eared bunny named Liberty Valance, but knowing the unfulfilled, and at times melancholic aspects of my father, maybe not. Something about Liberty Valance stuck with him all those years.

I'm so glad that you and Kirk found one another. What you have I only found once and I am certain I will never find it twice (JEAN). We still talk like most people never do. We may be apart but she is the only wife I've ever known. I didn't meet her until I was 37. It was a very good age. Much easier than now.

```
          FROST

     You know it's time to go when the   drift   is
just like snow and between cannot be mastered.

     I'm here on the side of the   road and cannot
be   quartered .  And here I will stay.

   Look's like I'll sleep in the woods
               Tonight

     That   ain't no big deal.

   If I could take you to strange ripply
bower and hold you one more time ,
     Would you forgive sometime andbemine.

   I'd opine that   Id   love you

               And feed ya turpentine,

                    Guess Who?
```

Letter from Daddy to my mother, dated April 5, 2000:

Anne,

This is for the two of ya per letter from Pooh Doll. I assume she and Kurt (sic) are there rooting about with ecstatic aplomb. I've gone to work with gruesome Thursday Friday Saturday nights shure and I'm loving life. I'm working for a grocery chain just walked in with loads of prior experience. So far so good.

I'm ready for all regarding matrimony and intend to purchase a deluxe tuxedo (cherry red and purple bowtie (correct me).

Tell K my latest dance selection be "Come Monday." Actually that would be better if you and I were to dance. (No, "By the Time I Get to Phoenix" - nyeh nyeh) Anyway, I'm glad the wedding is still six months away. I intend to help out financially in any way possible. We shall see.

That's about it.

I've not worked since August and my first night has just chewed me up and spit me out. More semi-lucidity in the near future.

Love Pancho (and his sidekick Liberty Valence)

"I've been sprung 10 days now and I've finally slept eight hours at a time. I hadn't done that since San Francisco," reads a letter to Jeffrey dated 'April Fool.' "Keep any interest in school and don't worry about girls and insects. It's time for a small garden; say cucumbers and green peppers and yeschh—sugar-snap peas if you get transplants...I'm trying to get to see you—if I can't get my license back I may go to Philadelphia. I will stay in touch. Love, 'Little Pop'"

My father wrote to me around the same time, he was piecing together odd jobs and doing what he needed to do, fulfilling on what he hoped would redeem himself in the eyes of Maryland law, to get his driver's license back and be able to drive a tractor trailer again.

> I'm hanging in; worked five days out of seven plus a day of hire and orientation. I don't think I'd survive as long in the chili and onion fields of El Paso (again). Mexicans are not lazy. I'm going with the state 100% to get back my license. I've enrolled in a six month alcohol treatment program. To start I hitch-hike three miles each way. With this I go to a medical advisory board (DMV) and petition them. If I can't get mercy (a reinstatement of license after 26 weeks) I'll be at your wedding and then depart for my city by the bay. There'll be nowhere else for me to be.
>
> S.O.T.
>
> On the nutty side, I left my alcohol counselor and bought the "Valance" a Rite-Aid $1.25 Teddy Bear 'plete with removable washable halter. After four hours you daintily pick up this stuffed victim by the ear. Hideous.

In a letter dated April 28, 2000, Jeffrey points out the optimism:

> Hi guys,
>
> It was so good to see you. You looked healthy, lean an mean. I pray that will last a millennium. I'm hoping I'm onto something good that I can physically handle. It will have me between D.C. and Long Island (non-driving) Monday thru Friday—inventory work with Sam's Clubs and Wal-Marts. I haven't been this excited about work in a year-and-a-half. Half of my first check will be yours.
>
> If I don't write Shannah by Sunday night tell her I didn't tear up her picture and I love her as I love you all. I'm

busy for really the first time in eight months. I'll see you as soon as I can—probably two weeks.

I know you believe in me (or you are trying) and I have totally faith in you. Don't let yourselves down.

Develop your interests. If ya gotta mess with marijuana do it with your brother, say in the treehouse. (or any other hopeless drug).

Honor thy mother. More soon. I love you.

Looking at these letters together, Jeffrey chuckles and shakes his head, reading aloud again: "'If ya gotta mess with marijuana, do it with your brother!' That was his advice for his 14-year-old kid."

It's funny though, the advice reminds me of my mother's advice to me. She was pretty filterless and matter-of-fact as well. Her advice to me at 14 probably had something to do with using condoms and not getting pregnant, even though I wasn't sexually active yet and would've been mortified by the suggestion. She was coming from reality vs. propriety—kind of like Daddy—and it actually makes a lot of sense. I was the only one of my friends (I could name half a dozen of them) who never had an unwanted pregnancy.

In the next couple of missives written to the boys, it's as though Daddy was trying to impart every ounce of fatherly wisdom ever—knowing he wasn't going to be there for them, physically or otherwise, throughout their teen years.

Occasionally, he wrote things like, "Don't give up on your dreams like I did," but that's as far as his introspection would go. There would be no more exploration or a deep meaningful look at why that was. Booze just made it go away quietly.

Like TJ says, "For him it was never even on the table—to ever stop drinking—not just denial, but no fucks given. That's not how it was for me. I don't know if he ever got the perspective he needed on himself to have the kind of life he had the potential for. I guess he could just make do with where he was and it didn't matter."

'This here is a tough world,
You only make it easy'
by your attitude. Easy 'for
one 56 to say to one eighteen
Not so easy for you.

Try fortune or fame,
Pick either but neither
are to be what they claim,
It all isn't that 'simple.

Try marine biology,
Try homesteading,
Try 'Zen and the art
of motorcycle maintenance",
Try reading Henry Miller,
"   "   Jack Kerouac
Be a forest ranger,
Raise Turtles,
Raise Lop-eared rabbits,
Play left-handed guitar.
Build tree houses for hire,
~~Be a Hebo~~
Always be true to yourself'

Love,
Dad

Dad called and said he was working at a rubber vagina warehouse. I don't know. Can't wait to see you! Love, Jeffrey

— Letter from Jeffrey to me, pre-wedding, August 2000

A wedding?! YESScchh! I shall grease the wheelchair and extract my special reception tiger suit from its mothballs. And I shant forget to pre-test the whoopee cushions. Ooh-la-la! I'm excited as a demented moose. Are you sure you wish to invite me? English goods were ever the best...Your father would be vastly proud...and delighted." - January 8, 2000

A gentleman of County Cork
who slung a humongous dork
Was graced to receive
A royal reprieve
For stuffing the duchess of York

(Fornication Under Consent of the King)?

From a letter written on July 2, 2000:

Regarding your letter and doubts and fears I hope to set your mind at ease. I've attended three weddings of Jean's sibs. Lastly was Julia, born Thanksgiving '69. Episcopal Church Eastern Shore Chestertown remote. Horrific thunderstorm and rain like cow pissing on a flat rock. I saved a few $200 gowns and drove a broken Honda 12 miles to the reception. I refuse to be drunk at your wedding. Trust me here. Everything with me is play by ear these days but as I live I'll be there for you. I am so proud of you and the choices you have made. I love ya, Daddy

When I did get married in October 2000, there were no arrests on the church steps. No heated interactions between family members. And although he was maintenance drinking for those couple of days leading up to the wedding, Daddy didn't draw too much attention to himself, although we were all holding our breath.

At the church rehearsal the day before the wedding, I walked into the parish hall where all the bridesmaids and groomsmen were gathered. Daddy was sauntering around with a 12-ounce can of beer in a paper bag. Apparently, he had sniffed out a couple of tall boys that were in the kitchen fridge at the church, left over from some event.

```
        Candy Ass Blues Revisited Twicee

So your down and all broken-hearted,
    And the thief of the night no longer remains
And your favorite son has just farted
    You wonder if you really  are sane

Out in the distance you're out walking
   And holding all the stalkers at Bay
They say you don't know the difference
    But I think I know I know  you sweet  Kay

Life's  somewhat of a bitch without  you
    Guess I 'll die in battle or in vain
When you want somebody you don't have to
    Speak to
Walk awhile and see me Queen Kay.

    I don't  how you are commissioned
But I fully understand your pain

    But I pray you  have the comprehension to
see me one more time again.

            Eddy Chowan

            Ed Clay
```

We all stayed at the Sleep Inn in Salisbury, which had a big field behind it leading up to rows of trees. The morning of my wedding, I looked out my hotel room window and spotted this lone figure. I pressed my face up against the window. Yup, it was Daddy. Oh God. He was drinking already. Tall boy with a paper bag in hand.

"Please God, let us get through this day," I pleaded. "Just one more day, please, please, please, we've gotten this far, we can do it."

I mean seriously. My father had been in jail all those months with no guarantee he'd be released before our wedding. And when he did get out, he somehow managed to stay out of trouble long enough to get himself on a Greyhound bus from my grandmother's house in Vero Beach, Florida, all the way up to Salisbury, Maryland, on the very day we had told him to be there. My mom and I went to pick him up in the middle of the night and took him to the hotel. Kirk had helped arrange for a suit for the rehearsal dinner and a tuxedo fitting for the wedding. It was looking like my father was going to be able to walk me down the aisle, but I knew there was only about a 24-hour window of safety. He could show up relatively clean and sober, well-behaved and mostly off of alcohol for about one day.

With Daddy at my rehearsal dinner, October 27, 2000

The times when Daddy did show up just sober enough to pull off the occasion, he was awkward, not the version of himself he was most comfortable with nor the one we'd come to interact with the most. There was nothing to say. It was as though we hardly knew each other. So we'd pussyfoot around with polite conversation until he'd adequately tied one on and we were back in step. By then it was almost like wishing for him to just be the same old drunk we'd come to know, like get on with it already. He didn't know how to be in that other skin and we didn't know how to relate to him that way either.

We were already well into our second full day with the wedding still ahead. Daddy's ability to keep it together would gradually disintegrate from there. But he knew I was counting on him for this one day, and I needed him to put on his best possible performance. Indeed, we did make it down the aisle with my mother on my left arm and my father on my right. None of us stumbled to the altar.

At the reception, when it was time for our father-daughter dance, the Van Morrison track "Into the Mystic" came on. Daddy had spent many months pondering the selection from his jail cell and finally announced it in one of his letters. "We were born before the wind," Van Morrison crooned as my father and I held onto each other and slow-danced in a circular motion. I was still wary of what he might do, so when he stepped away and attempted to twirl me—his own movements became a bit more Mick Jaggerish—I shook my head to rein him in. To all outward appearances, he was just father-of-the-bride having a really good time. The rest of us, though, hoped there wouldn't be a scene.

I found out the morning after the wedding that my in-laws had been last at the church before riding into town for the reception. They saw my father sort of roaming around the church cemetery with beer in bag and asked him if he needed a ride. He looked around and noticing there weren't any cars left, said, "I reckon I do." So they drove him to the reception. My husband and I always cracked up at that story. We couldn't imagine what the conversation was like, my father half-loaded in the back seat in his borrowed tux and tall boy in hand and my very proper in-laws in the front, making small talk about the union of their children.

Photos of TJ and Jeffrey at my wedding show two tall, gangly teenage boys.

"Seeing Dad at your wedding," says Jeffrey, "I remember TJ saying, 'I don't even like Dad anymore.' If you look at the pictures, he never smiled in any of them. He had that weird thing with the mouth, kind of like Dad."

Father's Day

Gentlemen...sooner or later
Sooner or later you decide what your "role" is. The world
is a bloody stage, gentlemen. Money is merely an exchange

*'twixt people. If you have a ton of it ye jest might drink or
drug or fuck yerself to death. I believe you each have the
wisdom to respect my thoughts. I have always lived HARD! I
don't recommend it. I have suffered until I thought being
down was being up. Then again, I can't wait to roll eighteen
wheels again.*

*Take your sweet time and learn. You haven't yet any
concept of what you are growing into. I'll tell you this. Your
attitudes are your ally. (Positive)*

Never ever despair or compare.

Comparisons are "nuts"

"Nough said"

I'll always help.

Eddy Chowan

Daddy didn't smile in photos, he just endured them. Most pictures
have the half-frown, half-smile thing Jeffrey talks about, as though
Daddy couldn't decide which way to go with it. If there were a cartoon
bubble over his head, it would say, "Well, fuck me!" like the line of neck-
ties Daddy said he was gonna launch.

"I think TJ's actually trying to hide how happy he is most of the
time," Jeffrey goes on. "He perfected that frown-when-happy face for
photos."

The day after my wedding, my father and Jeffrey went walking and
talking outside around the hotel. I'm on FaceTime with Jeffrey as he
tells me this story for the first time, kind of looking off to the side as he
relives the conversation. I notice his face turning a bit pink and I get
quiet so he can say whatever is there.

"He was talking about how he was gonna be taking off again,"
Jeffrey says with the tiniest shake of his head, still disbelieving. "He
could have done whatever he wanted to do, it would have been so easy at
that moment in time, if ever there were one. He could have stayed
around. Three out of his four younger kids were still in Maryland at the

time. He could've been around his family, even if it wasn't getting back together with Mom. He could've stayed. If he'd ever wanted to hit the reset button and be a family man, that would've been it."

Jeffrey's face looks about eight years old, showing betrayal and disappointment, the loss and rejection that was never made up for. He snaps out of it, a little too quickly perhaps, then shakes his head and smiles. "He chose booze over family." The same off-handed explanation we all use to cover up the emotional impact of my father's legacy of drinking and leaving.

"Unfortunately, Jimmy became our role model after that," Jeffrey continues, and there was an emotional trickle-down effect. "Of course Jimmy was never really a good older brother, so then TJ saw that was how you treat a younger sibling...and I was like Goddamn, I love all you guys, I just wanna hang out!"

I had never before considered that Jimmy became a father figure to the boys, so I let that one sink in a moment. We all love Jimmy, but even he would agree he was no fine example. One time when the boys were old enough to party, Jimmy invited them to come down to North Carolina. The boys took a week off school to go down and hang out.

"Dude, I'm supposed to be in school," TJ remembers thinking. "Unfortunately, we really looked up to Jimmy. That was our role model as far as Clay boys go."

But sometimes kids go opposite of what they grew up with. The way Jeffrey sees it, "I think it's made me a pretty good person. I care about people and their feelings."

When Jeffrey was 15, he had just been caught trying to steal a case of beer from Gibson's, where he was working part-time for minimum wage in Greenville.

"I didn't get fired but I was too embarrassed to go back," he says. "It was a shitty feeling, and it was the last time I ever tried to steal."

Daddy's letter from "Zero Beach, FL" consoled:

Jeffrey, So good to get yer message and Shannah's as well. I was working and elsewhere at the time.

I've been short on work hours which affects what I can send. Generally I'm earning only $1.50 above minimum wage *but carrying benefits ranging from 90% to 100%, including dental.*

Don't be discouraged by your wages. Every one starts somewhere. You, I assume, pay no rent, no food, no electric, heat, or water. You must earn to save when you are young. I'm proud of your job and always of your willingness to work.

How 'bout it for coincidence?! We're both storekeepers of sorts. You a liquor-deli; me with a supermarket chain. I look forward to the day when I can put you in a truck and show you the best working class job in the world!"

"I wonder if he knew he'd never be behind the wheel of an 18-wheeler again?" Jeffrey says. "Or did he have false hopes that he would get his license back and go back to work?"

Anyways; I'm fixing to re-pursue my natural trade. If I cant get back in I'll become a Troubadour\ street-singer, If that doesn't pan out I'll raise guineau pigs and lop-eared bunnies; Mebbe grow marijuana and run a poker-house. Or fight off the border patrol and infiltrate (OLD) Mexico with my bible, gun, medicine bag and medical books. Never be blue for long, gal. They's too many good things in life. Proverb from an ancient cynic

Whether it was the magical thinking or the stubborn streak in Daddy's optimism—a refusal to be beaten down by life or anyone else's rules—he always spoke with hope and promise, walking that fine line with delusions of adequacy.

"I guess it's kind of a good thing he wasn't all 'woe is me' and sad sack," TJ points out. "It would have been awful if he was always talking about how pathetic and worthless and miserable he was."

Occasionally, Daddy would sound morose in his letters. Rambling on, cursive handwriting a bit askew letting on that he'd been drinking. "I got a few that felt like a drunken pity party," says Jeffrey.

TJ, Jeffrey,

I should have been around but wasn't. I have always followed my heart. I had no selection.

Whatever I mean to you I love you and I'm gonna take a chance to save me and gives youse guys education. You must always follow your mind and spirit.

Your family (with few exceptions) is your only friend. Life is a struggle for you alone. Never ever trust a stranger. 'LIEVE ME—They don't care.

I've been thru' the jaws of Hell. I don't want to see you there. Do not be confused by the problems of others. God has given you your own mind. Cherish it. Do not cast your pearls before swine.

Whisky can't kill this baby. Heroin didn't make him crazy. Women won't put him in his grave. I learned to hold my liquor somewhere down in Costa Rica ain't nobody's business what I do.

Business IS REAL
LIFE IS SERIOUS

Attitude is 200% of everything. They's ups and downs but the good times will win out in the long run. (If you try)

You didn't ask to be born. I say it's better than nothing (I mean not be at all) you have so many possibilities and so much energy and good health: You must use it now. Time waits for no one. Save your dollars. Learn to build them. Eat safe pussy; that has money (HOPEFULLY). If it smells like cologne leave it alone. (My name is Rodriguez Jose I earn 15 pesos a day I met Miss Lucy; she showed her pussy, the pesos they ran away.)

Anyway, my sons, I have two missions to do and after this letter I'll try to do postcards. I guess the last word is to always, always believe in yourselves. I'm proud of you. Pop

P.S. The Heart is a lonely, lonely Hunter. Be easy on yourselves!! Drink alligator Piss for breakfast!

A letter dated Un Decembris 2 Thou written to Jeffrey and TJ:

'member that at seventeen your (greater) friend is a library. Use it. Open all these things slowly. You guys are fucking brilliant! (But never be arrogant)

I'm so tired and weary I could sleep for a million years. — HOWEVER—They's "Stones" to dance to and education to be had

I reckon I'll stick awhile.

Don't worry about girls.

" " insects.

" " parents.

" " dogs.

" " cats.

" " school.

" " cops.

" " *God.*

Be ye own boss and be good to yourself. You fucking deserve it.
Love, Your Daddy

A Holy Night card with a couple of bills enclosed reads:

My Sons,
You've got a long row to hoe. I'm glad I'm not a million-aire. Arrogance is often a curse. Always use yer minds first—then follow your hearts. Save all you can and you will thrive. Be sure you're right—then go ahead. 'William F. Burro' This ain't much but I've had a shitty year. I love you, Pop

Around that same time, in one of the "polar bear with Santa hat" series (I've got several of these in my own collection), on which Daddy drew a hand-rolled cigarette and a puff of smoke coming out of the bear's mouth:

TJ and JEFFREY,
You can't always get what you WANT. (repeat twice)
But if you try some time you might find you'll get what you need.
I was imagining yer lives at 20 or so. It occurred to me that to get yer own act in order could be a major priority. Be brothers to one another. Yer Daddy, with Love.

In reading these messages to his young sons, I wonder if Daddy made a conscious decision long ago to always uplift his children, having himself survived the beatings—physical and otherwise—by his own father as a child.

In a page out of TJ's spiral-bound book "DAD *Share Your Life With Me*," given to my father when TJ was a kid to answer all kinds of questions about Daddy's childhood, the response to one question: 'What happened when you got in trouble at home?' was particularly loaded.

"I will never speak of this as long as I live."

And he didn't. We never really knew. None of us.

But the physical violence was legend in our family, horrible things that nobody wanted to talk about yet were alluded to from time to time. Punishment inflicted by my paternal grandfather on my father, aunt, and uncle, but especially on my Aunt Sally, undeniably the mouthiest of the lot. My grandfather denied the abuse to his dying day.

But my grandmother confided to me over the years, from the time Aunt Sally was just a toddler crying in the crib, my grandfather would get so angry, he'd go in and shake her and give her horrible spankings—the kind of physical roughness that would get your kids taken away from you nowadays. My grandmother said she would try to stop him, but he'd push her out of the way and threaten to beat her, too. She often ended up sitting in the bedroom crying and listening while he beat her baby daughter, and she couldn't do a thing about it.

Before my grandmother died, she shared one incident that was particularly horrific. My aunt had only recently brought it up to her for the very first time since it actually happened. When my Aunt Sally was in high school, she had gotten in trouble for something. She and my grandmother and grandfather were outside of the school gymnasium. By this time, her rebellious spirit would have been well developed—probably starting with the first slap in the crib—and her mouth was one way she fought back. God and Aunt Sally are the only ones who know what really happened that day when my grandfather yanked her into the gym and locked my grandmother out. All I remember is Grandmother telling me how she was beating and yelling on the door for him to stop and she could hear Sally screaming inside. Once again, nothing she could do to help her daughter who was crying in pain and fear and outrage, wondering why on earth her mother wasn't protecting her—why no one was.

The incident had so traumatized my aunt that it drove a subtle wedge between her and my grandmother all those years. Keeping in mind once again that no one had ready access to psychotherapy or any language to even process this kind of experience, let alone call it domestic violence or crime. So it's not surprising it took decades for it to really bubble to the surface for my aunt. When it did come up, she wanted to know why my grandmother hadn't tried to help her. The way she remembered it, she was completely abandoned. She couldn't have understood at the time or imagined her own mother's fear and helplessness in the face of my grandfather's anger.

During her childhood years, Aunt Sally remembered coming home from school every day. My grandfather was running a couple of businesses while my grandmother worked at Eastern State, the mental hospital, as a psych nurse.

"Mom would leave a BILLBOARD on the pantry door: 'Daily Updates.' Sally—

- Take out and thaw dinner (wrapped in packages) in cold water
- Make salad with lettuce, tomato, cukes, no onion
- Set the table with plates and make sure napkins are beside
- Pick up laundry from all baskets and put into utility room
- Brush the floors off and empty everything in a waste can

Instruction for Eddie would be to sweep out the garage. Uncle Ray had to dump all the garbage."

"How do you like that?" says my Aunt Sally, pointing to the obvious extra work she was burdened with compared to her brothers. "My parents made sure there was never a wasted moment."

Then my grandmother would come home worn out from being on her feet all day, dealing with mental patients. She'd say, "Sally, hi, how are you honey?"

"I'm okay, I'm going to my room now," said Aunt Sally, aiming to disappear.

"Thank you, honey. You checked off everything I asked of you."

"Are you sure?" Aunt Sally would ask.

"Because if I hadn't done it all," she tells me, "my mother would report me and then I would've been restricted or whipped. Then at dinner, we weren't allowed to TALK. Ever. What do you think about this shit in a 12-year-old's life?"

Daddy on the farm

It's no wonder my father longed for summers at his grandmother's house down in Harrellsville, North Carolina. Grandma Clay (my great-grandmother) had a big farm where the 11 Clay children, including my grandfather, had grown up.

> As a child, what did you want to be when you grew up?
> GARBAGEMAN, FISHERMAN, MINISTER, Hobo, (Now called homeless person), Professional guitarist or musician, Bum, FREE (above all), Actor, Teacher, Shipmaster.

Daddy would spend boyhood summer days in the fields, trailing behind his Uncle Thomas, one of my grandfather's brothers. My brother TJ remembers hearing something about a Black woman who worked on the farm and Daddy trying to look up her long skirts when he was little. And then there was the castrating of hogs.

> I decided to roam with Uncle Jimmy. It was time to take the balls off the hogs and I thought I was young and able. I was done with the first squeal but hung on—puking like the siblings I'd guffawed on. Red-blue testicles and X-rated bottle, blue-sharpened pen-knife doing job. Great. Having shot these guys thro' the brains was the ultimate previous.

*(Same specie I mean.) Every morning, summer, slop and corn,
I almost kissed the poor bastards.*

Uncle Thomas and his family, including daughters Nancy and Bonnie, all lived there in the big house with Grandma Clay and helped work the farm. Uncle Jimmy (my brother's namesake) and his wife Bessie also lived on the property.

"From the front door there was a huge wide hallway. On the left side was my grandma's bedroom. Upstairs my sister and I stayed," Nancy reminisces. "My best memory is of my grandmaw's living room piano, and she and Uncle Ed would sit and sing and play in the living room and sing old songs, 'Meet me in Saint Louis, Louis.'"

Everybody in the Clay family loved to fish. Gracie's Hole was a well-known and favorite spot in Harrellsville.

"Grandmaw, she was so funny," says Nancy. "She and my Aunt Bessie would tell dirty jokes and you could hear them laughing all over the river."

My father always spoke highly of his uncles. Like Jeffrey says, probably because he got the affection and kindness from them rarely afforded by my grandfather.

"He loved my daddy, loved our whole family," says Nancy. "He just wanted to be out in the country; he really was a country person. Your dad was quiet and sweet, no trouble for my mother. We loved it when he came. He followed Daddy in the field and they talked. He had a very gentle way, around me anyway, and he was always so polite at the dinner table. He was just one of our family when he was there, always kind and respectful."

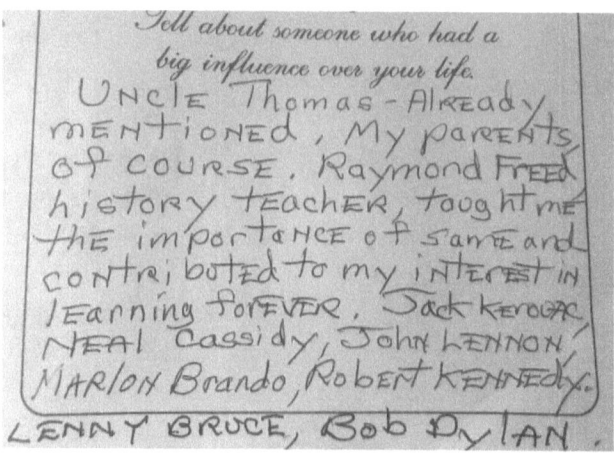

Tell about someone who had a big influence over your life.

UNCLE Thomas - Already mENTioNEd, My parEnts of COURSE. Raymond FrEEd history tEachER, tooght mE the importaNCE of sanE and contributed to my intErEst in lEarning forEVER, Jack kErouac NEAl Cassidy, JohN LENNON, MARloN Brando, RobErt KENNEdy, LENNY BRUCE, Bob DylAN.

Twas '57. My father and Bob Boyd and I traveled 80 miles to Harrellsville. It was a brisk and windy day in April. When we reached the Clay farm we shifted to a pick-up and transferred our goods, bamboo poles and fishing bait. Instead of boating we parked and walked to the river. I was following Uncle Bob. His ass-end was large and his jeans displayed "POWERHOUSE." I began to laugh uncontrollably. My father asked why. I was too amused to speak.

We arrived at a small beachhead on the Chowan River; north of "Gracie's Hole." All I recall then is fishing. The yellow-bellies, white perch, speckled too, an occasional English perch. We had a mess in a short time. To my surprise my father produced a cast-iron skillet, cooking oil, cornmeal and a wood fire six feet from high tide. As I feasted on fish and cornbread, a 1-1/2 pound yellow-belly ran into the lily pads with my worm (I caught him)."

- excerpt from a Father's Day card written from Daddy to Grandfather Clay, 1989

Gracie's Hole, Chowan River, Harrellsville, North Carolina

Drums Along the Chowan (Eddy Boys' Insomnia)

The Clay house was built in 1923. My father was born that year.

She was magnificent. Built on brick supports 4-feet high a child played freely under this great house. It was heaven on summer days. Kicked the hell out of 105-degree summer days.

Huge potbelly stoves. Five bedrooms and a parlor. Precious hardwood flooring. A kitchen nook for 3. (All farting at once.)

Anyways — my grandfodder knew what he was doing. The river was over a mile away but he had his house on stilts. He also produced the finest hog in North Carolina. Hickory smoke in a tradition older than the Civil War.

Kinda makes me wonder what it was that got under my grandfather's skin so bad that his children could never measure up. Especially since Nancy tells me how completely normal her childhood felt.

"My parents had level heads," she says, not a hint of violence.

Yet I held onto the belief that my grandfather—I swore he'd once told me this—had an older brother who used to get drunk and beat up on the younger ones.

But Nancy never heard anything like that.

"They fought a lot, played awful tricks on each other," she says. "Like getting in bed at night, one person would always have to be the one to get up out of bed and flip the light switch, then run and jump back in bed. The other boys would move the bed while that one was up, and they'd all laugh. They fought like crazy living out on a farm."

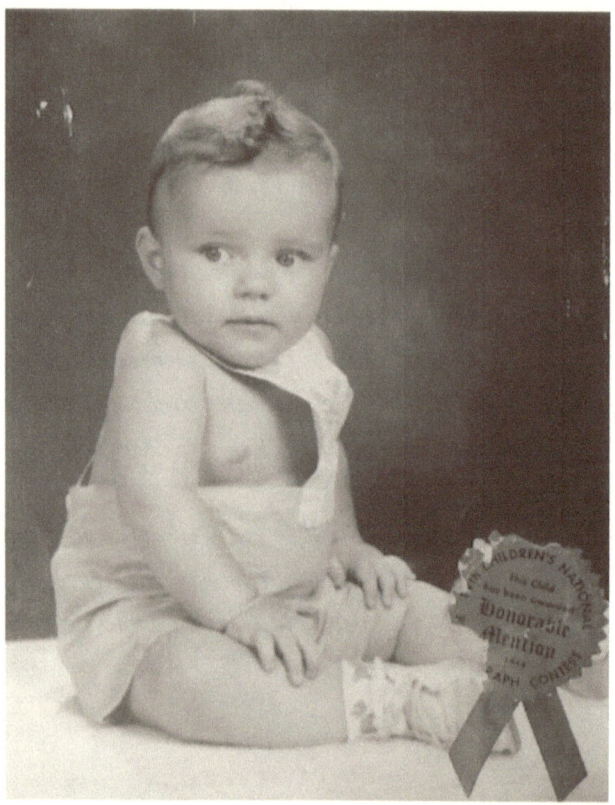

Daddy as a baby (cute baby contest)

Her father Thomas didn't drink, and neither did another brother, Charlie, who lived in Danville, Virginia, she says. She and her sisters never drank, and neither did Grandmother Clay.

"Now Jimmy, he was addicted to morphine. I remember this my whole childhood. He kept a pan on the stove of hypodermic needles. Whoever the doctor was kept him supplied with morphine. He tried to get off of it, but instead of morphine he would drink, which was worse than morphine."

Uncle Jimmy was another of my father's favorite uncles. I wonder if his propensity for drugs and alcohol is where the affection came from, and if he were the older sibling my grandfather was referring to, the one who got ornery drunk and beat up the younger ones.

"When he was a boy, your father, Eddie, just adored his father," Nancy continues. "He would do anything to please him."

My father as a boy

I had never imagined my father trying to please anyone, let alone being a young boy, trying to please my grandfather. Perhaps that's right where it all stopped, him giving a good goddamn what anybody thought because nothing he did made a difference anyway. We either prove them right or prove them wrong, what we've been told about ourselves, and Daddy teetered his entire life between proving he was no good and proving he was worthy.

A fictitious picture suddenly pops into my mind of a 1955 scene. My father at eight years old sitting properly at the dinner table, being as polite as he can be, trying to do the right thing.

"Eddie was very sensitive, he wanted to please him so badly," Nancy says. I can tell she is leading up to something. She hesitates, then comes right out with it.

"Uncle Ed belittled him. He would tell Eddie he was no good."

I suck in my breath.

"Wow," I respond. "I've never heard that before."

"He loved his dad, but he could never live up to what Uncle Ed wanted him to be."

Young Daddy

I'd never heard these actual words uttered from my own father, so somehow I have been shielded from the idea that Daddy had been put down or never thought that he measured up. It's almost as if Daddy was too defiant to let on how low the put-downs had been. Plus, as children ourselves, we don't often relate to our parents as children.

As the realization of my father taking in the hurt as a child sinks in, my eyes start stinging hard and heaviness overcomes my body—a burden of sadness, of being that kid. I feel fucking heartbroken for my father. Not that he would ever want an ounce of pity or sadness, but I feel sad for the little boy who was trying to please and never could, and who endured the belittlement. I'm suddenly sad for all the kids on the entire planet who ever have to experience that. Even sad for my own children, for the moments I dishonored them in some way that would leave them feeling less than as they got older. Such a burden (of belittlement) has never been mine to bear, and I am grateful for it.

The thought also crosses my mind that while my grandfather humiliated my father as a child, my father humiliated his children in a different way. Not that he ever did it to be cruel, but he did it. And he never once took responsibility for it, ever.

I imagine Aunt Sally or Uncle Ray reading this and going, *Duh, wouldn't you assume we were belittled along with beaten?* I can hear all the times Uncle Ray said he could never live up to his father's expectations, well into adulthood regarding just about anything, that he was never good enough. Uncle Ray just got used to that dynamic with my grandfather.

My paternal grandparents on their wedding day

"We were told we were nothin' and would never amount to noth-in'," my Aunt Sally shares with me, "but we all rose above what our father thought of us, even though he carried those thoughts about us his entire life. My mother spoke of this to me many a time and we hashed out his issues to overcome our own inferiorities."

"Uncle Ed was a tough person," Nancy adds kindly, about my grandfather.

It's not easy for her to talk about my grandfather in this way. He was her favorite uncle from the time she was a young girl. He loved her and Bonnie like daughters. She sighs heavily with the weight of it, and we are both present to things families don't talk about but affect everyone, one way or another.

"I just want you to know this doesn't change the way I feel about my grandfather," I assure her. "I loved him. He never laid a finger on me, and I always had my own relationship with him, regardless. But there were things that happened. And that's just the truth."

"Yes, it just happened," she agrees. "Your grandparents were such a beautiful couple," she goes on.

My grandmother, a tall, slim, brunette with green eyes, and my grandfather, who epitomized tall, dark, and handsome, both had magnetic personas.

"They were like a Hollywood movie couple," she says. "That's what it was like whenever they came to visit."

I imagined my grandparents pulling up to the Clay farm in their shiny automobile, stepping out into the dirt with their fashionable shoes, poofing dust all over them.

My Aunt Sally says my grandmother hated going there because of having to use the outhouse.

When Nancy was 17 years old, going into her senior year of high school, she went to live with my grandparents in Newport News, Virginia. Nancy was born in 1939 so she was about eight years older than my father and 10 years older than my Aunt Sally.

"Uncle Ed got me a job. I saw their family life and it was very—" Nancy sighs, searching tactfully for the right words. She is a lovely, gentle, refined Southern woman.

Clay family portrait early 1960s

"It wasn't a happy home," she concludes. "It was a beautiful family, but they just couldn't bring it all together. They were physically beautiful, had a beautiful home, they all had music lessons, they had everything. They just couldn't bring it together. It was sad."

According to Nancy, my Aunt Sally was left out and the boys were favored, something my aunt has always contended but my grandmother brushed off, insisting it wasn't true. It drove my aunt batshit-wild that 50 years later my vagabond, nearly-wet-brain father with all his wreckage would still garner such favor from my grandmother, let alone live in her house, play guitar on her patio all night long, and have the cops come multiple times in her nice little neighborhood she'd been in for 20 years.

"My dear cousin Sally, whom I adore and still love to pieces," Nancy tells me, sighing, "I felt bad for her. I was so drawn to her, and we spent a lot of time together. We had so much fun one time when we went on vacation to Virginia Beach. Aunt June and Uncle Ed went out to dinner or something. I was messing with Sally, and Eddie was running up and down the hallway. Ray was just three or four years old, so he was quiet and good, of course. I was just a little country girl observing family, but I do think Sally was not favored." She sighs again. "After that, there were so many problems. There was always conflict. It was really sad. I think

Aunt June and Uncle Ed loved each other, but they just clashed and were very different people. Uncle Ed was very ambitious and outspoken, and so was Aunt June—and the children were brought up in this."

I imagine my grandmother being outspoken with my grandfather back then. I always had it like she couldn't really stand up to him—not enough to make a difference anyway. Thirty years after their divorce and after they'd both been remarried and widowed, he moved back in with her. By that time, she certainly had no qualms telling him exactly what was on her mind and what she would and would not be doing.

"Gee," she'd sing-song to me on the phone. "Ed Clay here is always tellin' me how to live my life. I am way past all that. I live my own life. I have my church and my women's bible study. I have my friends. I have my homeless children's center. I dance. I do all kinds of things. And to think he's trying to tell me what to do."

Then she'd giggle, lightheartedly, which made me think she was playing at complaining more than it was truly driving her crazy. It must've been something, to be sleeping in the same bed with the man you married in 1947, had three children with, were divorced from, both remarried, lived separate lives from all those years, and were now reunited, spending your time together in big fat white leather La-Z-Boys watching the news.

Excerpts from TJ's *Dad - Tell Me About Your Life* book

When on car trips, did you play car games?

Yes. But all in the mind. Gameboards or books or cards would make me nauseous. Counted cars and their make. Broke wind silently to see who would get blamed. Mostly Sally and I would sit in the back-seat and avoid swinging at each other. (A fight meant a roadside "switch.")

Tell of any other nicknames in your family.

Ray to Mom - "Vittles"
Dad to Sally - "Tha-lly"

Me to Ray - "Fartblossom"
Dad to Me - "Fartblossom"
Ray to Me - "Little Brother"
Me to Ray - "Big Brother"
Me to Sally - "@#$!*&!"
Sally to Me - "**&*#^$#*!"
Me to Sally - "Butterfield 8"
Sally to Me ? "A_ _ _ _ _"

Share a memory of going to church as you were growing up.

I'll merely say that I hated every damned second. (Why?) As I know so well (now) - a sermon is horseshit; anyone can give one. I know that life is loving, forgiveness, and being true to yourself. You don't need a church - you need a caring community.

Describe a very proud moment in your childhood.

I was too ordinary to have many. When I was fifteen I chased down Charles Miller who had set himself on fire; got him wrapped in a blanket and kept him from 3rd degree burns.

By all accounts, the move from Newport News to downtown Williamsburg was a promising time. My Aunt Sally was 10 or 11 and my father two years ahead of her when they both started at James Blair High School. They moved into the historic Griffin House, in the heart of Colonial Williamsburg, down the street from the George Wythe House, the Blacksmith Shop, Bruton Parish Church, and the Governor's Palace.

"Our parents rented this place to make sure we were in the real hub of history," Aunt Sally told me.

The Griffin House was built around 1770 by Colonel William Allen. It was later acquired by Samuel Griffin, after whom the house is named. The Colonial Williamsburg Foundation acquired the Griffin

House in the late 1920s and it has since been used as commercial and residential space.

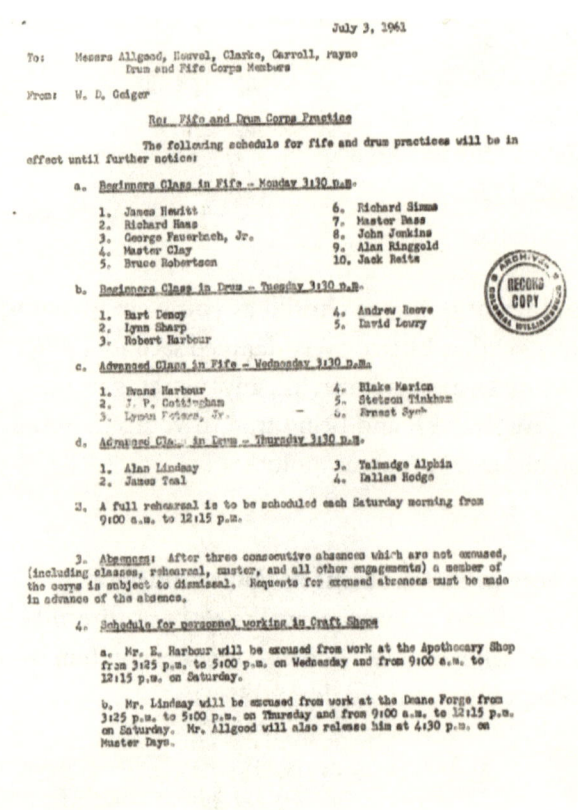

Master Clay, Beginners Class in Fife, 1961

In 1961 my father joined the newly established Continental Boys' Fife and Drum Corps of northern Virginia, something my father did that my grandmother remained especially proud of throughout her life. She told me how the boys in the corps would travel all over to different events, even Philadelphia one time for a special July 4th week celebration.[1]

In 1962, the Corps received its first set of standard "dress uniforms" consisting of brown rifle shirts, black britches, white belts, and hats with white trim.[2]

By early 1963, there were more than 50 tunes and drum beatings in the corps' repertoire.

"The cadence of the ancient style is slower than modern marching bands. The slower pace accurately recreates the marching speed of 18th Century armies, which would be marching to the beat of the drummers. The slower tempo also reflects the "open" style of rudimental drumming authentic to the period, in which the rudiments (drum beats) are carefully and fully executed. Because drum beats were used by armies (from before the American Revolution through the Civil War) as signals to the troops, the drum beats had to have distinctive sounds so they would be understood by the troops. As a result, distinctive rudiments were developed. Rudiments to the drum are like scales to musical instruments."[3]

Having made the cut and receiving that training, surely Daddy had more musical ability than my brother Jimmy gave him credit for. It also took a level of commitment and sacrifice as the practice and travel were pretty demanding.

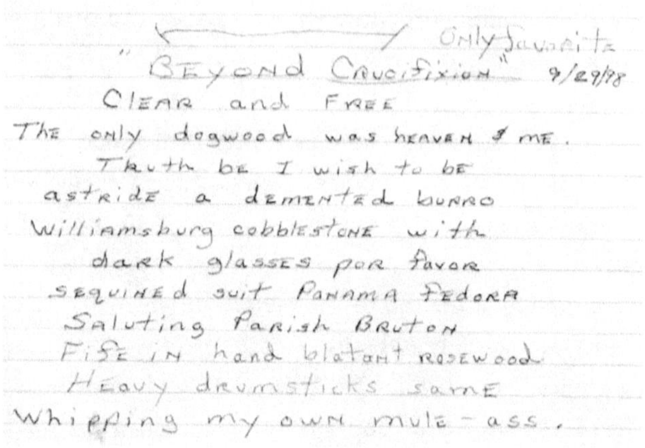

The handwritten note reads:

"BEYOND CRUCIFIXION" 9/29/78   Only favorite
CLEAR and FREE
The only dogwood was heaven & me.
Truth be I wish to be
astride a demented burro
Williamsburg cobblestone with
dark glasses por favor
sequined suit Panama fedora
Saluting Parish Bruton
Fife in hand blatant rosewood
Heavy drumsticks same
Whipping my own mule - ass.

According to the Colonial Williamsburg Fifes and Drums Alumni Association,

"Such performances and schedules demanded excellence and both units established rigorous training and rehearsal schedules. Unlike other fife and drum corps in the early 1960's, Colonial Williamsburg and the U.S. Army had the financial resources to equip and maintain their units and, significantly, the members of both units were paid musicians. The CW Corps musicians were high school aged boys employed part time to perform with the CW Militia and the Old Guard musicians were full time U. S. Army soldiers. Within a very short time, the two corps became prominent on the national fife and drum scene and joined leaders in the then re-emerging return to the ancient style of fifing and drumming in America."[4]

My father was a great lover of American history. My Aunt Sally remembers one special day when he came to her.

"Tha-lly," he said. He had a lisp when he was young, confirmed yet again by my aunt. "We're going to tour Williamsburg together on a bus, alone, and you can NEVER tell our parents where we're going, ever. Promise me? Because you know we'll have to lie and they would restrict us forever if they found out."

"Okay, I promise," she told him over and over.

"We were so fearful of our parents because they were so very strict," she tells me.

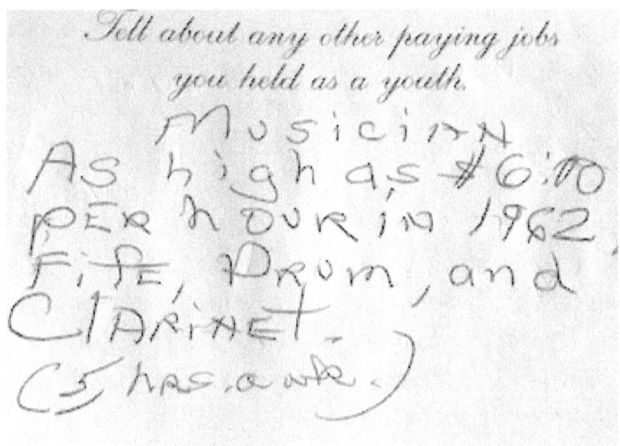

Back then, Aunt Sally and my father could look each other eye to eye because they were both tall and about the same height.

"I prommmmm-isssss," she said to him again.

The two of them ended up going on the Williamsburg tour bus for free, all over town for more than an hour, ending up at the Williamsburg Motor House Theater. So many things were free back then, including the movie that would play.

"Your father led me down to the front aisle and we sat down. Then when the lights dimmed down, he motioned me to crawl down to the pit, and so we did. And I remember it to this day, watching *The Story of a Patriot*. The movie featured Jack Lord, who became famous for his role in *Hawaii Five-O*. Oh my goodness. I was so, at that time, overwhelmed, mesmerized, by all the colors, the people, the real story of Williamsburg. I was so in another world as a young child, to see and feel and know that history up close. He kept whispering to me, 'Tha-lly, listen to every word, okay? And don't say anything, promise me forever, you will not tell Mom and Dad.'"

I decide to watch the movie with my husband to see what it's all about. Almost immediately, a spoken line jumps out at me. One of the characters in the film says they're "vastly proud" about something.

Vastly proud? My father used that expression often to describe his children! I mean, who says vastly proud, for God's sake?

"One Sunday after church," my aunt continues, "our parents allowed us to go off alone. We grinned and said, 'Sure, we'll just walk around through town and see you back home in a couple of hours.' We headed right for the tour bus and went out again to see *The Story of a Patriot*. Many times in our lives we would speak about that and our mutual understanding of what life was really like for the early Americans in Williamsburg."

Aunt Sally wonders if Daddy would remember the crackling of the paper when the barrel was opened, or the Patrick Henry speech.

"In due respect, my brother and I were really kindred spirits," she concedes. "At the time, he was smarter and wiser, and he gave me that gift of really knowing about history."

As a child, what did you want to be when you grew up?
GARbagEMAN, FishErmAN, MiNisTER, Hobo (Now called homeless pErSon), PROFEssioNAL guiTAurisT oR musiciAN, Bum, FREE (above all), AcToR, TEAchER, ShipmasTER.

Understandably, my aunt's feelings towards my father are mixed. As the years went on and his drinking worsened—and its impact was more widely felt by my grandmother, for one—Aunt Sally resented him more and more. Mostly because he was always my grandmother's precious "Eddie Boy," even when he was a godforsaken mess.

"The truth is that EDDIE BOY"—my aunt always wrote with sarcasm—"was an abuser towards my mom. He not only threatened her constantly, but he knocked her around. Over the years, she would call me in distress and I had to call the cops constantly. He threatened me, but I was the stronger bitch that threatened him back. But I have forgiven him over and over."

> *When you played make-believe, what did you pretend?*
>
> I was always a character before my own time; Such as A Pirate, Robin Hood styled outlaw, Western gunfighter gangster, Actor (Bogart, Cagney, Mitchum, Gable.) A Knight, such as Sir Lancelot. At 11, a Methodist Minister.

---

1. https://www.cwfdalumni.org/wp/chapter-5/ Chapter 5—The Colonial Williamsburg Fifes and Drums Alumni Association (cwfdalumni.org)
2. Ibid., Chapter 4
3. Ibid., Chapter 5
4. Ibid.

worn out welcomes

"My whole wretched life swam before my weary eyes, and I realized no matter what you do, it's bound to be a waste of time in the end, so you might as well go mad."
— Jack Kerouac

In his hobo years, Daddy was barely tolerable for a few days at a time if he came to visit. He wore out his welcome at our place in Philly within 72 hours, was politely asked to leave Jeffrey and Olivia's place in Maine, and was cussed out and possibly even accosted by Jimmy for overstaying his welcome in Charlotte.

Nonetheless, we were happy to see him for a brief time in Philadelphia. Except when I came home from work one evening and Daddy was sitting all sloshy on the front step, drinking beer and deep in conversation with Esther, this gorgeous, exotic-looking girl with black hair who lived next door. She was the pseudo-girlfriend of a well-known DJ neighbor of ours, Robby D., and I think she was some kind of high-end call girl. I'd see her leaving all decked out in black from head to toe, cute miniskirts, kinda punky-chic, striding to a waiting private car and driver.

She was always cool and friendly until one night when we had

friends over for a party. My husband popped over next door to visit
Robby D. and Esther came accusing in my ear that he and my husband
were having some kind of affair because why else would they spend all
this time alone together? I assured her my husband was straight as a
fucking arrow and I was sure it wasn't the case, but happy to bring it all
out in the open if she wanted.

Anyway, wackadoodle. Then along came my father. Dear Lord, I
thought to myself when I saw the two of them engaged in conversation
on my Center City front stoop. This is not allowed to happen.

I somehow coaxed my father inside as Esther protested, "He was just
about to tell me a story..."

"I know, I'm sorry, he'll have to catch you next time, we have plans.
Bye!"

A day or so later, Daddy figured it was time for him to move on.

Whenever he wrote about leaving, there was always something exciting
at the beginning of the journey, but something sad and tired and desperate, a sense of going nowhere, at the end of it. In one missive from San
Francisco dated August 26, 2002, out there on the run from a bench
warrant on the East Coast, at the bottom of page "DOSH," Daddy
wrote to me:

> *Anyways, back to the point. Society has stripped me of
> my capability to earn $50,000.00 a year. I've done manual
> labor since I was twelve. Until I can ply my trade again I am
> 'chillin' and writing. I couldn't give a cow's fart what anyone
> thinks. I'm a hobo at heart and a Cherokee in my soul. I'll
> hunt my own knowledge, I'll drink my own whiskey, and die at
> ninety-three with my moccasins or boots on. 'NOUGH SAID."*
> *141 Eddy Street, San Francisco, CA*

Daddy was staying at the West Hotel in the heart of the Tenderloin,
home to drunks and junkies, ne'er do-wells, down-and-outers and

people living rough on the streets. Otherwise, he wouldn't have been able to afford the skyrocketing cost of living in the City by the Bay.

"Serving 106 individuals with low incomes, including people who experienced homelessness and are currently living with health challenges...a home for a community of seniors, persons with AIDS and persons with mental health and substance abuse issues."

I knew he was staying in the Tenderloin and that he could very well take care of himself, and I was glad, really, just knowing he had a reasonably safe place to stay. Frankly, Daddy was meant for the Tenderloin at that point. He was one of them. Though I'm sure he never would have imagined living right there in the dregs after all these years.

Back when we were living in San Francisco in the late Sixties, he would have been dining nonchalantly on buffalo stew at Tommy's Joynt a couple blocks away. We were poor—as in hippie poor—but not Tenderloin-poor.

"Kendra a saintress of Tenderloin desperate for heroin—or any high. Registered nurse. Left $10, no blow. <u>Too much life</u>."
— letter from the Tenderloin, 2002

One of the times Daddy stayed down in Charlotte with Jimmy and Leslie, his artist girlfriend we all stayed friends with over the years, my father stayed up all night drinking vodka. Somehow Jimmy was actually sleeping even though he was usually up all night himself. He woke up to Leslie shaking him and saying, "Don't freak out, don't freak out."

"Oh shit, what did he do?"

My father had found some black paint and poetic inspiration.

"Some goddamn Robert Frost shit, at one point I had it written down, it was foot-high fucking letters, floor to ceiling, 'always remember stay forever fucking young.' I had told him when he came to visit, just don't fuck up anything, please, I gotta live here. It was like he did it to spite me."

Crashed
3/15/06

I have tried to eat
In my wretched state
I have tried to
Work
It may be far too late.
I have loved you strong
God knows how you wait.

I am only me.
I live with that alone.
I must here survive
We're always on our own.

I guess I'm out of gas and rolling
Like a bloody stone.

We shall be fine
If we can
East of Nowhere.

"One time when he got out of jail over by Annapolis, Jessup County Detention Center, can't remember when or how old I was," TJ recounts, "he had written a poem in the back of a book. It was the best poem I'd ever read of his. I ripped it out and was gonna read it at Jeffrey's wedding but I lost it. I was shit-faced that whole weekend. It sounded Neal Cassady or Bukowski. He had hitchhiked to this 404 empty storage unit."

A smile creeps over his face as concentration turns into memory. TJ generates the poem:

Route 404 Blues

My home be an empty storage locker
My mailbox be an empty bottle of port
The Asians sell it for $4.50
They were here before us and they'll be here after us
They have the adaptability of sharks.
Don't worry Chowan
You will drink alligator piss again.
And deep down I was never at want for anything
Except for those who felt they had not.

"It was kind of Buddhist," TJ expands on this one piece of literary legacy left to him. Any other letters were tossed or lost at some point. Since his early 20s, TJ's own drinking had culminated in too many incidents and failed trips to rehab to mention.

He was on borrowed time more than once, including the time Shannah and I got the call from Jeffrey. TJ had come back from Colorado and was living in Jeffrey and Olivia's basement in Maine, holding a pretty good housepainting gig. It was perfect for alcoholics; the work crew and boss were either drunks themselves or in recovery.

"You gotta get him outta here," was the plea from Jeffrey. "He's been drinking down there for days. I've got a kid now, and Olivia's been putting up with a lot."

Shannah and I bonded like so many times before—anything to do with taking care of family and we were on it. Like the time Grandmother was moving out of the old house on 39th Avenue in Vero Beach to the new townhouse and we flew down to help her settle in and get organized and trim some items from the rummage sale at church that kept showing up every time she was working the booth. We rented a car at the Orlando airport and cruised into Vero that night. The next morning, we were off buying shoe organizers and bins and space savers to transform Grandmother's closets.

Shannah is someone you want on your team. She's smart, she hustles, she gets shit done. She's reliable and generous. And she's much better with directions than I am. You couldn't ask for a better partner, whether cleaning out a closet, going on a road trip, or trying to save your brother's life.

She picked me up in Pennsylvania within 24 hours and we were in Maine that very next day holding an intervention in Jeffrey's living room. TJ emerged from the basement, puffy, pink-skinned, bleary-eyed. He knew exactly why we were there. It wasn't as though he and I hadn't spoken of this before, his drinking. I was honored to be on the call list from time to time, and I knew that *he knew* that he could count on me as a sober example in the family. Still, it was always painful to hear through the slushiness the desire to stop—something you never heard in my father, ever—and yet the utter grip of the disease on my brother. It seemed as though his had progressed far worse and faster at a younger age.

Now he's perfectly lucid. Sober for what I presume to be one year or so—more months sober than he's ever put together since he launched his career as an alcoholic. I am present to how brilliant his mind is. He's dauntingly articulate, continually beats my ass to embarrassment at Scrabble Go, and some of his literary leanings are closest of all to Daddy's—Charles Bukowski, Hunter S. Thompson—as are some of the personality traits of a drunk that he despises about himself. The selfishness, the lack of accountability, he says, the unwillingness to look at one's own impact on other people's lives.

Lest all this talking about Daddy results in too much admiration given to someone who tore through our lives with zero regard...TJ's voice gets louder, his latent anger activated and showing up as irritation and disgust on his face. I realize he's probably been holding back for a while out of politeness and respect for me.

"If anybody is a hero, it's my mom and Shannah. They're the ones that always came through. We shouldn't be hero-worshipping him." I feel the same about my mother, but my mom and I have talked through these things for years.

I quietly take in TJ's concerns and let them land. I'm thinking, yeah, I do have a tendency to go easy on our father. I'm having this whole conversation in my head, thanking TJ for the reminder of that, but also judging him—wondering if he has to say that in order to distance himself further from the man he doesn't want to be.

When he comments on the Route 404 Blues poem, I see it as an act of generosity, considering.

"The poem's optimistic given he's just out of jail, says he always had enough, always had what he wanted, felt sad for others who didn't have that kind of fulfillment—'wherever I am, whatever I'm doing, whatever I have, I'm good'—only so others could have this sort of enlightenment."

Then a flash of recognition comes over him. *"Journey to the End of the Night!"* says TJ. "That was the book, the one the poem was written on the back of. By Céline. This nihilistic existentialist book that I found very funny, this bottomless well of despair." He laughs.

As usual, TJ is more erudite than I, at least in this literary genre. I'll have to look this one up later.

"Yeah, later in life, the guy was so anti-Semitic even the Nazis thought he was too extreme!"

> "When you stop to examine the way in which our words are formed and uttered, our sentences are hard-put to it to survive the disaster of their slobbery origins. The mechanical effort of conversation is nastier and more complicated than defecation. That corolla of bloated flesh, the mouth, which screws itself up to whistle, which sucks in breath, contorts itself, discharges all manner of viscous sounds across a fetid barrier of decaying teeth—how revolting! Yet that is what we are adjured to sublimate into an ideal. It's not easy. Since we are nothing but packages of tepid, half-rotted viscera, we shall always have trouble with sentiment. Being in love is nothing, its sticking together that's difficult. Feces on the other hand make no attempt to endure or grow. On this score we are far more unfortunate than shit; our frenzy to persist in our present state—that's the unconscionable torture.

> — Louis-Ferdinand Céline, *Journey to the End of the Night*

Céline influenced the likes of Charles Bukowski, Kurt Vonnegut, and Henry Miller. Jim Morrison served up his own inspiration, hauntingly serenading us with: "Take the highway to the end of the night..."

Reading excerpts from *Journey*, I find myself darkly humored by it as well, my own cynicism with life having accelerated since peri-menopause and multiple physical setbacks due to car accidents. Thankfully, Céline didn't find me at 20. My depressive personality emerged victorious at 52, and I'm still having a hard time shaking it with an ongoing cocktail of antidepressants and weekly therapy. I can see exactly why TJ finds Céline a bit hilarious.

Then he softens a bit, going back to Daddy's poem.

"There are definitely words of wisdom seen in there. A lot of it is practical and relevant, and maybe I didn't get it at the time, but I kind of get it now."

A little more than a year later, my cousin Kelly texts during COVID when I'm at a family gathering in Maryland, socially distanced, visiting my mom and stepfather and mother-in-law for the first time in months. It's urgent, she says, wanting to get me on a three-way call with TJ. He's been drinking again. I know he's been drinking for some months because he's not responding to my texts. I figure he doesn't feel like facing me.

Not wanting to let Kelly down, or TJ, we get on a three-way. It's obvious TJ is being polite with her through his inebriation—knowing she is deeply committed to his welfare. As a therapist, she keeps reminding him, she knows his blood alcohol level has had him danger-ously close to death within the last 48 hours. I can tell how much she wants me to help make a difference.

But how can I?

I've been searching the internet for Xanax and how to have my own lethal cocktail in my back pocket so I could knock myself off the next time I just can't take it, which seems pretty often. I'm tired of not wanting to be here and still having to be here. So me on the phone with TJ is like, "I got nuthin', dude."

But I know he knows I love him. So I stay away from anything inau-thentic like, "You know you want to live" or "Don't you want to live?" —because as soon as Kelly says it, he laughs and says, "Clearly, I don't!"

I even find myself a bit envious that I don't have alcohol to take me out. I have to come up with some other gruesome plan. Meanwhile, he says he'll call me later. I tell him I'm going back to Philly. A few years earlier, I would've made myself available. This time, I'm tired and worn and self-consumed. He knows what to do and has a choice to make. Live or don't. I give myself the same advice.

Twenty-four hours later I get the message: TJ is in the hospital, detoxing. He's on the mend again. I always have faith he will get sober and stay sober, because he's *willing* to want to.

I'm not privy to how many times Daddy fucked up at my grandmother's house in Vero Beach. She was too embarrassed most of the time to let on how bad things were when he stayed with her. He lived there on and off for a number of years and surely contributed to her mental and physical decline.

"Your father just sits out on the patio and strums that ol' guitar and drinks all night long," she said, resigned. "I don' know."

"You've gotta get him outta there," I pleaded. "He's killing you."

"I know. And would you believe the police were here again the other day? He was out carrying on in the front yard because they told him he couldn't drink and ride a bicycle."

"Oh God," I groaned, imagining my father defending his goddamn right to drink vodka and ride a bicycle in Vero Beach, Florida.

"It was awful," my grandmother said. "I was ashamed. The neighbors were all out. He was so ugly. And he said such ugly things to me after that."

This was the kind of stuff my aunt had to deal with. The older my father got, the worse his drinking, the fewer the filters, the more reprehensible his behavior. That's one of the reasons we were so grateful when Zora came along and rescued him, rescued all of us, really.

Sad Boy Blue
2006

Sad Boy BluE
Just Like mE
Just like you.
STRAFING
PARADISE.

LOVE it or lEavEit.
Such is LifE.

FoRgivE mE foR
bEing born
Ishouda taken
thEwoRld by
the fucking hoRNs.
HEY ---- Kid
HERE's thE Easy NEWS
YouR life is youRs
IN a world
bRokEN apart
Follow yER hEaRt.

Tony Turtle, Vero Beach, Florida

I always called Zora an angel. Without her, my father would have died in
a ditch somewhere between Florida and Texas, I'm sure of it. Her accent

gives away her Kentucky upbringing, but she's quick to let you know, "I may not be educated, but I'm not stupid."

Her middle name, "McCoy," heralds her descent from the legendary family that feuded with the Hatfields. She's been married twice to alcoholic husbands, both deceased. The last one was particularly abusive. When my father came along, she fell right in love with him. Overseeing an aging drunk was old familiar territory to her, especially since charm, humor, and good looks came with it. When she smiles, there is no pretense, no judgment, no self-consciousness. Just a wide, happy, pure, downright angelic beauty from a woman who has every right not to smile like that. She lost her son the same year I lost my father.

Without a wince, she says, "I was raped as a little girl by mah daddy—all mahh sisters were—but I still loved him. He was mah daddy."

One June—coincidentally, two weeks before my grandmother died in Vero Beach—TJ and Kelly and I stop in to see Zora at her home in Vero Beach. Sitting across from each other at her kitchen table, we talk about Daddy, family, life stuff.

"Your daddy used to bawl when he was drinkin' and writin' letters. He cried every night."

Zora pronounces "night" drawn out with an "a" sound like "nah-hht" and it somehow makes you wish everybody said night like that.

"He regretted leaving his kids. He loved kids. The tears would fall down all over the paper and he'd have to stop. He always said he had no regrets, but I don't believe it. He cried every nahhht."

I am certain Zora is the only person ever to experience this version of my father.

Then she gestures at me. "Especially you, Kennerly. He'd lie in bed and hold my hand and tell me what it was like to have to leave you when you were just a little girl, and he'd lie there and cry and hold my hand just like that as he was tellin' me."

Until Zora shares this with me, I have never actually considered what it was like for my father to have to leave me, and the sudden sorrow for him rises up in my throat and comes leaking out my eyes. I remember those same times. My bedroom in our house on Quantico Road had a single bed against the wall to the right as you came into the room. When I took naps, I could hear a rhythmic thumping sound in my ear against the pillow, which I never knew until years later was my own heartbeat.

As I'd be getting ready for a nap or bed, Daddy's hug would signal a send-off to sleep as well as a send-off for him. "Will you be here when I wake up?" I can still hear myself asking the question, expectantly, because I remember the answer was always the same, always a goodbye, never a repeat in the morning.

Leaving Zora, then Florida and back home to Pennsylvania, I am left with such sadness at all the loss between me and my father. During another energy release work session, I tell my practitioner that I can remember what it was like to be that two-year-old child and for my father to always be leaving. Now for the first time I can actually feel the pain of it so bad, it's like a gaping hole opening up in my throat so wide I can't swallow or breathe. I have built up layers of protection from it for a long time. I couldn't even remember it enough to know that it was there. This is what we're all walking around with underneath life itself. Deep, deep pain and sadness that nobody gets to escape and few of us are ever willing to examine fully.

Thank you, Girl - Zora (IE) Yoko Perhaps

All I can say
Is "Thank you Girl"
Thank you Girl
Ooh yeah
Ooh yeah (Harmonica)
Thank you girl
For loving me
The way the way that
You do
That's the kind
Of love
That's too be good
To be true
SEEMS
All I have to do

Is thank you girl
Thank you girl
Oooh Yeah
Oh yes
(REPEAT)
Thank you girl!

4th de Marco

Jeffrey,

After we spoke I was compelled to write ye. I was in Topsham in that fine frozen cottage at your very age. 1973 early. I got a chance to turn my life around. It gave you and brothers and sister a better life.

Your only limits are those you create for yerself. Life is a struggle at best. Believe me - I at 63 kick my own mule-ass for not having the persistence to become a doctor or teacher. 'Member - if you have a child you might limit other possibilities. This is no lecture. I am very proud of you! Proud of you all. Give your mother full credit.

Leaving your mother was the biggest mistake of my life. When you gets a woman who loves and believes in you don't take another. She's gonna have complications too. Just hang out and be friends. Then you'll avoid the pain I had.

In the spring of 2010 when Daddy would have been 62 years old, he had been up in Maine visiting Jeffrey and Olivia.

"Pops was here for 13 days sleeping on our futon in our one-bedroom apartment, so suffice it to say we collected our share of tales," Jeffrey muses.

In preparation for Daddy's initial arrival, Jeffrey got a two-hour head start at the bar. "To prep myself and get on a level playing field with him."

The bar, along with the Bull Moose record store where Jeffrey worked and the 7-Eleven where the bus would be arriving, formed a triangle. "You could hit any of them with a rock from any of the three parking lots."

Jeffrey was talking with the bartender when he got a ring on his cell phone. "It was my co-workers informing me that Pops was across the street at Bull Moose. So I squared up at the bar, the bartender wished me luck, and I rushed outside only to realize it was raining its dick off! Absolute downpour. I got over there and of course my co-workers, who were all good friends of mine, were aware of what was going on. Pops had strolled in dripping wet, declaring, 'It ain't a fit night out for man or beast!' My co-workers looked at each other and knew: This must be Jeffrey's dad."

Another night while Daddy was staying at their house in Brunswick, he was in the kitchen making a pot of beans. "He was explaining to me and my buddy how to de-gas them so you wouldn't get farts," says Jeffrey, "so I asked him, 'Isn't that the best part of eating bean soup?'"

Daddy didn't answer but could be heard a short time later saying "Mmm, beans" under his breath. "My buddy and I both heard it and looked at each other with matching, shit-eating grins because we each had some smartass remark to make. My friend let me go first.

"Everything alright in there, Sling Blade?" Jeffrey said. "We both died laughing."

Sling Blade was one of Daddy's Top Five Favorite Movies of all time. He was always parodying Billy Bob Thornton with the deep, growly "Mmm-hmm."

I can still see Daddy now. "Some calls it a kaiser blade, mmm-hmm. I calls it a sling blade." Daddy'd throw his head back and laugh, like he was hearing it again for the first time.

Sometimes when he and I were speaking on the phone, if I said something particularly wise, he'd pause and say, 'I like the way you talk," all drawly-like, imitating Thornton's character, Karl Childers.

"Yeah, Pops was actively pursuing work up here because he was ready to make Maine his last home. He even got a call back from

Hannaford, the local grocery store here. I wasn't opposed to the idea, but made it clear he'd have to find another place to live. Olivia is the sweetest thing in two shoes, but she was wondering how long our scenario was going to last."

One night they had all gone over to a friend's house. "Pops said he liked hanging with us young'uns because we had something new to say. When my friend said he was looking for a roommate, Pops suggested himself. 'I'll be quiet and keep to myself,' he said. 'If you decide to bring a chick home, you won't even know I'm there. Wait, that's not true, I might stand in the corner jerking off while watching.'"

My father could be particularly crude, becoming more embarrassingly obscene and inappropriate with age and drinking. That night after everyone bade farewell, Jeffrey and Olivia started walking home a good bit ahead of my father.

"Suddenly a cop threw on its flashers and pulled a quick 180 degrees," Jeffrey said. "'Uh-oh,' I heard Pops say, and I remember thinking to myself, what could he possibly be doing wrong this close to home? I turn around and see Pops strolling across Maine Street, double-fisting, with two drinks in his hands. So I told Olivia to go home, we'd be there shortly, and I hung back to do damage control. The cop asked for our IDs and ran our names. Pops was getting agitated but I assured him we didn't have to worry, we had no warrants. The checks came back clean and the lovely young officer explained, 'Mister Clay, I can't have you out here walking around with two open containers.' Pops was a prick. He proceeded to dump the beer out with his one hand while chugging the wine with his other. He finished doing both and threw the empty beer can at the cop's feet. I picked up the beer can, assured her we would recycle it, and pointed out how close my apartment was. I promised her she wouldn't see us again that night.

"When we got back to the apartment, I said, 'No wonder you always get arrested, you're an asshole to cops.' To which Pops replied, like he was passing on some great wisdom, 'Son, son, son...I wasn't going to waste good wine.'"

"Joy of Cooking is a fine cookbook. Even if I'm doing something new with another book I'll have it open as a reference. Try the

**U.S. Senate Navy Bean Soup, p 149? Be sure and de-gas the
beans or you'll be talking divorce before marriage."
— letter from Daddy**

* Bring beans and water to boil. Remove from heat. Add 2 table-
spoons or so Arm & Hammer baking soda. Let sit two hours. Drain and
rinse twice.

Savannah 5/26/10
Now I's sitting by railroad track with dreams of a tent
and kerosene lamp. It's alright here but dealing wid mosquito
is a priority. Along wid souther rattler, copperhead, moccasin,
black widow, ticks, deerfly, skunk, possum, racoon, and two
leggers on crack. Gonna buy a bowie, a machete, and a .38
revolver. Maybe a can of mace. (So's I don't have to kill
nobody.) Wouldn't know how to clean 'em and cook 'em
anyway. Thons of bitthes.
    'Midst the poplar trees I've found perfect site. Now I
need 100 aluminum cans, an ice pick and 60 feet of wire.
Camping is fun but it's hell these days. I swear speed and
lousy crack take all the good out of things. - Letter to Jeffrey

Guess I'll close writing shop
soon. I've done 10,000 miles
in sixty days. I'm almost 63.
Never go greyhound, buy a
wooden nickel, nor kick a fresh
turd on a hot day. Amen.

Daddy's welcome wore thin in Colorado in later years as well. "The
worst thing was the deception," says Dick Losh, "and that he knew that
I knew. I thought he was becoming delusional, predementia, this whole
Eddie Chowan thing. What's wrong with Ed Clay, for God's sake? He
was in a fantasy world. He would say, 'I'm writing,' and he'd scribble out

this stuff. It would be nonsensical. He'd have all these pages and I couldn't make any sense of it. And it was just that, he was getting deceptive as a defense mechanism."

For years, the two of them would talk on the phone as old friends do, about life and music. My father would often pass through Denver and pay Dick a visit en route from one coast to another.

"The last time I saw him, he was a bit suspicious, staying out all night and sleeping all day, running up bad credit charges, leaving doors open, and coming home at 4:30 or 5:30 in the morning. I told him I'd set him up in an apartment or with a car. He'd say no."

When they'd go out to eat, my father would boldly stride into a convenience store, then come out again and announce, "Okay, I can get a job in there." But then of course he never would. That was just a way of saving face.

"He did tell my brother one time, he regretted how he left here," says Dick.

For many years, Daddy would call Dick every Sunday—"stewed"—and they'd even planned to get together in Florida one time.

"At the last minute, your grandmother had to call me and tell me not to come, that your father was too sick to see me." Drunk sick, of course.

But before my father was deeply into alcoholism, he never seemed that far out from reality, from Dick's perspective.

"That is, until he left San Francisco in the later years and was homeless for a while, camping out on rooftops in El Paso, panhandling, and sending postcards that said, 'Living the life.' Towards the end, it just became plain that he wasn't the same person anymore."

Dick tells me that a new Dylan album called *Tempest* came out not long after Daddy passed away in 2011. "I even thought about sending a copy of the album to each of you kids."

Through the pause in conversation, I can hear the bittersweetness of memory catch in his throat. "'Duquesne Whistle,' 'Narrow Way,' and my favorite, 'Early Roman Kings.' I think your father would have really liked it."

"We understand each other," Daddy said of hanging out with my firstborn.

eleven
endings

"I'm the one that's got to die when it's time for me to die, so let me live my life the way I want to."
— Jimi Hendrix

My grandmother called my cell one morning while I was at work in early November 2011. My father was in the hospital, his distended belly foretelling how this was all going to end.

"He's dying," she said, which was enough for me to take a few days off work and fly down to Florida. If this was going to be it, I wanted to be there.

As I stood by his hospital bed, Daddy's eyes rolled by in a medicated haze. He mumbled through the meds, "K? Is that Kennerly? You came all the way down here for your old man?"

From his semi-reclined position, his belly swelled through the sheets. Knowing his lean frame all my life, I found the protrusion grotesque and could see why he had stopped calling. This thing truly had him and it was soon to be over. I pushed aside the random guilty thought of what a relief it would finally be for him, for all of us. No more worrying about him dying in a ditch or causing my grandmother pain and grief and embarrassment or putting any more drunk-and-disorderliness on Zora than she'd already been through. It was time for him to go, and I was preparing to let him know this before I left Florida.

But lying there in the bed, his color looked good, his face shaven. He was my father, handsome as ever, even in this pathetic condition. In hushed conversations outside the hospital room door, my grandmother and I talked with the doctor about the drinking, explaining that he was just going to go home and keep drinking himself to death. I implored the doctor to read him the riot act because he wouldn't hear it from anyone else. With all of us gathered around the bed at one point, the doctor talked to my father, trying to penetrate the dopey high from medication to ensure Daddy was really getting the message.

"You're going to die if you keep going like this, Mr. Clay—" And then something else about getting him into detox and rehab.

"I will NOT be going to any GOD-DAM rehab!" my father roared from the hospital bed, suddenly coming out of his stupor to assert his right to drink himself to death.

Grandmother and I laughed awkwardly with the doctor, realizing that my father was still *compos mentis* enough to make his own decisions, and we had heard his wishes loud and clear.

My brother Jimmy had been staying with Daddy and Zora for some months leading up to that point, and he was there in the room with us. I made sure he heard what the doctor was saying. I wanted to tell him that when Daddy came home from the hospital, this would not be the time to be handing him a beer and kicking back together. If he drank, he would die. That's where we were. Jimmy got it, but at the same time he was probably thinking the same thing we all were on some level. Who cared at that point? Hell, let him drink. What did it matter?

Still, I found myself admonishing my father about what would happen if he continued to drink. It was my last day visiting before flying back to Philly and I felt responsible for somehow getting through to him and ensuring he followed the rules. I was also cognizant that those moments in the hospital room might be the last ones we'd ever spend together. Still, I wanted to be straight, uninhibited, nothing left unsaid.

Instead I came away feeling as though I'd been too harsh on him, a dying man. I was conflicted with that age-old fear of driving him away when I chose to say what was really on my mind. Plus, I never asked Jimmy and Zora to leave the room so I could say my own personal goodbye, a vision I had of just Daddy and I holding hands and not having to say much of anything. Like listening to Quicksilver together in San Francisco. And making sure he knew all was forgiven and how much I loved him.

As soon as I left Indian River Hospital that day, heavy regret came over me. Two weeks later he was dead, having drunk of his own whiskey and knowledge until it killed him at 64 years old.

But no one could mess with his choice, that's for sure. It was the way he chose to live and die. Maybe it was my grandfather telling him he was no good. Or the perfect storm of coming of age in the 1960s and the Civil Rights movement and protesting Vietnam. Maybe it was the stubborn Clay gene and alligator piss for breakfast. Surely the decades of alcohol had my father fighting for (or against) something that he would never win but would surely die for. Like Neal Cassady along the railroad tracks in San Miguel de Allende.

The ultimate diagnosis from his autopsy was hemochromatosis, a genetic disorder affecting iron metabolism. The system gets overloaded by iron, which attacks organs such as the liver. It is closely associated with alcoholism as alcohol aids iron absorption, and together alcohol and iron do a double-whammy on the liver.

"Ingestion of 30 grams or more per day potentiates hepatic injury due to iron overload."

In the United States, one alcoholic drink has about 14 grams of pure alcohol. My father drank a jug of wine or a bottle of vodka a day, at least. I wondered if my brothers had hemochromatosis, too; it was an inherited disorder. Alcohol just made it worse.

Two days before Daddy died, he told Jimmy, "If I had it to do all over again, I wouldn't have had any of you."

Jimmy took this to mean Daddy didn't like the thought of bringing us into this shitty life and was sorry we'd have to experience the same thing. (It was so like Jimmy to interpret life like that.) Jeffrey thought it was because Daddy felt he'd let us down and disappointed us so much. TJ always thought it was that Daddy's greatest accomplishment in life was his children, but also his greatest regret. My own interpretation was the one where Daddy got to be somebody else, completely unencumbered by any of us.

"The last conversation I had with him, I was lost in a vodka bottle starting to get the DTs," says TJ. "I was hitting all my lows, and I was living at home."

Over the course of several attempts at sobriety and doing the necessary fourth step work, TJ finds there isn't anything left unsaid and no lingering resentments that he can identify.

"Last time we talked, I remember he kinda asked me, 'Would you say I was a good father?' kind of thing. I don't think I ever gave him that. Maybe it was a little selfish. I didn't want to give him that peace of mind. Also, I did have a chance to go see him before he passed, but Jimmy and I were on bad terms and I was drinking at a pace I couldn't manage—it would've been a bad scene all around."

Besides, he'd already had enough conversations with Daddy before he died, so TJ was not left at a want for answers.

"I even yelled at him a little for stuff that happened in the past, but there was nothing very satisfying about that. He never said he shouldn't have done whatever. He probably should have regretted a lot more," and here TJ laughs, "but I don't get the sense that he did. As I've been involved in the program and got in there to figure out why I was resentful, I didn't find anything there after all. If he died thinking I was resentful, that sucks. It may have come up in my speaking and the way I acted, but resenting him and hating him has not been part of my emotional state."

So while Daddy was dying from a lifetime of alcohol, TJ was doing the same, waking up with fierce DTs and sick all the time.

"I couldn't have gone down there to hang with the boys and be like, 'Hey Pops, why'd you drink yourself to death? I'm doing it right now and I'll continue to do it for the next however many years.' My own misery kind of superseded anything else there, including when he died. I was still living in my mom's basement. I went to work the morning he died."

TJ hesitates, obviously uncomfortable with too much credit given to our father for anything.

"He fancied himself an iconoclast, whatever it was, like this wasn't his time in society. Couldn't have been six or so years before he died, he'd been out in San Francisco for a time and still had this grandiose ambition: 'I was going to study and pass the bar, but you lose your ability to learn.' He was approaching wet brain by then. I'd hate to think I ever got to the point I lost my ability to learn and only grandiosity was keeping me going."

Worst of all are the traits TJ recognizes in himself that are reminiscent of our dad's.

"There's a part of me that doesn't find him that interesting, because I've been a lot like him, that is, being very self-centered, prone to grandiosity, egotistical. If that makes him some sort of hero, then I should keep drinking. It was way more heroic for a mother to be there raising four kids on her own, and for her and my sister to continue to be there."

My brother Jeffrey, on the other hand, stayed in touch until the end. "If I wanted to call at 2 a.m. drunk, we'd talk about anything," says Jeffrey. "'Rod Stewart is badass,' and Dad said, 'Yeah, I played some of that for Zora the other night and she cried. Wanna go fishing? Let's get a case of beer and go fishing somewhere.'"

Aside from the $10,000 life insurance policy Daddy left us—which paid for a big house for a week at Nags Head where we scattered his ashes—we inherited personality traits and characteristics quintessentially Clay.

"Mostly, we're pretty loud and obnoxious," according to Jeffrey. "Then you got the Clay girls' laugh. Kennerly and Jimmy, love of traveling. And we all got the fuck away from that place, the Eastern Shore. It does wonders for a person's soul. Now the big Clay ball and chain landed in my fuckin' lap. It used to be Jimmy and TJ, but I just realized I'm now the biggest Clay drunk left. Shannah doesn't count. She's rich and successful."

A letter from Daddy to Shannah:

You're a fantastic daughter and I'm very proud of you. 'Specially for sticking out a tough situation and making it bear fruit. It seems you're happy with what you're doing. All I know is that ten percent of a life is what occurs and 90 percent is one's attitude towards all these things. ERGO Keep Life Simple. I Love You, Dad

For many months leading up to his death, Daddy and Shannah had been writing frequently, making plans for her to bring her little girls down to Florida to meet him. In spite of everything, she was including him in her life as a mom, sending him photos and sharing stories about her children.

Mebbe you wonder why I do what I do. Don't wonder!

— letter to Shannah

But when Shannah got married a few years earlier, she didn't take any chances. Although she did invite Daddy and Zora to come to the wedding, she asked a special uncle to walk her down the aisle. I had just given birth to my second child weeks before, and there was a moment where Daddy was striding across the wooden platform floor that had been erected outside for the dining area. As Daddy was stepping out, he missed the drop off and stumbled and nearly fell—with my three-week-old newborn over his shoulder. You could hear the collective gasps of the wedding-goers. I was just thankful Daddy stuck the landing. Even though he'd been drinking and we'd have blamed it on that, several people had done the same thing that evening, missing that step.

But it came out later that Daddy had been beyond inappropriate that night.

"I could've gone the rest of my life without knowing my father asked my husband at the wedding how I was in bed," Shannah says.

Hello Shannah,
Yer little girls are almost 'yond comprehension. You are

doing one hell of a job! And I'm proud! I hope everyone knows I am a virtual cripple. House and yardwork at best. Anyways I'm a writer and a good one and that's my focus; probably forever.

I hope to see you in the spring, when the chill don't cut so deep ; I've come around and give the "shore" another crack at me. Going to Maine somewhere thereabouts. Certain.

Life is tough at best but the toughest get going when it does. I always have and you will too. Enclosed be a pittance for the babies.

I love you,

Dad

P.S. If you ever get a note from me minus dinero - call me.

Tropical Song

I drink alligator piss for breakfast
Eat crocodile cunt at noon.
I'll shoot off both yer legs for fun on a Florida afternoon.
Some folks say I'm crazy
But I am just a tune
Going nowhere, East of Nowhere.
Well me I hoe a rough row;
Preacher Weems he rides a mount.
It doesn't matter very much
'Tis doom alone that counts.
East of Nowhere
(sha-la-la MAN)

2/14/11

Call it Valentine

Well things went bad. Things got worse and money didn't change a thing. Anyways, I thought I'd drop youse a line.

The calendar is fantastic! A great piece of work. I desire one. Do what you feel. I'm sending a little bread. It's been a good month for me. That means a surplus. I don't need anything 'cept life itself, never did.

Through Mom I hear you are thriving and I am glad. 'Member this: Money cannot buy fresh air or snow geese. Give my darlings a goodnight kiss from Grandpoppy. I hope to see you in the spring.

Always, Dad

2/16/11

Hello Pooh #2,

Just got our valentine and the lovely pic! I coulda thrived without the booger story. Oh well.

It be unhealthy to eat snot. It is part of the human ecosystem, shure as a turd; a way of eliminating poisons.

Teach your girl Kleenex or sheetrock; she can collect boogers on her wall. Even paint a bit. You destroy her artwork wid a warm washrag.

I'm sliding into retirement gracefully. In my condition you accept things you never imagined six months ago. (Got a sit-down job for me?)

Please support TJ. I'm going to call him daily from now on.

Here's a late valentine.

Huggs, Luvs, Pampers, and you do the Kisses. I'd love to see the girls. Love to all, Dad

3/29/11

Shannah,

I trust this finds you alive and well and in good health. I marvel at your ability to deal with an eighteen-year stepson and two little girls. Well - you're me daughter! (slightly amazing)

/-------------/

I talked with my best friend Al Miller today and we agreed to get together in May 'round the 26th. With your permission he'd drive me over and I'd see you guys and those beautiful girls! (and quickly haulass) At my age babies scare me.

/----------/

I know that you are the best mother any child could wish for. Hell I'm coming home. (Joke)

- DOS -

They's two lobsters sunbathing.

"Honey, please fetch me an ice cream cone. Waldo Lobster goes to the ice cream store, gets two cones and being they melt and he eats, Lad Lobster say, "Where's my ice cream?"

"I'm sorry honey."

"You know what you are...you're a shellfish slob."

/-----------/

*Hope the snow goes and ye dine on fine blue crab. I wish
I lived near you. The Chesapeake is my true home.*

Kiss my grand-daughters.

I love you all.

Dad

From the way Daddy wrote to Shannah, it seems to me he was grateful
to have her attention and was reveling in grandfatherliness, while at the
same time there's a tentativeness, perhaps him sorely remembering that
in my sister's eyes, he had royally fucked up for a lifetime, she had not
forgiven him, and this was as good as it would ever get between them.
When I ask her about this she says, "Funny you say that. Maybe towards
the end, my letters were definitely not as vulgar. He started leaving some
of the stuff out. I think I got the CUNT word once and I might have
said something, like I don't wanna read about alligator cunt. Around
the time I had children, I was about done with him and he could tell
that.

"I was like, couldn't you see all that when you become a parent?
Couldn't you see that you needed to be a parent and all that responsibility? I think there was an apology hidden in each one of his letters. Or an
acknowledgement. Take care of your brothers, some admission that he
just couldn't do it.

"He loved us but he just could not do it."

'Round May 2011

Howdy Pooh,

*I'm sitting outdoors soaking up the last remnants of
Florida springtime wishing it were winter instead. It heats up
here in mid-May and stays that way 'til October. I hate
Florida sun like an s.t.d.*

*Gas has jumped $1.25 per gallon here in nine months,
utterly removing the wind from my sails. I had intended to*

come north in May. Oh well. Maybe I'll learn how to manu-
facture gas!

Aside from the return of MLB things remain very ordinary. I feel like the coach in a donkey baseball game.

DOS + EASTER -

I was 'membering when you were 4 or 5. It was 7 pm
and I had to work at 8:00. You asked me to demonstrate the
"Easter Bunny hop."

I went a hopping from the front door landing down to
underhalf and the third hop cracked my skull on the over-
hang. I had to cancel work and received five stitches.

/-------------/

Sorry for the negligence. I had a kidney infection for a
week and I was only good for biting off people's heads.

As usual - there's a bit here for my granddaughters.
Look forward to summer, blue-crab and friendship.

I hope all is well.

Dad

August 2011

Hi Pooh,

Sorry I neglected you. A lot of my time has been taken up
with health. It has cost me a bit. Therefore, I've had short-
ages. Anyways, here's a bit for the little one. Shure wish I
could be there.

/-------/

At this point I cannot travel. (Can you believe that?) I
got a fragile heart. Gotta stay put as it were. If you live long
enough, crappy things happen.

/---------/

I'm so glad you're 30 years behind me. Look at all the good you got coming! You'd best make the most of it. (I know you will.) I never thought or imagined I'd get this old. You are warned. Take care of yourself.

/-----------/

Your grandmom is slowly but surely recovering (she prefers slowly). I'm sure you are e-mailing so I shan't elaborate furtherly.

Tips from Mama Ed:

1.Extreme diaper rash - cornstarch.

2.Colic - walk her till your legs fall or strap her in and take a ride in the countryside.

3.Diarrhea. Use heavy towel and feed it raw to the washer.

4.Booger-eating. God help you.

5.Cough - insomnia. Whiskey and honey.

That's all for now.

Love, Dad

September 30th (2011)

Hi there Pooh.

I'm behind this month. Blame it on your brothers. I enjoy them so much.

Jimmy is still here. I'm hoping he'll find work he enjoys. What does a poor boy do? Ain't no rock and roll band hereabouts. I think he'll do fine but he's most likely a drifter like me.

Jimmy, Zora and I just returned from a night-time

fishing expedition. I think I caught a small cold. Oh well - it's always good to be on the water. AND, congratulations to Chuck on the commercial license!

Hope there are oyster beds nearby. I loved that work when I did it. My grandfodder was a waterman. Good luck. It's a great sideline.

Tangier Island it's the only line.

Shannah! I'm short-winded for a change. Literally. Little dose of c.o.p.d. I pray that you smoke rarely. "Where y'all from anyway?"

Hope Monday is a great day.

Love,

Dad

Try to guide your brothers. I know that their hides are only half-Clay. Clays drink alligator piss for breakfast. Wellingtons and Marshalls do not. If TJ and Jeffrey drift they'll be eaten alive. (Jimmy was lucky.)

Halloween 2011

Shannah,

Thank you for the card and those wunderbar pictures. The pictures made my day. Am I really 64?! You tell me. (I feel 80)

The weather has made its October turn here which means a month or more of "Indian summer." We're loving life.

It makes you want to pitch a tent, toss in a line, and sip
good wine.

/----------/

I was all packed up to head your way - via US 17 and
the Outer Banks, tackle box and all. We has to get a bottom
seal for the car tranny instead.

Just got yer message. Sounds like you've been smoking
Chesterfields. (Where y'all from, anyway?)

No elongated letter is expected. Just stay tired and busy
- in short, a good mother!

I've given a lot of thought to a visit down here by youse
guys, say between Thanksgiving and Christmas.

I am certain I can help a great deal. Jimmy can be your
taxi shure. You know computer. Dig up some rates.

Gotta run now.

Love, Dad

Daddy died on November 28, 2011, never able to meet his two granddaughters and reconnect with Shannah as planned.

"The thing that bothered me the most," says Shannah, "I was so ready to see him. I really wanted him to see my girls. I had bought the tickets, but he could not hang on. It was the only time I could've introduced them to him. I couldn't have done it when they were older."

Long ago and far away your grandfather would roll around
on a Sunday wid a brand-new used car. I'd think God loved
me after all.

— letter to Shannah

The first time I had energy work done, my practitioner asked me if there was anything I'd like to look at. I said, "Well, my father died a year ago and I'm sure there's some residual stuff there."

And so, sitting in the chair across from her that first session, we tapped into pain—mine and my father's—and I felt profoundly lonely. That's why I so wanted to connect. It felt like he wasn't around, like his spirit was not present in my mortal life as I had hoped or expected it to be.

"Your father is still healing," the woman said, after checking in with Spirit. Then she alluded to him needing a lot of time to heal from this life he had lived, and it would take several more years to do that.

It made sense. It always seemed like his life was so hard or he just wasn't meant for this world. Sounds cliche, but because of his idiosyncrasies and the way he went about his life, he just never meshed entirely with cultural and familial norms. The alcohol drove it all home. So hearing that my father needed time was comforting. Like he was there somewhere in the stratosphere, licking his mortal wounds, and I shouldn't be so worried about looking for signs.

Daddy playing guitar on Zora's patio sometime in 2011

twelve
legacy

"A chain is no stronger than its weakest link, and life is after all a chain."
— William James

Reflecting on the paradox that was my father, my mom puts it like this: "It comes down to—just like the Bible—someone in ancient days was given all these talents, something like gold coins. But instead of using them, they buried them. The meaning of the parable is that if a person was given some real benefits, such as a musical ear, poetic nature, ready smile, loving family, good education, you were smart, had a good personality—and somehow buried all these gifts, almost literally in the ground—then the person hasn't chosen to use his talents. Just like the bible story, those were all gifts that your father was given. I wouldn't say that they were misused, but they were buried."

A few years ago, my mother and I did our DNA tests and had been talking about going down to Harrellsville, North Carolina to explore my paternal grandfather's birthplace and research historical records that might give clues to the "Cherokee blood" my great-grandmother was rumored to have had.

As I pushed further back on the genealogical timeline on Ancestry.com, deep into the Clay lineage where no one in my father's family had interest in going before, I kept following the name: Clay—held onto by male offspring, spectacularly through the generations. On and on it went, with a fascinating stop in West Virginia in the late 1700s where my fifth great-grandfather William Mitchell Clay was an early settler of the land. His name lives on in horrific infamy, as the family camp was attacked by Shawnee Indians. Two of the children were scalped, and another was taken off to Ohio and burned at the stake. Historic placards and stone monuments still mark the area. I read in horror at the plight of my ancestors, yet with conflicted hindsight at whose land it was anyway. I couldn't get enough of this genealogical time machine; it just kept going. I thought for sure it would stop abruptly with some parent hailing from the distant shores of England or Ireland under some other name, sometime in the early 1700s, certainly no later than the late 1600s.

But it continued. 1672, Henry Clay I, great-grandfather of Henry Clay, the famous American statesman. 1638, Charles Clay, a soldier in Bacon's Rebellion. 1613, *Captain John Clay*, arrived at Jamestown Settlement just seven years after the first colonists arrived, after hundreds had already died of starvation, disease, Indian massacre and saltwater poisoning—or never made it across the sea in the first place.

Once he set foot, John Clay himself endured.

He endured the lack of supplies and organization that was Jamestown at that time. The same year he arrived, his boat, *The Treasurer*, was used to kidnap Pocahontas from the Powhatan Indians and her father, Chief Powhatan, as retribution for past attacks on the English and as a bargaining chip for any in the future.

Out of the 6,000 people who settled in Jamestown between 1607 and 1625, some 4,800 died from starvation and disease. Another 300 settlers were massacred in 1622. And yet John Clay survived. In 1635 he received "headrights," land in exchange for having brought immigrants to the colonies: 1,100 acres for 22 people and 100 acres for having been an "old planter," which was someone who had arrived before the government of Sir Thomas Dale.

He married a woman named Ann with whom he had one child. He later married a woman named Elizabeth and from that union, we are descended.

In light of this discovery, I found myself connected with my ancestors in a way I could never have imagined, perhaps akin to what Asian people feel when they connect with those who've gone before them. I couldn't help but compare our pilgrim ancestor's mettle to our own. Like there was something of Captain Clay's genetic blueprint, perhaps the memory of a pioneering spirit, maybe even a brain pattern or two that's somehow been passed down through the ages, manifesting as distinct Clay traits. Doggedness, stubbornness, restlessness, industriousness, and resilience, to name a few. Then there are the darker aspects of our nature, such as what my father wrote in a letter to my grandmother just after he received an unlikely note from my grandfather. Whatever my grandfather had written, possibly the kind letter he wrote the first time Daddy really landed himself in jail, left my dad with "a great sense of peace and purpose"—not likely to have transpired between the two of them for years before.

"Probably the Clay's greatest weakness is disliking themselves," Daddy wrote Grandmother.

Self-loathing is a familiar trait although we've all done our best to disrupt patterns that no longer serve—patterns of abuse and violence and addiction. At the very least, we're all watching and noticing when these symptoms of dysfunction creep in.

I'm enjoying morning coffee with my mom and stepfather and my eldest son at a coffeehouse overlooking a sparkling pond in Salisbury, Maryland. My mother, in typical fashion, has a stack of newspaper clippings to share with me. (Isn't it great that we still have moms around who still read newspapers? She drives me nuts with her piles of black-and-white print wisdom, but I know I'll miss it someday.)

She also holds three slim scraps of paper on which she has written random notes. While she's introducing news clippings about screen time and digital addiction for kids, she casually mentions that my Aunt Sally, my father's sister, told her on the phone the night of my 93-year-old grandmother's passing that my father had in fact sired two other children, one in Maryland and one in Michigan or Wisconsin. And then my mom hands me another clipping about how to prepare for college tuition and continues chattering on about the next topic.

I stare at my mother in disbelief, though I'm not exactly stunned. I mean, none of us kids would have been, I don't think, to hear of such news. I know my mom and I had often joked over the years that my father had "five children—that we know of."

And here it was, eight years after his death, and nearly two weeks since the death of my grandmother. I guess my aunt was good and tired of holding onto that one last family secret. I don't imagine my grandmother knew. I say that only because I think she would have told me. She told me a lot of things that would have been considered secret at one time and none of it seemed to matter much anymore. If she did know about these two children, and chose not to tell me, I don't think it would have been out of protection of me. She knew that I could handle just about anything, and we talked openly about so many family things. But I imagine she would've known I'd eventually share it with my sister Shannah, and it would get to my stepmother Leia, and that it could potentially be hurtful to her, and she wouldn't have wanted that, and neither would I.

But I am assuming my aunt acted alone. I don't think she gave this info to my mother out of spite but rather out of cathartic relief of grief and sadness at my grandmother's passing and years of troubled relationship that was complicated by love and longing. My aunt had access to legal records anywhere in the country, since my uncle was a lawyer and she worked with him in his firm. I'm guessing she may have dug up that info at some point in light of what must have seemed like "Eddie can do no wrong" adoration my grandmother had for my father, in spite of his drinking and even the humiliation and embarrassment he brought on my grandmother at times. My aunt felt like he had always been favored, and I imagine she may have had to discover it for herself, if only to confirm her own suspicions that he was living the lie she knew he must have been living.

Thing is though, about my father living some kind of "lie," it's not really big news. Of course, him having two real live new children is pretty big—now that it's potentially more true than ever, though at time of writing, no one except me amongst my siblings knows this information. Although I haven't actually seen the evidence, I have no reason to doubt its truth. My father had many fine qualities, but fidelity to women was not one of them. It's actually *unlikely* that he didn't sire other children, regardless of what my aunt brought forth.

That leaves me with the next obvious question: who are these kids? Grown adults by now. The last thing anyone needs at this stage of life is to dredge up old pain caused by my father. At the same time, we could all be facing the truth at any moment thanks to Ancestry.com!

I am, oddly, not that curious, given my close connection with Jimmy, Shannah, TJ, and Jeffrey—and the fact that we have shared memories and family that I can't imagine a biological half-sibling now being a part of, especially now that our father is deceased. I do wonder, though, at the idea of some woman who raised his child on her own. Was she after him for child support like my mother was, when he could barely cough up support for us? And if she was, what a nightmare that must have been! Did he ever see the woman in Michigan again? Did he ever pass through and know that he had a child? Did he see the kid? I mean, how much of this was even known to him? Was he even cognizant, or did the women go off and just deal with it on their own?

Wow. I guess I do have questions, the answers to many of which went to the grave with him. And then again, I might wonder, just a little bit, do they look like us? And are they alcoholics? Do they want to know? Will they get curious?

I've since scoured birth records in Wisconsin and Michigan, comparing to my father's 1974 trucking travels in that part of the country and estimating times of conception and birth and wondering if a child would have been named "Edward" or "Francis Edward"—or perhaps never had any connection like that at all and was given some other man's name as the father on the birth certificate and we will never know for sure unless somebody shows up in a DNA match.

People continue to find such surprises every day by logging into 23andMe and Ancestry for the first time, so I check regularly for new DNA relatives, just in case.

Whether evidence or just drunken written ramblings, a notebook of Daddy's from Zora's house talks about a trucking jaunt in Wisconsin and the luscious "Marcia" awaiting him, who would never require a wedding but wanted his manhood when he rolled into town. I looked for every Mom named Marcia who had a kid in 1974/1975 in Wisconsin and nothing magically jumped out at me except for this one dude I secretly stalked on social media whose half-smile looked just like my brother TJ's and much like my father's.

I even saved his photo so I could compare them side by side. Uncanny, really.

But naahh, couldn't have been. Looked like he was named after his father, whose name was also Francis, just like my father's first name—and I was just grasping at straws.

thirteen
love lost, such a cost

"Ever has it been that love knows not its own depth until the hour of separation."
— **Kahlil Gibran**

Riddle from Daddy (letter dated April 6, 1999)

Q. What's difference 'twixt black and white?
A. "Me"

My mother once told me the only time she ever saw my father cry was when Martin Luther King was assassinated on April 4, 1968. It always stuck in my memory as something noble and compassionate about him.

All the more jarring then, at the height of racial protest in cities across the country in the summer of 2020, to have this text exchange with my sister Shannah late one night.

> Me: Hey!! I've been making the rounds -
> meant to get up with you last week when I
> was on vacation in New York but wanted to
> see if you're around to talk maybe Friday
> evening if not maybe Sunday midday? I also
> wanted to set aside interview time - can we
> do that?

> Wrong Shannah?!

> [checking the number and the name and
> what I wrote, genuinely thinking I had the
> wrong person] Wow I guess my sis changed
> her number sorry!

> This is Shannah Kennerly is this you?

> Um yeah

> You're devoting your time to defending BLM
> now? My kids didn't even know about
> racism until last year.

I suck in my breath, taken aback. My sister has never talked to me like this before. And given how this text started out, there is no mistaking what her tone is.

Since I'm eight years older than she is and we didn't grow up together, our friendship, our sisterhood, was formed in adulthood. We had never squabbled or fallen out over anything—ever. Not even a cross word that I could think of. And we even had a half-spoken agreement to not talk about politics; that is, ever since she declared that her family was "riding the Trump train all the way." So we just didn't cross that line, which has always been friendly. This time my guard goes up.

> Me: Dude, if you and your kids don't know
> about racism then you / they don't know
> what's up on this country.

> Dude, we do. And we practice daily. Why did
> you move out of South Philly?

What's the concern with being curious about
racism? BLM? (I'm texting over her.)

Because it wasn't safe (She's texting
over me.)

Um no 2008 and school cachement We
failed"

(I'm defending our decision to get out of Philly when we were underwater with real estate and a toddler and a baby and living on credit and didn't get into any of the school lotteries we wanted.)

I check in with myself about this. If we had been having a give-and-take conversation, I would readily admit we had wanted our kids to go to Greenfield Elementary at 22nd and Chestnut in Center City, Philadelphia, where a bunch of our friends' kids were going. It was a good school, reflective of city diversity, with good teachers and reputation. But we were just a block or so outside the catchment area, and it looked like we would have to go to the school in our neighborhood. And yes, my kid would have been one of the few white kids there.

We had moved onto Catharine Street at a time when you could still buy a three-story, red-brick colonial for $150,000 or less and flip it for at least double, usually more. The added benefit was, we lived on the block so Kirk could go work on the house next door or down the street. We invested in the community, and we loved it. We shared a block with white families just moving in as well as Black folks who owned their homes free and clear after 50 years of living there. There were Section 8 families right next door to homeowners, Black and white, as well as renters. We were nestled nicely between all the gay guys—we called it Rainbow Row—and I was a block captain for two years. Together we beautified the block and planted trees with the Fairmount Park Commission, had block parties, bouncy houses, and fire truck visits, and danced in the streets—all of our kids "step-sitting" (a Philly tradition) and growing up together on the sidewalks of Philadelphia.

The only other option for elementary school was to put in for lotteries at different charter schools around the city—which we did, and none of which we got accepted into—so with that disheartening news, along with all of our failed businesses and near bankruptcy in 2008, Kirk insisted that we leave Philadelphia. "To change the molecules," as it were. But clearly my sister had made her own assumptions.

We text over each other back and forth about Black Lives Matter and then go quiet for the night. When I indulge again the next day with my own long-winded text response, I get this back:

> Shannah: Was slamming wine last night because half of my kids' friends are testing Covid positive. My kids had no idea what racism was until this year and I'm tired of it being shoved in everyone's faces

Admittedly, I have to wonder if she is also a hoaxer or COVID denier or downplayer. Rather than my first concern being for my nieces, I'm thinking about what's in the background and wondering if Shannah is a new believer in COVID or, given that she is highly intelligent and educated—with a science background to boot—she would be taking the virus more seriously than the president. In another time and place, I presume we would have been able to have had a normal, neutral conversation about things like this.

> Me: and you're upset with me why?

> you could actually shift your entire context from "it's being shoved in our faces" to " wow— i had no idea it was this bad - let's see what's going on..." and your experience will change...

> Btw it's not lost on me that this was the first time you ever actually commented on anything ive ever posted on facebook unless you were tagged - seems like there's a lot unsaid

I haven't heard from my sister in months. It feels like a piece of my foundation has been kicked out from under me. Something I could count on and lean on suddenly not there, and a feeling of dread that I might never have it back. In the weeks that go by, I examine it in so many ways, with a friend, with my therapist, with a coach. In one session I'm completely overcome by fear of being cut out—like if Shannah were to write me out of her life, somehow I would also lose my brothers because they're all "family" with each other and of course they would "go" with her. I don't actually believe this is what would happen, but seven-year-old me feels it viscerally, and I'm freaked out.

Already unmoored by six months of COVID, still reeling from a mental breakdown the previous December, and no-exaggeration-struggling to go about each day, passionless, with little interest or hope for the future—this thing with my sister has seriously darkened my path even further.

(Sat, Sep 12)

> Me: Shall we find some time to talk

(Tue, Oct 6)

> Me: Did you get my September 12 text?

Shannah: We can talk anytime...about family, your boys, life. Just don't want a debate about any issues

> Shannah i didn't debate you about anything - you attacked me via text and we haven't "talked" since - and I've never had that kind of vitriol coming from you and it's been really upsetting for me - it's not okay to leave it like this and it's not okay for us to not be able to communicate - AND we both know that we don't exchange political views however, there is a mess to clean up that requires mutual understanding of some sort - what do you propose?

> Sorry to upset you. Not mad at you. Just
> don't understand your passions. And don't
> need to. I usually try to keep my opinions to
> myself and will from now on.

> You could always ask about my passions (in
> order to understand) and we could always
> have a conversation but blasting me in a
> cryptic text message when you're drinking is
> totally uncool and then being silent about it
> and leaving it like that is really shitty of you -
> frankly - so I've been angry and shocked
> and taken aback and hurt and afraid - I've
> never had that experience with you and I've
> been in a fucked up place with it ever
> since...

My long-winded text continued, pointing out that people had made politics personal but I didn't feel any kind of way about her, personally, because of my politics, and wished the same from her.

No answer.

November 7, 2020. President-Elect Biden gives his speech in Wilmington, Delaware, while Trump and Giuliani and Barr and Graham ramp up with allegations of voter fraud and lawsuits. All along I've been thinking of my sister and this crap. Not a peep from her, but she may be feeling like she can't deal with talking to me until all of this is over. In moments of heartfelt generosity, given my own mental and spiritual state, I totally understand that she's probably going through her own stuff while also trying to homeschool her girls, manage a business, and deal with the stress of a pandemic and the volatility of the country, just like everyone else. Just like me.

Still, one of her biggest criticisms of our father's family was how crazy that somebody was always on the outs with someone else for some real or perceived slight. The next time you'd talk to Grandmother, you'd hear how Uncle Ray and Aunt Sally would be talking again but they'd both fallen out with my grandfather, or my grandmother and Aunt Sally were on the outs, and my father was pretty much on the outs with everyone most of the time (well, they were with him), so there was never harmony in the family. I've been wanting to call my sister out on this, still in shock that it's even at play in our relationship.

Shannah calls me on the other line while I'm still talking to Jeffrey. It's January 6, 2021, and he's just told me my brother Jimmy is dead at 44 years old. Died in his sleep, most likely due to severe (and untreated) sleep apnea compounded by obesity after having had the best year of his life and seeing his mom, brothers and sister, nieces, and nephews just weeks before up in Maryland and Maine, as if making the rounds.

Jeffrey gets off the line and I switch over to Shannah. We have a phone cry together for everything that's there, the Jimmy-ness of it all. Then I joke, "I guess he's kind of giving us a gift too, to have us talking to each other."

Shannah laughs. "God, I would have called two weeks ago if I knew this was gonna happen!"

We're cool again, sisters, dealing with family and sadness and grief. We've done it before and it brought us together. Familiar. Everything else goes away. Whatever our political differences, they're insignificant, especially now. And the abrasive interaction we've had via text, we'll just talk it out sometime soon when we finally get to see each other in person or when the dust settles enough to do a FaceTime call or something.

Jimmy's passing leaves me feeling oddly peaceful and at ease. I screamed and cried when Jeffrey called, knowing that something terrible was going to come out of his mouth and it was going to be Jimmy or TJ, one or the other. A few years back at a family wedding, we were all dressed up, having fun. But I noticed Jimmy's belly—swollen well beyond what my father's was in his dying days—and I remember thinking to myself, "He's going to die." As in, he would die young. Who knew when, but he would probably be first. I just wasn't sitting around expecting it to be right now. But why not right now? It's so perfectly orchestrated. After having been laid off because of the pandemic, Jimmy had been receiving unemployment like many others. The times that I talked with him over the last year, he was loving not having to work his ass off for the first time in his adult life. I told him he deserved every penny of it. He paid into the pot; he should enjoy its benefits. Without having to work so much, he was less stressed and had more time to enjoy making music and doing whatever he wanted to do, feeling like a really good version of himself. We all knew at some point everybody'd be getting off unemployment and going back to work. I doubt seriously Jimmy was looking forward to going back to Red Lobster, where he'd worked on and off for two decades. What if somehow he was able to say, "You know what? This is the perfect stopping point for me. It's as good as it's been and will ever get, and I'm ready."

Whenever I think of Jimmy leaving, that's what I keep imagining.

Then a Fleetwood Mac song comes on and it pierces my heart, holding me hostage with snot and tears for the next five or ten minutes as I commune with the music and my deceased brother. I always have it that Daddy talks to me when our songs come on, so that's when I have little conversations with him. Now I'm having them with Jimmy too, especially when four songs from *Rumours* come on in one playlist from Amazon, which seems particularly random.

Jimmy was born the year the album came out, and it played on the turntable like the air we breathed, over and over again in their apartment on Bay Ridge Avenue in Annapolis, every line of every song deeply ingrained into our childhoods. Despite his death metal preferences, Jimmy was a die-hard Fleetwood Mac fan.

Since his death, I keep evaluating who he was for me, what made our connection special. In some ways, it all starts with age and simply having more shared memories together, being able to remember back further to times shared only by us. Or like the time my father brought him and Shannah up to New York City to see me when I first moved there after high school. It was a big adventure for them, and I remembered telling people, proudly, that my little brother and sister were coming up. Remembering my own adolescence when I would visit sometimes, it was a happy feeling having a little kid brother so excited I was coming. He'd be waiting at the door to meet me, then drag me down to his room to show me his latest toys. Shannah was shy as a child, so she was less insistent.

I worried about Jimmy on and off throughout the years, mostly due to alcohol and periodic situations that he seemed to wade through, some of it pretty dark. But he always triumphed. And he saw early on that it would not be a good idea for him to bring children into the world, not intentionally anyway, so we were all pretty grateful that Jimmy wasn't somebody's dad.

Still, he became a larger-than-life uncle to his nieces and nephews.

The last couple of years, being in touch more often on Facebook, Jimmy shared music clips with me and my sons. We'd watch him playing bass alongside his head-thrashing lead singer in the metal band in some dim cave, or out under a canopy of leaves in the tranquility of a cemetery, just plucking acoustic accompanied by a friend on drums. I loved being "with" him like that and was happy to see him develop his musical talent—that gift from Daddy that not everybody got.

I realize I haven't reached out to my sister much since Jimmy died, so I text her one evening.

> Me: You doing okay

> Honestly I can't get past who you really are to what needs to be. Good luck with your book

I look down at my phone and shake my head in disbelief.

> What?

> Kennerly, whatever you choose to publish, you know your dad wouldn't suppor your current views, dad would support Trump He would support that over...

My mind is now racing a thousand miles a minute, devouring this response and wanting to crush it all at once.

I'm dying to break it to her that Daddy liked Obama, he voted for

Bobby Kennedy, and he hated Nixon. He was against anything that took advantage of small, weak, or poor. Having been on the wrong side of the billy club himself so many times, he identified with the underdog. His soul and spirit flew with the Cherokee, so he would not have supported a pipeline through his Dakota brethren's territory and would not have been a fan of drilling in the Arctic Wildlife Refuge. He knew how much Black lives mattered and he would've known the difference between using the words versus identifying with a radicalized few. About the only thing Daddy and 45 had in common was getting out of going to Vietnam.

I am determined not to let this shit go back and forth again. We're gonna talk, dammit. I dial my sister's number and leave the bedroom where my husband and I are watching every news channel there is, just after the attack on the Capitol and in preparation for the inauguration. The phone rings a few times before her voicemail picks up, "This is Shannah..."

I hang up and text her:

> Call me now please

No thanks

> What are you doing with me? What is going On with you ? And why can't you have the courage to get on the phone with me and have a conversation if you think you know so much about everything that I believe and everything that our deceased father would believe why don't you tell me

Because I don't want drama, good night

(I find that last statement slightly hilarious. It reminds me of the time I told my father on the phone, tongue-in-cheekedly, "I don't like drama, unless it's of my own making," to which he guffawed heartily.)

We text-spar a bit longer and then I recognize the futility—and the alcohol—and know I don't stand a chance against a whole shit-swirl of personal jabs that are either collapsed into the book, the daddy issues, the bottle of wine she must be drinking, and some as-until-now-unleashed lifetime of resentment towards me.

But don't think for a minute that doesn't leave me completely torn up all over again, feeling more alone because now I'm down a brother *and* a sister. I don't want to triangulate with Jeffrey and talk about Shannah. TJ has his own Shannah issues. So I'm just sitting here frantic in my mind again—like how's it all going to turn out? Because if it keeps going *this way*, guaranteed we won't be a family like we have been. I am shaken.

I start thinking to myself, maybe I should get in touch with her husband Chuck. I'll reach out to him, maybe he knows what's going on, maybe he can just help me understand or he can talk to her or bring us together or something. I don't freaking know.

Looking through my phone, I discover I have no number for my brother-in-law. That's how out of touch we've become over the last decade with kids and life. Maybe even politics, now that I'm falling into the gaping divide between us. So I message Chuck on Facebook. Some desperate plea for him to intervene with me and Shannah so this whole thing didn't go to shit because my sister feels like she doesn't know who I am, and everything that I am seems to be some personal threat to who she is.

My eyes start to open. She doesn't know who I am. She doesn't know who Daddy was either. She has no sense of the cultural and political ideology I was sprung from, grew into and was raised in. I'm still baffled though. I had assumed. Assumed that she knew. But now I understand maybe all she knew was "hippie" and not much else that came along with that.

As I got older, I started to notice how much my father's earlier life had been tabled. Obviously, he chose that, so that he could have a family and home life. Like my own story, however, it seems to have hung back in the shadows, never called upon to speak. No one had interest and therefore no one got to know that part of him...that part of me...that she got to see...on display...that made her...so mad...she didn't want any part of my passions.

I wanna shake her. Bitch-slap her even. Doesn't she see that so much of the ground gained in the hippie Sixties is what we stand on today?

The counterculture revolution led by long-haired-freaky-people pushed eco-consciousness to the fringes of our minds and eventually into the mainstream.

There was no environmental protection movement until the hippies of California got loud about it.

Dolphins? They were drag-netted and drowned, mercilessly. There were no "Dolphin Safe" labels and promises.

Vietnam? Who else was questioning, if not the hippies and the Left? How far would the war have gone if not for the protests against the government? (Democratic and Republican presidents to boot.)

And you're welcome. Marijuana now available for medicinal use in all but a few states and recreational use in many. Duh! Let alone psychedelics like psilocybin (mushrooms) for mental health disorders. Duh again, not to mention all manner of holistic therapies and treatments that have become mainstream thanks to hippie-leftist-countercultural-thinking.

Self-improvement and personal development are now practically integral to daily life. Think self-care and meditation. Thank you, 1960s California hippies. Women's lib, as such a full expression that the next generation mostly takes it for granted. That was the 60s, modern feminism, Betty Friedan, Gloria Steinem.

Gay liberation? Throw that in there, too. There would have been no Stonewall without Woodstock, women's lib, and Black Power. And let's be clear: most of these voices and this evolution/transformation did not come from the Right.

And the music, well, if you're singing the lyrics to a '60s protest song that doesn't strike a single political chord for you, then I assert the music doesn't belong to you at all.

In my cynicism, I've reflected on the year 2020 as one in which I lost a lot of people in my life—not to death, but to major loss of love and friendship. I lost a best friend of 30 years. I lost someone who'd coached me for a decade. I lost a friend and mentor who'd been a beacon in my life since my early 20s. And now it looked like I might lose my sister as well. I never imagined in a thousand years she would turn on me, utterly unprovoked, in this way.

In one last attempt to help her understand how destructive this has been for me, I send a video articulating my ache and asking her to get it. She replies by email, shallowly. "Sorry you're hurt" and something about strong genes and being a mean drunk.

P.S. - This card will have perhaps an Orlando post mark. In any conversation do not mention the fact I was in and out of Floreida. My immediate family is clinically insane and trying like hell to put me in stir. Don't help em. Thanks, Dad

Note from Daddy to Jeffrey

In one of my posthumous conversations with Jimmy, I find myself driving home one night and coming up to a red light. I start talking to Jimmy about the situation with Shannah and how I really need his help, to intervene, and see us all through this. No sooner have I formed the words then Fleetwood Mac comes through on the radio, singing *"Listen to the wind blow, watch the sunrise..."*

I laugh out loud and choke through a cry, "Hi Jimmy."

"Run in the shadows, damn your love, damn your lies."

The light changes and I accelerate, tears causing my vision to blur.

"Thank you, Jimmy, for being with me," I sputter, "and I really, really needed you to stick around."

"And if you don't love me now..." the song continues.

I pull up to another light and come to a stop, giving me a moment to wipe my face and blow my nose. As "The Chain" fades away on the radio, Van Morrison begins to croon, *"We were born before the wind..."*

Holy shit, it's Daddy! Our father-daughter dance song at my wedding. And the song we later played on the beach in Nags Head as the boys took his ashes out to sea.

"Oh so younger than the sun."

I laugh out loud again, sputtering with tears. I'm convinced that my father and Jimmy are out in the ether together, sending me a sign.

I drive the rest of the way home, crying into the mystic.

Turns out I'm not exactly okay with Jimmy gone. The gap is feeling really wide. Even though I'm the oldest child, Jimmy was the oldest boy, so in a way he was like a rock for me, too. Not that he ever had to stand up for me or anything, but because of him I got to feel like the big sister I became. With everything going on with Shannah (and the world), nothing feels safe or certain anymore. Jesus, fucking family doesn't feel certain for the first time ever, and it is so fucked up and scary and awful. And isn't it ironic that I'm writing a book about my father who was always leaving and there was never certainty with him?

I don't want to be left out here alone again.

What's happened between Shannah and me is not something easily repaired. I had hope that for this book, we would cry and laugh and share things we'd never talked about before. We would become closer than we'd ever been.

Here we haven't talked once about anything at all. One of us may as well have dropped dead for the distance between us.

I'm sitting at Shannah's kitchen counter eating breakfast. It's been just over a year since Jimmy passed away. Today, it's just us and her husband Chuck, hanging out, no kids, no other family around. I happened to be in the area for a family memorial and asked if I could spend the night at their place afterwards. It's nice to hang out on the farm like old times and nothing in the space. A perfect time for me to say what I've been wanting to say.

"So, I have a little speech to make."

"Uh-oh."

"No, it's nothing bad."

Chuck looks my way over breakfast of eggs and recently slaughtered bacon.

"I just wanna say that I don't want politics to ever come between us like it did before. You know, things are going to heat up again soon, and I need you to know that I really love you guys, forever and always, and I don't care what your politics are. You can dislike my politics and I can dislike yours, but that doesn't mean I don't love you, you know? I like you, I want you to be happy and successful, and I never want politics to come between us, no matter what."

Tears well up in my eyes and I'm grateful to finally be in a quiet moment where they're both present and nobody's been drinking and there's no distractions. Just us, connecting like family and I know the message is landing as intended.

"I couldn't agree more," Chuck says, between mouthfuls.

Shannah comes around the counter and tells me not to cry, gives me a hug, then belts outs like a guttural Clay girl, "Trump 2022!" with a fist in the air.

"We knew that was coming," Chuck says, shaking his head.

"Fucker!" I laugh.

As I pull out down the lane that morning, I think to myself, *I got my sister back.*

fourteen
explain me

"Study me as much as you like, you will not know me, for I differ in a hundred ways from what you see me to be. Put yourself behind my eyes and see me as I see myself, for I have chosen to dwell in a place you cannot see."
— Rumi

I discover this "Hiway 60 Blues" poem in the composition book that Zora—my father's caretaker, girlfriend, Kentucky woman, landlady, driver, chef, hospice nurse, angel—handed over to me that time TJ and Kelly and I stopped in for a visit. In it, Daddy is thumbing to California again, escaping arrest, paying homage to Neal Cassady. In 2006 he would have been a year shy of 60. Still running. Still chasing. Gone.

Now his words speak louder to me in a letter dated August 7, 2007, with "East of Nowhere" and return address of Zora's place in Florida:

As we continue to grow together I hope you'll explain me (event of death) to your half brothers and sister. You know me well!

In digging up all these letters, I start getting a distinct communication, heard within a new context. Like a higher calling to tell a bigger story, to widen the lens and discover something more, to give my father some breadth and depth that perhaps my siblings and I never gave him or only had some glimmer of.

"My find in this world has been myself after a veritable ton of bullshit and piss-poor advice. Everyone seems to want to get you down in the hole they are lodged in."
— Eddie Chowan, East of Nowhere, 2006

(with a nod to Dylan, "It's Alright Ma I'm Only
    Bleeding")

(Day One) 4/1/06
Hiway 60 Blues

Leap-frog it were
Crazy sign in hand
East of somewhere I'd rather not be.
[SOT]
Every ounce of misery befits me well.
Ancient palm a-waving
Neal Cassady in my
Brain.
'Member you silly
Car thief and great
Man and visionary.
You must know
This man followed you.
With utter faith.
I owe these things.
As you know and I know
There is no ass-kissing
Whatsoever.
R.I.P. shure

Guadalajara D.F.

Note: My father's reference to Guadalajara may have been intended as San Miguel de Allende, which is where Neal Cassady dropped dead on the train tracks.

When I come across the poem, I decide to get interested in Route 60 and find that it runs from Virginia Beach right on the edge of the Atlantic Ocean, launching westward for 2,655 miles by way of Kentucky, Missouri, Oklahoma, and landing somewhere around Brenda, Arizona (pop. 676). Los Angeles is about four-and-a-half-hours due west, while San Francisco—where my father would always end up—is a good 10½ hours further north of that.

Highway 60 would have been like an old familiar friend to him, traversed both ways numerous times by car, truck, and motorcycle, and with thumb or "palm a-waving" many a time, in all kinds of weather, trying to get east of somewhere he'd rather not be. The poem invites me in, allowing me to be in the moment with Daddy, letting him be just himself, someone other than our father. Letting him be Neal Cassady, living with wild abandon on the road with nothing to tie him down and no one to answer to. Just the call of the highway, the warm smell of colitas rising up through the air in dingy rooms with *mamacitas* to drink and lay with and never see again.

> **"I was surprised, as always, by how easy the act of leaving was, and how good it felt. The world was suddenly rich with possibility."**
> **— Jack Kerouac, On the Road**

In another letter to my grandmother dated June 25, 2002, my father writes from San Francisco:

I'm finally free. Because finally it's just me. Far from any grandchildren. I only had to work for forty years (I'm still working!). Some aren't so lucky.

The grandchildren reference would have been for her benefit as none of us had children at the time. I take it not so much as a comment on not having to be with us kids, but rather a freedom from any sort of familial obligation to anyone. Perhaps since 1968. Since I was born, really.

In another letter, he writes he's enjoying the beauty of San Francisco like never before, and that he's doing a lot of writing. From Seal Rock, just off the westernmost promontory of San Francisco and a popular spot near the famous Cliff House restaurant and vista, he writes to my grandmother:

> Incidentally, Point Lobos, where I am sitting, was where John Steinbeck's last rites were held in 1968. I was busy trying to halt troop trains in Berkley and Kennerly was growing in her mother's womb. Perhaps you understand why I live here. Nowhere else do I have a past. One day for fun I visited over a dozen addresses I'd lived at. All gated and locked 'cept for the one Kennerly was conceived at. It had been demolished and a park was in its place. That night, I dreamt she was with child. You've gotta be wild to live here and love it, and I do. There is so much here that even an old man gets inspired.

In a letter to me, later that summer with return address Gen'l Delivery, 101 Hyde St, S.F., CA, 94142:

> 8x10 2002
>
> Pooh Doll
> I'm sitting two rock throws from your old abode on Stanyan Street, digging the morning sun with a McDonald's coffee laced with a Southern Comfort dollop, obviously hating life. It's good to be home, after all. Except for the good money

I earned in trucking, I can honestly say I might have never left California.

This was the trip he was headed from Florida to Charlotte to see Jimmy and ended up switching his bus ticket to Fargo, North Dakota. From there he thumbed west, "finally seeing the badlands (goodlands!) and Montana," he wrote. "I experienced a peace I'd never known. Montana is a country that no one has fucked up. (YET). If I were 62 I'd spend summers there; then return to the coasts."

True to form, my mother resurrects additional letters. This time, chronologically saved from 1998 to 2001 and a few that trickled in through that decade and up until the last few months before my father died. I had no idea he had continued writing to her in such a way and their friendship had so ensued through letters.

He wrote her melancholy, reminiscent poems, like:

Long Gone Rain
3/16/99

Fades thru' matured San Francisco shades.
Tiny world no blades.
Sweet mist of dew.
Me and you.
Long long ago.
We certain kicked ass.
Naturally ran out of gas.

And some wistfully, lost-romance items, like:

The Beat Who Never Let Go

Long long ago

There was a song
Pudding of Cassidy (sic)
And Kerouac.

It was named freedom and Ginsberg feet
Rump a bum bum
On this weary drum
And we fell a bit.
I smoked a Chesterfield
And was lit.
You can't lay a hand
On this. No! No! No!
We simply stroll
Without abscess
We lay in ditches with
Total contentment
And abandon
We are not crushed
By laws or standards.
We heed our natural
law.
With a beer can twixt' legs.
Loving life (down the freeway)
Fish tank of our
Imagination.

For what it's worth
1998
Pome

I awoke and wrote quickly all that
I knew.
1968 running blue.
Huggable - Loveable
Might been
True

File this somewhere
For sure
Love is an open door.
Wish I'd gave you 3
more openchance.
21 and couldn't dance.
I'll always love you.
Clay

And sometimes he was just sort of thinking out loud about what they once had:

Anne 1997
We met round 'bout '65. I think I'd just turned 18. She smiled and laffered a bit. Byrds concert. Sexiest woman ever seen (at the time) Rambled round - burnt out '56 Volkswagon. Sex failure
Sometimes try Prince George Palace outroom for pleasure. (Can anyone make love in a Volkswagon.) You are 18 and she be 22. Hell of a mess. Anyways beautiful child.

And a letter dated April 21, 2000, just after he was sprung from jail and would likely be walking me down the aisle.

Anne - Lily,
I was writhing and dreaming of all on Ken's half-birthday and got up and wrote this little song - perhaps for all the sad days or good days gone by. I was dreaming 'bout "Freewheelin'" and "Spanish Boots" and how life "kicks butt" so eloquent and hoping I'll see October. Tell yer mum I pray for her. Even as I couldn't care less if I dropped. (IGNORE ALL NEGATIVES) Your card was a delight and is displayed on my cypress-knee lamp base. Thank you for caring about me. As I see it one takes one

child at a time and focuses. You can't be everywhere at once as much as ye wish you could. Your work in AA makes you a minor saint and makes me thankful I'm not sponsored. I'll do what I can. I've always loved you.
Pancho

My mother always corresponded in turn and must have thanked my father for the gift of "me." A card dated December 18, 2000, has the word "Yessscccchhh!" scribbled in, coming from the mouths of the manatees on the front.

To the wife I should have stuck with (HELL OR HIGH WATER) you thanked me for Kennerly," Daddy writes. "Now I thank you for Kennerly. We weren't all bad were we. I wish we had three like her. I pray you have the content-ment I have. I'm alone and it's good. I'm glad you are not. (ALONE) Steve seems remarkable to me. A very good man. Funny how time slip away. Give me love to all of yours and have the best the Big Man can give. I love you,
Manatee Ed

A birthday card arrived in September 2011—two months before he passed—wishing her well on the solemnity of turning "68" and alluding to the potency of that number (the year I was born). "Imagine doing that one again," he writes.

I find the latest round of missives telling. The inspiration for writing his novel "East of Nowhere" started with his time at William & Mary with my mother. Their shared youth and that volatile, exhilarating, fantastical time and place when music and culture and ideas coalesced, and they forged their way in and through it together. And his sharing of perspective on their relationship, though not wholly responsible given he never became transparent about the role alcohol played in his behavior, nonetheless was kind, conciliatory, and loving.

It's been delicious for me to see the love my father had for my mother, yet frustrating to see my mother's indifference to it, given all the years of hardship and distance she had to create, just so she could survive as a single mom.

In these later letters though, she admits something new.

"I was still using the old lens," she says of our prior conversations. "Looking back now, I can give credence to what he felt and said. It was so beneficial to me to read him with a different lens, and in later years see that he was a real gentleman to me. I think now I am seeing the real thing rather than what I thought here or there, which is very helpful."

My mom tells me she would never have come to such realizations had it not been for this book and the unfolding of the stories we never knew were there to tell.

"Not that I wish I'd ever done this or that," she clarifies. "It's just: Where are you now, and where are you coming from? It's like by living the life that he did, he has become a champion for you and for me. Seeing him in a more positive way, it's not that he set out to do that, it's just that, like Jesus on the cross in his suffering, it came out as something else for us."

My father and "champion" are not words often used in the same sentence, so I sit with my mother's generosity, but most of all, I am curious to know. "So, after all that, can you hear how much he loved you? Can you let it in?"

She concedes, while still pointing out that alcohol won over any love my father had for either of us. She later tells me she has cried many tears over these letters. Not because of some long-lost feelings for my father, but because of the tragedy of observing the alcoholic grip on a person we all loved so much.

It is the same heartache I have for my brother TJ. You see it all happening and you can't do a damn thing about it. And you know it's all a crapshoot. One roll of the dice and the alcohol may win for good.

Letter to me written on Daddy's last trip to the West Coast in 2010:

I caught a ride back with a 25-year-old drifter. We

*shared driving and I saw Seattle for the first time. I was
impressed as usual by the night sky. 'Jack' was hell-bent for
San Francisco. After Portland I toured him down the Oregon
coast, passing Yachats and stopping briefly at the forest
service road where you, I, and your mum stayed in a cabin
when you was an 'infink.' Down past Eureka, yea, to Bodega
Bay. And back here.*

'And here I'll stay.'
'Here I'll stay.'

Rereading this letter, every word is richer now, every memory more
evocative. I imagine what it must've been like for Daddy to be at the
very service road he'd been at when we'd gone up the Oregon coast,
camping when I was a baby. My mother has spoken of that Oregon trip
many times, and it was the first time I'd ever noticed my father writing
the word "infink"—a silly expression for infant that my mother always
used. I find myself wanting to be there with him, with them, in 1969,
the three of us together on the Oregon coast, just to have one good
memory of what it was like when we were together.

I have not a single one.

The letter continued with news of a 20- to 25-hour a week job as a
breakfast cook ("all my legs can stand") as well as eight hours at
Hamilton House in the Haight, a community outreach of sorts that
helped families get back on their feet. Daddy probably got free meals in
exchange for keeping the place clean.

"'Tis a bit like say the San Diego Zoo," he wrote, "but I enjoy every
single second. (Why not?)"

———————— ✦ ————————

If Some God Ran Here

He'd drink himself silly
Kinda like Santa Claus.
Cherubic.
Amazing.
Distracted.
Honest.
Compassionate.
Loving.
Giving.
Having.
Holding
Being his silly self.
Heading for the
WOODS.
Letting things happen
After all.
E-O-N

(E-O-N: East of Nowhere)

fifteen
epilogue: the briefcase

While I was writing this book, my brother Jeffrey unearthed another batch of my father's writings in the most unlikely way. An old buddy of his from Maryland was planning to attend Jimmy's memorial service at my sister's house. In fact, the guy had dated my sister back in the day. Turns out, he happened to have this worn out, soft-leather satchel my father had given him that was full of random poems, scratchpads, stories, first drafts, letters from family members, and miscellaneous thoughts and wisdom.

How on earth this transpired was even more odd, but so bizarrely believable we all had to laugh. At the time the guy was dating my sister back in the mid-90s, he had pulled up to the house and was waiting in the car. He was actually waiting for my brother Jimmy to come out (he was friends with both of them). My father sauntered out to the car, got in on the passenger side with this satchel, then said to the guy, "Son, I don't know that I approve of what you're doing with my daughter, but this may help you some day, and I want you to have it."

Daddy handed him the satchel, got out of the car, went back into the house, and the guy held onto this stuff for 25+ years. Without having any idea that I was writing a book based on Daddy's letters and writings, he tells my brother out of the blue he has all these writings and asked Jeffrey if he wanted them.

"Hell yeah!" said Jeffrey, and thus unfolded new clues and messages from a fragmented past.

There are two particularly poignant poems written to and about TJ. If he interprets them the same as I do, they sound like the most amends I could ever imagine Daddy having made. He wrote of letting him down —an apology, even if he never said it.

A letter from my grandfather written to Daddy when he went to jail for his first long-ish sentence for DWI is so loving and supportive you'd never know there was so much murky water under that bridge.

A poem about alcohol even uses the word "alcoholism"—a truth that never seemed to make its way from Daddy's lips, but it was there on paper.

Weirdly, there's a folded map of Germany (never heard him talk about going there); vivid memories about hog castration on the Clay farm when he was a child with his Uncle Jimmy; and the fear of God event he always talked about, which was the one time he went hunting and was convinced his father was going to kill him. The whole story lies within these yellowed, legal pad pages, along with simple wisdom blurted on the pages of a small scratch pad: "Always look for the good in things," "Never leave the one you love (you can't run)," "Midnight sun abound. Existence. Pray for Barry," and "Life of mind so unkind. Nancy made me believe" (a nod to his loving cousin during the dark time when her son was at Johns Hopkins).

Aside from the content of the writing and whether or not any of the poetry is any good, the satchel holds hints of what Daddy had to say to the world that never got expressed fully or in the way that he wanted to be heard. There was a lot going on in that mind of his. In his writings, even the sloppy drunken ones, you can see what might have been if the glaze of alcohol were not in the way of his thoughts and imagination.

In writing this book, I recently wrote to Steve, my parents' old friend and roommate from Williamsburg who also lived in San Francisco and was a great support to me when I lived there myself. He even hired my former boyfriend in his landscaping business when we were living out there together.

My last communique with him perchance had been a thank-you for a wooden garden bench he sent me and my husband for our wedding in

2000. Although he and my mother have kept up through the years, I had stopped writing due to my own self- and family-absorption. I wanted to reconnect with him and also let him know I was writing this book. He wrote back:

I am so very pleased to hear you are making the effort to write about your dad. I've never shared with your mom, but he has been an open sore within me for a very long time, a regret and disturbance that life never allowed me to be there for him in the way that I think he so desperately craved. He never wrote to me, to my recollection, but very occasionally he would call drunk of course - but reaching for connection and support; maybe wanting me to tell him to come out and live with me. I did what I could over the phone, knowing it wasn't enough and cursing my own dire circumstances preventing me from doing more. I hated it then, I still hate it today...it haunts me.

I suppose you know he, your mom and I all lived together for nearly a year (late '65 and most of '66). They both drank, especially your dad, and he would often tell me how much he loved me - at that point I sort of assumed like a brother, a male bonding thing; but have since sometimes wondered if it was more?

I think Ed had a deep need/feeling for connection—really deep connection—something God knows, I was certainly looking for...but circumstances just didn't play out too far. I think we both felt it, hence the occasional phone call.

I know whatever it was, he never found it. I think the first connection he made, the first time he found his "language" was when he discovered Bob Dylan...he was and stayed so excited, "besotted" if you will, with those lyrics. At 18, he couldn't articulate that well and Dylan was an explosive opening to expression for him. That's why Bob Dylan appealed to him so much and I expect some like Kerouac and company would have too.

There is a segment of humanity who have for whatever reasons almost too much sensitivity (you will know what I mean I think) - perhaps from having seen too much too closely over a long period of time (multiple life experiences) that creates kind of a void in them, a hole that doesn't have to be there, but with it and alcohol/drugs at least take the edge off for awhile. I never went there because I've wanted some truth.

———————————— ❖ ————————————

August 4, 1998
Letter from Grandfather to Daddy
at Caroline County Detention Center
(first major incarceration for DWI)

Dear Eddie,

Ordinarily this would be a very hard letter for me to write but as I go along you will surely understand why it's not hard at all; for the first time in many years my heart is light and a very dark cloud has left its position above my head and dissipated into the unknown.

First let me say that I know being confined is very hard for you; a free spirit! And I with full heart feel sad for you, but Eddie I feel that God has laid a hand on the Clay family, like my ordeal and then your mom wanting to and then coming down and looking after me. Surely God had a hand as I am now happy at last and I believe she is too.

Then knowing that we could not afford treatment for you and now you have it free. I know that you have it hard but think Eddie what could have happened and then surely what would have happened as you were going on your way to sure destruction.

I shall never forget our last visit. How happy you and the boys were; you have so much to live for, and so many people who love you. What I would give to be your age and be in your physical condition. The whole world is before you; you only have to get your head on straight.

Eddie now I finally have lots of hope for you and you will

be amazed how the world and everyone else will accept you as you are.

Please read this letter carefully and realize how much we all love you and we will all be waiting for you with open arms and loving hearts.

Most sincerely,
Dad

FACT: I would gladly take your place for however long if you could be cured of your problem!!!

Booze

There be a certain truth to all
What we speak of is Booze.
We were prepared from the cradle.
Vodka is me only Magic.
Alcoholism one can never dodge..

Somewhere back in time you knew you had it beat
Nowadays you retreat
Nothing like total craze - Rampage

Got Lop-eared conspirator in full heat.
Nothing to eat.
Fissures abound. We stroll around. Whiskey Bound..

We walk air We cross bear
Always on the lam
I be ham
We be no lie. Ever.
We will always run the James.

Sometimes we just be a hymn..
Insanity ain't nothing new.
We'll never know...
There must be the sweet hand of God
Tokyo beyond.
Christian Magic...
Idling Trucks...

Purity Life and Sound
Let me not bore you.

Mother of Jesus
I shain't implore you.
The Rumble and Rustle of freight trains
sometime be essence.
We're always best going away.

Someday Never Comes.

———————— ✾ ————————

EON 2001 POEM

Somewhere
East of Nowhere
Elsewhere
Frozen niceline
Free of pain
Free of gain
Mississippi thaw
Running raw
Like La Crosse (Wisc.)
What do we do?
Start anew?
All right then.

SOT

I believe I heard
    One time
    That the heart is a very lonely
    Hunter
    It took me 50 years
    To know mine
    It is so sublime.

I 'spose these are finally the good/s
    times. I never knew
    that many that
    bad.

It's just life.
    It's toil; it's strife.
    Job is job.
    Ye gotta love it.
    You must fill it.
    (It might help to love it.)

There are matters
    Of the heart that
    Rule the mind.
    (what's new)
    My heart is my matter (<u>master</u>).
    I am one mad hatter.
    Torn in two.

My Pooh (doll) Bear; Life is a long time and a short time. You must realize that you can't always get what you want. (I

never did.) I getting what I need. I understand your pain
and disappointment. But

It's just life.
You didn't ask to be here but you
IS IS IS
THEREFORE

If writing ain't working
Scrub a floor
Have total faith
In yourself
Always.

I love you,
Daddy

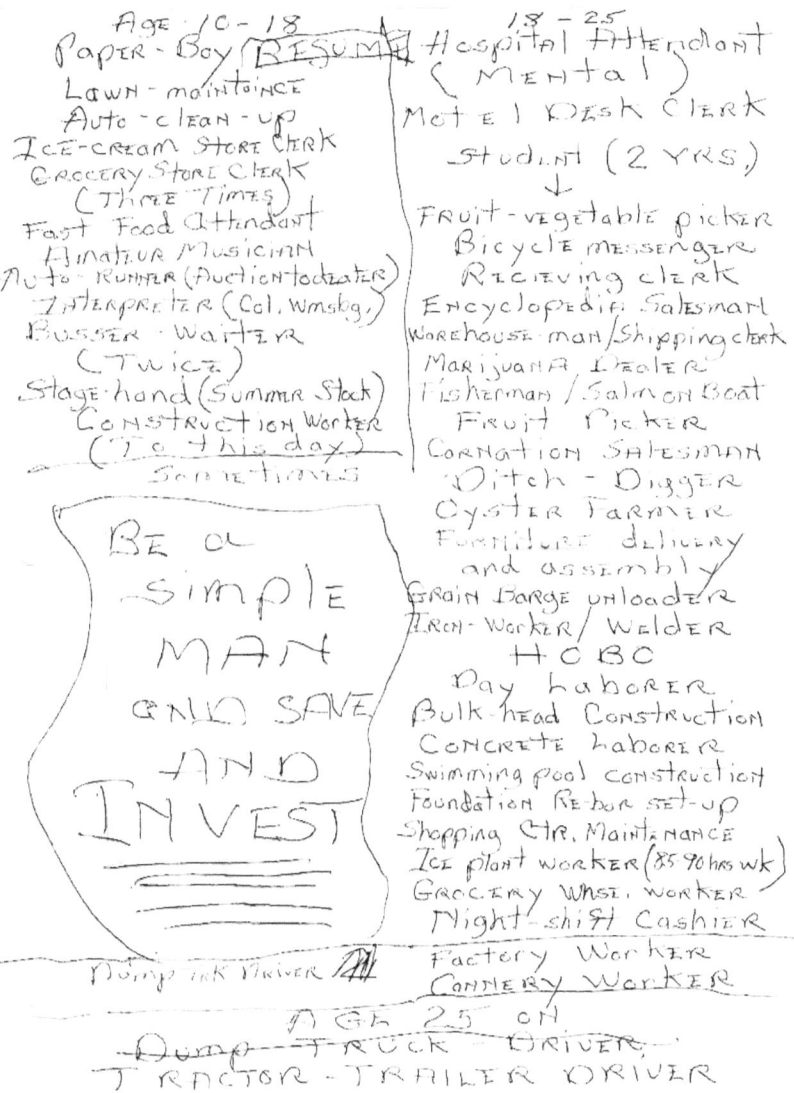

My father's list of occupations starting at age 10 and advice for my brothers on work

Part-time Tire-Recapper
    Land-scaper
Bartender - Bingo Hall Operator
Vacuum Cleaner Salesman

    Firewood sales

---

                these
All of jobs are true,
I may have omitted four
         or five,

    If you study the list
you might notice the
absensce of "professionlism",
That absensce is the absence
of the need for Education for
the job,

    Ninety-percent of these
jobs a trained chimpanzee
could have done, I could
have alleviated my blisters,
scars, splinters, backache,
toxic fumes, aching back,
and feet, not to mention
worn-out bouncy busses hauling
you to fruit and vegetable
fields out of Skid Row San
Francisco to the fields of
Milpitas, California at 3 A.M,
Gentlemen (and may you be
always), The three of us are
way beyond this needless
         suffering,

After all these things, I urge you to educate yourselves. Challenge your minds and not your bodies. My course in life could have me in a walker at 60. SHIT. I wanna live to be one-hundred, nyeh, nyeh.

DESERVE is a false word. I will quote Master Jeffrey: "It's my own damn fault."

What you should note in all of these jobs is (I know I repeat this) an absence of being anything other than a swinging dick.

OR - do what you like to do and do it well and stay in one place. You will surely thrive.

If you want an easier life you must have education. Or a technical school. Or maybe you two come up wid a bizness of your own.

My work-life is trucking. I'll never regret it.

I love you,

Dad

Search for the *Letters from East of Nowhere* playlist on Spotify

The Dolphins	Tim Buckley
Universal Soldier	Donovan
Positively 4th Street	Bob Dylan
Duquesne Whistle	Bob Dylan
Reflections in a Crystal Wind	Mimi & Richard Fariña
Bold Marauder	Mimi & Richard Fariña
Darling Be Home Soon	The Lovin' Spoonful
Crying	Roy Orbison
Last Night of the World	Bruce Cockburn
If I Had a Rocket Launcher	Bruce Cockburn
Wondering Where the Lions Are	Bruce Cockburn
Into the Mystic	Van Morrison
One (Achtung Baby)	U2
Take Care of All My Children	Tom Waits
On the Nickel	Tom Waits
100 Years Ago	Rolling Stones
Under My Thumb	Rolling Stones
Paint It, Black	Rolling Stones
Street Fighting Man	Rolling Stones
Before They Make Me Run	Rolling Stones
Jungleland	Bruce Springsteen
Do I Have to Come Right Out and Say It	Buffalo Springfield
Broken Arrow	Buffalo Springfield
Only Love Can Break Your Heart	Crosby, Stills, Nash & Young
End of the Line	Traveling Wilburys
Walkin' After Midnight	Patsy Cline
Femme Fatale	Velvet Underground
I'm Waiting for the Man	Velvet Underground
Sweet Jane	Velvet Underground
Crazy Wind	James McMurtry
Painting by Numbers	James McMurtry
Light Your Windows	Quicksilver Messenger Service
Gold and Silver	Quicksilver Messenger Service
What About Me?	Quicksilver Messenger Service
Sittin' in Circles	Electric Flag
Coney Island Baby	Lou Reed
Crawl Back (Under My Stone)	Richard Thompson
By the Time I Get to Phoenix	Glen Campbell
The Chain	Fleetwood Mac
Never Going Back Again	Fleetwood Mac
Come Monday	Jimmy Buffet
Harvest Moon	Pondside (instrumental)

sixteen
east of nowhere, chapter 2 - 1966

By F. Edward Clay, Jr.
Written early 2000s

Activism arrived in the nonperson image of a huge Navy fighter jet towed onto campus and planted directly in front of the Student Union building for the express purpose of stimulating recruitment. What it initially recruited was a motley crew of ten or so lonesome demonstrators who lined the plane oh, some with signs, and more than 100 counter demonstrators who had looted the cafeteria dumpster and armed themselves with outdated eggs and fruit.

Colin Kaid happened onto the scene. Egg yolk was running off the plane and demonstrators alike. He recognized a friend, James Bard, and, always loving the underdog, joined the group by climbing up and straddling the plane behind the cockpit. The head of the fine arts department came out of a nearby classroom building, commenced cursing them, calling them faggots and cowards. As he yelled and gesticulated, a campus stray dog charged and was trying to strip him by a pants leg. The pandemonium was hilarious. Bard was half smiling, holding a "Funeral - No Parking" sign five-feet-tall with pedestal. He and Kaid shared a firm handshake. The school's war resistance movement was born.

By nightfall a rally took place under the plane's shadow. Kaid was off work and found Kate there. There were now 30 or so people; he knew most through parties. It was determined that the "warbird" must go.

After a smattering of ad-lib speeches the group adjourned to party. They were pleased, believing this anti-war tremor truly would have its role in affecting campus opinion. Amongst those Kaid knew, neutrality in the face of this war was impossible. All were intensely opinioned and vocal. He saw it in philosophical rather than moral terms. After all, what war wasn't immoral? Vietnam was plain stupid and his elected government was lying about it, escalating it, and killing his peers in vain.

One could latch onto an 2-S exemption (provided he could muster money for college), maintain a C average, and ride out the war while acquiring higher education, as long as he kept a credit load of fifteen hours. (This exemption was withering away in some states as the military's need for fresh meat was increasing.) You might knock up your girl-friend (Joan Baez was currently advising girls to say "yes" to boys who said "no") and be the sole source of family income, securing a "3-A" deferment. You could be "1-A" and haul ass to Canada or Mexico. Or join the Coast Guard. Then again you could do a tour of Vietnam and be an unsung hero, or perhaps come home in a bag, or both. Maybe you'd shoot yourself in the foot or show at your induction physical wearing a dress or high on LSD. Lastly, you could be a genuine consci-entious objector, register as such, and be an object of scorn because of the ensuing FBI investigation. There were no easy choices. Kaid contested the draft as a CO, was discouraged by the ensuing harassment of every imaginable person who might harbor knowledge of his convic-tions, and finally dealt with the SSS in Ken Kesey style, which stated in essence that to stop the war you turned your back, walked away and said "fuck it." To hell with an intellectual approach!

Over the weekend the Navy moved the plane a half-mile cross campus, plunking it in the middle of three mens' dormitories. Monday the recruiters were doing a brisk business. Kaid espied the plane and recognized Gorsch, an ROTC veteran, aiding the process. Gorsch's combat experience consisted of blowing the wall out of a closet in his apartment with a 30.06 automatic. They had different takes on Vietnam but the friendship remained solid. Gorsch was to go to Southeast Asia as an officer at the end of the school year, more out of curiosity than patriotism. Kaid was convinced he was out to sample Asian cunt.

Dave Bard, whose dormitory window overlooked the plane, wandered up. The uniforms took careful notice, remembering the previous Friday. The trio talked and smoked. Bard appeared extremely upset, balanced only by practiced self-control. Kaid suggested morning coffee at Kate's. When they arrived he extracted the house key from under a loose brick and let them in. Kate was in class. Soon the apartment was swaying to "December's Children" and smelling of espresso. The men were easy to please. Colin wondered why life couldn't remain as simple as this morning gathering; food, shelter, music and conversation. The war at times like these was a dream.

With sharpened wits they left for classes at 9:30.

Kaid spent a restless hour under the sway of Orlovsky's modern European history lecture, musing that contemporary events should be the focus. Even Joan of Arc could be a bore. Thank Christ Patty Polar was sitting up, behind, and to his right, with her luscious legs spread as usual. They had been in classes together since seventh grade but this diversion was the ultimate in temptation. In keep with the times she was without panties, which further enhanced his pleasure. His studious neighbor sported a football letter jacket, and was chortling at his pencil drops as though he were a demented spastic. Colin was aroused and wickedly self-amused. Patty coyly caught him once, winked, tittered, and widened the spread. Colin, now beet-red, feigned interest in the lecture.

At 10:55 the bell-buzzer sounded and one-hundred-fifty-eight hungry hearts poured out of the lecture hall. As Kaid reached the double doors of outside and free, he felt a tug at his sleeve and turning found himself looking into Patty's mischievous blue eyes:

"And how have you been, Mistuh Colin Kaid?"

A blush. "Fine Patty, and you?"

"Marvelous. When are you coming over?"

"Over where?"

"To see my apartment, of course."

"Really."

"Ireland Street, next to the firehouse, 2nd floor."

She reached into her pocketbook and gave him a key.

"Be seeing ya," she winked and walked away.

And a damn fine thing because seconds after Kate burst upon the scene. She and her friend Miriam were talking mile-a-minute. He was inclined to run. When the two women were ten feet away a resonant splat was heard and Kate's ebony hair was host to a greenish-white plopping of goose shit, from forehead back. This set the entire gang into a howl and Kate embarked on a sailor's round of cursing, her tiny fist in defiance of a formation of Canadians making their passage. Kaid produced a humongous red bandana from hip and directed "Miss Kitty" to the nearest ladies room. Miriam went along. Then, with only an internal explanation, he felt an overwhelming urge to Simply quit the scene, and did just that.

He strode on air across campus, past the blue-winged monstrosity to Greeks Pub and ordered a pitcher of beer. It wasn't noon but Mickey was a chum. He placed him in a well-concealed rear booth with the beer. He and Colin had been friends at sixteen. The drinking age was twenty-one but the elder sensed a boy he could infinitely trust. One winter's night removed any doubt. 'Twas a weeknight and Mickey had given a horny barmaid the night off and had sent little Alexis home at eleven. This lent Colin talking with Mickey about Greece and some rednecks shooting pool on two tables. Towards closing they were rowdy and menacing. Kaid as rowdy ex-classmates knew half or more had trials pending for assaults or robbery. He had gone to school with them, sadly dropped out as they did, and knew their resentment and penchant for violence.

He had gone to the men's room and while there heard a heated argument growing in volume. It seemed the good ol' boys wouldn't cease, or cover tab. He slipped through a door in the restroom into the kitchen and seized a loaded double-barrelled shotgun Mickey kept standing behind the door. Freeing the safety he leveled the gun and re-entered the bar just as Gerald Joyner was breaking the neck off a Bud bottle and advancing with four other fools.

He did pump-action on the shotgun and stepping into the middle of the scene, sixteen years old, aimed gun at Joyner's head, "Hold up Geary or I'll blow your head clean off."

Joyner laughed but froze, staring back and forth at Kaid and bottle weapon. A half-minute of growling and grumbling ensued. Kaid's stance never wavered. He held the gun until the men paid up and left.

"Whew," said Mickey. "He was going to cut me."

"They intended to mess you up and steal the house. Joyner's middle name is Bowie and he's used one."

They were friends and soulmates thereafter.

Kaid proceeded to get slowly sloshed on the draught. After a time he fed a half-buck to the jukebox. Chuck Berry and Bo Diddley were kicking serious ass. At this point Eddie Chowan rolled up, mini-chained his Harley-Davidson to Mickey's weighted "Specials" sign and lumbered into the pub.

"Well damn me if it ain't the 'Chowan.' Sit down Eddy, have a pitcher."

"Hello Colin, do mind if I don't."

He sat down, facing him in the booth. Mickey brought a mug and a beer-fest began in earnest.

"Christ - where've ya been?"

"Surveying and night classes."

"I haven't seen you in weeks, guy."

"Busy my boy, busy. Are you still with Kate?"

"Always - sometimes; you know how it goes."

"Good. Here's to ya and the great goddess of beer in the skyway."

They clinked mugs and guzzled.

By three p.m. when Kate and Miriam finally discovered them they were high as loons. The girls coaxed them out of the bar and homeward to Kate's with Chowan stopping to extract a pint of Jack Daniels from a padded compartment under his bike seat. At Kate's they shifted into high with shots and beers. The girls were into some leftover Chianti and had teamed up to concoct the world's greatest spaghetti. Things were into the mystic with the Beatles' "Rubber Soul." Time was standing still.

Miriam, a reserved traditional woman and daughter of a southern baptist Minister, was slightly aghast at daytime drinking but the attraction of the others was irresistible. Kate's zest and laughter were contagious and the two rowdy men looked like Roman gods. The thought led her to suggest a toga party. Kate made a mental count of available sheets.

"So anyway, where are you staying?"

"Two blocks past the Catholic church, Col."

"I didn't know there was anything to rent there."

"3rd floor, one-bedroom, classic huge bathtub, and, best of all, an open porch off the kitchen. I love it!"

"I'll have to check it out."

"Anytime. What's mine is yours."

John Lennon's "In My Life" filled the room. Colin caught Kate in a bearhug and they began to slow-dance. When Miriam wandered in from the kitchen, Chowan graciously and mock pompously proposed to dance. When the song ended the embrace lingered. A crazy chemistry was taking place; a biker, surveyor, Vietnam vet and newly a student, and a preacher's child majoring in sociology. C'est la vie.

While the sauce savory simmered on Kate's ancient gas stove the four lovebirds tossed the world about like a child's balloon. Jovial conversation served as an appetizer. As evening's shadows fell upon the flat, Kaid laid a fetching table and lit plain white candles. Kate produced pasta, sauce, salad and garlic bread, and a chilled bottle of cabernet sauvignon. Wine glasses were brimmed and feasting ensued. It was an evening and dinner the group would always treasure in memory.

At ten Eddie and Miriam said goodnight and strolled arm-in-arm back to Mickey's. Jesse Hogge, a town policeman, was waiting curbside with a parking ticket. Chowan gave the officer a Cheshire smile and stuck the ticket in his pocket. Nothing could raise a frown tonight. He freed the bike, climbed on, secured "Mimsie" (as he was already calling her) and roared off. Straight to his apartment.

All talking and giggling to the third story where Chowan ushered her into his humble abode, smelling faintly of fresh paint and incense. Eddy poured himself a nightcap and they chatted at the kitchen table.

His Siamese cat, Koko, brushed Miriam's legs and suddenly leapt right into her lap, surprising all three. Miriam gently stroked his head.

"Tell me all about you."

"Oh God!"

"I mean it. Everything. Anything?"

"More music and louder whiskey, lassie. I can't do that."

"Vietnam?"

"'Twas in another lifetime. I am not the same person I was then."

"How do you mean?"

"I find it hard to talk about. I spent three months of my tour sniping at night."

"What?!"

"Infra-red lens, shooting anything that moved. I killed Cong, snakes, a tiger, even shot a damned water buffalo once. I was a hell-of-a-shot and a nervous one. My C.O gave the village a replacement water buffalo at Uncle Sam's expense."

"That's funny, I guess."

"Yeah. But shooting people like flies isn't. I actually got used to it. It became easy. The reality sank in and I flipped. I was given a medical discharge."

"I see," she said.

Chowan arose, walked to the open porch door, and lit a Lucky Strike. Miriam followed and unfolded him, hands clutched deeply into his stomach. Both sighed deeply.

"You're not a killer," whispered Miriam, "and I'm in love with you."

He led her into the bedroom.

acknowledgments

I wish to thank...

The writers in my life who spurred me on: Pat Montandon, whose beautiful home in Beverly Hills is where I first put words to the page; and Sophia Demas, whose priceless wisdom to "get it all out without judgment" helped me do just that, and never have a moment of writer's block.

My brother, Jeffrey, for his boundless enthusiasm for the book, for my own story to be told, for the full embrace of all of it to come flowing out, and the love, love, love. I just can't thank you enough for keeping me going with your kind words.

My Aunt Sally, Uncle Ray, Cousin Nancy, brothers Jimmy and TJ, sister Shannah, Dick Losh, Steve Skinner, Al Miller, and Andy Crockett, for the memories mustered about my father. Your thoughts and reflections shaped the narrative and helped me discover the many facets of him I was looking to explore.

My sons and husband, for the space to indulge in my story and sometimes get away for a weekend of writing and crying, writing and crying.

My mother, for finding all those precious letters and sharing her love and wisdom as I sought to understand who my father was as a young man and through the years.

My editor, Dave, for being "the one." You so got it from the start, and I am forever grateful for your humor and friendship, and most of all your ability to weave the most important threads of this story into a beautiful fabric.

With deep gratitude,

Kennerly

about the author

Kennerly's adventures include mingling with Zapotec Indians in Oaxaca, drinking bilos of kava under the full moon in Fiji, skydiving in New Zealand, koala snuggling in Australia, riding elephants in Thailand, trekking Nepal's Himalaya, shooting an AK47 in Cambodia, and dancing in the streets of Chau Doc to Santana tunes with a toothless Vietnamese grandmother.

She now lives an adventurous life with her husband and two sons in the Philadelphia suburbs.

Find her at kennerlyclay.com.

also by f. kennerly clay

Calling of Ancestors: Finding Forgotten Secrets in My DNA (ebook)

The Ketamine Diaries - A Sober Psychonaut Explores Psychedelic Medicine for Depression (blog series)

The Buzz on Travel (co-author)

from the author

Thanks for reading!

If you enjoyed this book, I hope you'll take a few minutes to post a review on Amazon. It helps my book get found by others.